INTERP   ND

Interpreting Northern Ireland

JOHN WHYTE

Foreword by
Garret FitzGerald

CLARENDON PRESS · OXFORD

Oxford University Press, Walton Street, Oxford OX2 6DP

Oxford New York Toronto
Delhi Bombay Calcutta Madras Karachi
Petaling Jaya Singapore Hong Kong Tokyo
Nairobi Dar es Salaam Cape Town
Melbourne Auckland

and associated companies in
Berlin Ibadan

Oxford is a trade mark of Oxford University Press

Published in the United States
by Oxford University Press, New York

First published 1990
First issued in Clarendon Paperbacks 1991
Paperback reprinted 1991

British Library Cataloguing in Publication Data
Whyte, John
Interpreting Northern Ireland.
1. Northern Ireland. Social conditions
I. Title
941.60824
ISBN 0–19–827380–0

Library of Congress Cataloging in Publication Data
Whyte, John Henry, 1928–
Interpreting Northern Ireland / John Whyte.
p.   cm.
Includes bibliographical references.
1. Northern Ireland—Politics and government—1969–
–Historiography.   I. Title.
DA990.U46W47 1990   941.60824'072—dc20   90–35277
ISBN 0–19–827380–0

Printed and bound in
Great Britain by Biddles Ltd.
Guildford and King's Lynn

Foreword

Garret FitzGerald

In his earlier career John Whyte wrote the seminal work *Church and State in Modern Ireland.* Following his return for sixteen years to the part of Ireland where his roots lay he dedicated himself to research into the problems that had led to prolonged conflict in that area, and in particular, as the years passed, to a study of the rapidly growing literature about this conflict, which he estimated had attained some 7,000 items by 1989.

This comprehensive and balanced work, fortunately completed just before his sudden and tragic death en route to a Conference in the United States on the Northern Ireland problems, to which he was to have been a major contributor, is the outcome of these years of study, which continued after his return to Dublin in 1984.

However, the analysis of the literature of the Northern Ireland conflict in this book goes far beyond a bibliography because the 500 works to which he has chosen specifically to refer are deployed with great skill to illustrate a series of different interpretations of the nature of the community divide in Northern Ireland and of the conflict itself.

This process in turn entails a carefully-judged classification of alternative interpretations of the conflict—a classification of which he himself, typically, provides an objective critique and to which, indeed, he offers some suggested alternatives, thus displaying his usual objectivity and his dispassionate capacity for self-criticism.

For his own part he describes himself as being happy with any solution to this conflict that would bring peace, and, while having 'at different times held different views about the ultimate solution to the troubles' he tells us that he had come to doubt 'whether any solution can be applied to Northern Ireland as a whole'. But in his view more important than attachment on his part to any particular settlement is a presentation of the issues on a basis not of wishful thinking but of 'vigorous unemotional investigation'.

And that is what this work provides, without, however, falling into the trap of limiting the analysis to the fruits of academic research; the views of engaged participants are also employed to illustrate the various theses and theories, political as well as

academic, that have at different times been put forward as explanations of or justifications for the conflict in Northern Ireland.

His is not a sterile objectivity; on some controversial issues where
he judges the balance of the argument to be in favour of one
interpretation rather than the other he comes down firmly on one
side. An example—in relation to which I not unnaturally agree with
him!—is his evaluation of the Report of the New Ireland Forum. He
challenges Clare O'Halloran's argument that this report is fundamentally a restatement of old nationalist attitudes, pointing out that,
despite 'fudging' in some of the language of the Report, required to
bridge divergences between Party attitudes, the core of the Northern
Ireland problem is seen by the Forum as lying in the clash of two
identities and not the British presence. The Forum Report is
accordingly treated in this book as belonging to the 'internal conflict
interpretation' of Northern Ireland's crisis.

The book is, however, deliberately confined to an analysis of
different interpretations of the Northern Ireland problem that have
so far been put forward by researchers or protagonists and to
'proposals or approaches which I have found in the literature'. In his
view these can be categorized as arising either from the traditional
nationalist and traditional unionist interpretations, which, he
points out, shared the same paradigm—viz. blaming the problem on
an 'external actor' (although, of course, a different one in each
case)—or from an 'internal conflict' paradigm, which he sees as
having replaced during the past twenty years the earlier, traditional,
approach.

This 'paradigm shift' he sees as having been certainly an improvement, because it led researchers to look into aspects of the problem
that had previously been neglected. But, he adds, the fact that
disagreement has nevertheless persisted about the nature of the
conflict shows that this second paradigm has not solved all difficulties, and he adds, significantly, that 'perhaps the time has come when
we should start looking for a new paradigm'.

He disclaims knowledge of what shape a new paradigm might
take on the grounds that the exponent of the 'paradigm shift'
concept in the philosophy of science, Thomas Kuhn, has suggested
that 'the fundamental innovations of a new paradigm are almost
always due to either very young men or to men new to the field'.

Nevertheless in this context he draws attention to one factor that has recurred in the course of his analysis—viz. the contrasts that exist between different parts of the 'narrow ground' of Northern Ireland, as a result of which the nature and intensity of the conflict have varied widely—and he concludes that the nature of a settlement likely to bring peace may vary widely too as between different areas.

I share his view that this factor has been underestimated hitherto; thus what might work for people in many small towns and rural districts of Northern Ireland, and in middle-class areas of Belfast or North Down, could prove quite irrelevant to the problems of three areas which are themselves quite different in character from each other—viz. West Belfast, South Armagh, and Derry City.

It is a tribute to the comprehensive and objective character of this work that one can say with assurance that no one is likely to be able to write intelligently about the Northern Ireland conflict in future without having first taken account of John Whyte's last book.

July 1990

Preface

Since the current troubles in Northern Ireland began in 1968, there has been an explosion of research on the area. Hundreds of books and an even larger number of articles have been published. The invaluable *Social Science Bibliography of Northern Ireland* (Rolston *et al*. 1983) listed over 5,000 items, the great majority published since 1968. If it were brought up to date the total might now approach 7,000. There are other conflict-torn parts of the world, such as South Africa or Israel/Palestine, where the total volume of research done is greater, but then the populations involved are larger too. It is quite possible that, in proportion to size, Northern Ireland is the most heavily researched area on earth.

In these circumstances, the most useful contribution which a specialist on Northern Ireland can make is, not to add yet another item to the already daunting pile of research, but to provide a guide through it. That is the purpose of this book. My object is to survey and appraise some of the research on Northern Ireland. The book is divided into three parts:

Part I examines the nature of the community divide;
Part II examines interpretations of the Northern Ireland problem;
Part III, entitled 'Conclusions', does two things: it examines possible solutions, and it discusses some of the implications for research of the findings in preceding chapters.

When discussing each subject-area my usual pattern will be to summarize the state of knowledge as it stood on the eve of the troubles, and then discuss how research has developed since. I hope, first, to give readers an idea of the spectrum of opinion among researchers in each area; and secondly, to indicate where (if anywhere) consensus lies. If consensus is limited (as happens rather often) I shall make suggestions about the relative merits of the different points of view.

I have picked out these three fields because they are ones in which conclusions are relatively unlikely to go out of date. My original intention had been to appraise the research that has appeared on all aspects of the Northern Ireland problem. I had intended to include chapters on the historical development of the problem, and on the course of events since the troubles began in 1968. That would have entailed appraisals of British government policy in the fields of the economy, security, and politics, and of the policies of the other actors—the government of Northern Ireland (before its dissolution in 1972), the political parties and paramilitary groups in Northern Ireland, and the government and opposition in the Republic of Ireland. I came to realize that this was an impossible task. There was so much coming out that it was beyond the power of one researcher to keep up with the literature. I decided to omit the detailed discussion of the course of events, because this was the part of the enterprise that would be most quickly superseded. It is not just that more keeps happening, but that the stream of memoirs and of newspaper revelations means that the picture of events in the recent past has continually to be redrawn. For example, British newspapers during 1987 published fresh revelations of the activities of British intelligence during the mid-1970s. The areas which I have selected for examination, however, are ones where scholarly discussion moves more slowly, and findings take years—or on some topics even decades—to become out of date.

One implication of my choice of subjects should be made clear. This is not a book for absolute beginners. It assumes an outline knowledge of the nature of Northern Ireland society, and of the course of events. Anyone who does not have such knowledge would be well advised to read first some introductory work such as Lord Longford and Anne McHardy's *Ulster* (1981), or Paul Arthur's *Government and Politics of Northern Ireland* (1987). On the other hand, neither is this a book only for experts. I hope that it will be intelligible and helpful even for readers whose knowledge of Northern Ireland is quite limited.

I might say a word about my qualifications to undertake this task. From 1966 to 1984 I lectured in political science at the Queen's University of Belfast. From 1968 till the end of that period I was responsible for the teaching of courses on the government and politics of Northern Ireland. Since 1984 I have continued to teach courses on Northern Ireland at University College Dublin. While teaching these courses I have always interpreted my brief widely, and have drawn on material from every relevant discipline—not only political science, but also history, sociology, economics, anthropology, geography, law, and social psychology. In 1975 I was asked to set up a programme for research into the Northern Ireland crisis, instigated and in part funded by the Committee for Social Science Research in Ireland (the CSSRI). Details of this programme, which is now virtually complete, can be found in Appendix A: suffice it to say here that organizing it gave me a further motive to re-examine literature in the field. Many researchers have examined particular aspects of Northern Ireland more deeply than I have, but there can be only a handful—if any—who have been under the same necessity to study the literature so widely.

Readers may reasonably ask for some indication of my point of view. I consider myself to be near the centre of the spectrum of opinion on Northern Ireland. I would be happy with any solution that would bring peace. If some form of a united Ireland is likeliest to do that, then I would favour it. If some structure within the United Kingdom is likeliest to do it, then I would favour that. If some fresh structure, neither simply Irish nor simply British, were to give the best chance of promoting peace, then I would prefer that instead. At different times I have had different views about the ultimate solution to the troubles, and at present I am inclined (for reasons that will become clear in the course of this book) to doubt whether any single solution can be applied to Northern Ireland as a whole. However, what I feel is more important than attachment to any particular settlement is that solutions are offered on a basis, not of wishful thinking, but of rigorous, unemotional investigation. My hope is that this book will do something to bring that about.

A word should be said about my choice of books or articles for discussion in the following pages. I have not discussed anything like all the items that I have read. There are three possible reasons for omission. The first is that the item, interesting though it may be in itself, is not germane to the subject-areas examined in this book. The second is that the work is too mediocre to be worth discussing. Such works are not many, but they do exist, and—unless they are important as representing a particular point of view—I have usually considered it more charitable to draw a veil over them than to dissect their weaknesses. The third reason is that the work, while competent, belongs to a cluster of items all of which say much the same thing. Where this has happened, I have chosen one or two of the best examples of the genre for discussion, rather than spending time examining them all. Even as it is, I refer to over 500 items.

There is of course a further reason why a publication may not be discussed in this book. This is that it appeared too recently for consideration. I have not been able to discuss works which appeared more recently than the end of 1989.

When I discuss a publication, I can do so only in summary form. I appreciate that this means over-simplifying an author's thought. I know from personal experience how irritating it is to have one's thought distorted when summarized by other people, and I shall do my best to avoid the same provocation. I hope that the authors whose work I discuss will feel that not too much violence has been done to their ideas, and that at least the discussion is in good faith.

One problem must be adverted to in writing about Northern Ireland. This is the question of what name to give various geographical entities. These names can be controversial, with the choice often revealing one's political preferences. I shall try to be as neutral as possible. For instance, I shall describe the region as 'Northern Ireland', which is its legal title. I shall eschew 'the six counties', preferred by some nationalists, and 'Ulster', preferred by many Unionists. An objection to using 'Ulster' for 'Northern Ireland' is that the term is ambiguous, for it also refers to the historic nine-county province of Ulster. I shall use it only in the latter sense. Again, some refer to Northern Ireland as a 'province'. That usage can arouse irritation particularly among nationalists, who claim that the title 'province' should be properly reserved to the four historic provinces of Ireland—Ulster, Leinster, Munster, and Connacht. If I want a label to apply to Northern Ireland I shall call it a 'region'. Unionists should find that title as acceptable as 'province': Northern Ireland appears as a region in the regional statistics of the United Kingdom published by the British government.

Another name that causes constant difficulty is Derry/Londonderry, the first form being preferred by nationalists, and the second by many unionists. I shall adopt a compromise which has been employed by a number of academic writers. I shall use Derry for the town, and Londonderry for the county. After all, the county is an English creation, dating only from the seventeenth century, so the use of a term which is of English origin can be defended. Derry city, on the other hand, grew out of a settlement which existed long before the English came to Ireland, and the indigenous name is more appropriate. (I also find that, in everyday conversation, those who actually live in the city normally call it Derry, regardless of their political persuasion.)

A further term which causes difficulty is 'British Isles' as the name of the archipelago to which Great Britain and Ireland belong. Nationalists generally dislike it because it might be taken to imply that Ireland belongs to Britain. The alternative term of 'these islands' may sound unneutral because it is the phrase preferred by nationalists. I shall talk simply of 'the archipelago'.

University College Dublin   J.W.
January 1990.

Acknowledgements

In the first place I must thank the Committee for Social Science Research in Ireland, a body which was set up in 1973 to administer a grant from the Ford Foundation for the development of the social sciences in Ireland, and which subsequently obtained further funds from the Ford Foundation and from other quarters. The Committee financed a year's leave of absence for me in 1980–1 during which I worked on an early version of this book. It is not the Committee's fault that the book has taken so long to come to fruition. One difficulty was that, as explained above, the task proved much bigger than I expected. Another was that my change of job in 1984 put a dead stop for eighteen months to my writing: I found that the teaching and administration that went with my new post were so overwhelming that I had to put everything else aside for the time being. However, the task is now at long last complete.

I owe an especial debt of thanks to the friends who were kind enough to read part or all of the draft for me: Ed Cairns, Bob Cormack, John Darby, Michael Gallagher, Attracta Ingram, Michael Laffan, Liam O'Dowd, Brendan O'Leary, Bob Osborne, Jennifer Todd, Karen Trew, and Frank Wright. My text has benefited greatly from their comments, but as I did not accept all their suggestions they cannot be blamed for the shortcomings that remain. I also have to thank David Smith, Edward Moxon-Browne, and Ian McAllister for providing me with unpublished survey data, and Liam Kennedy for allowing me to copy maps which he has constructed.

I have to thank the Netherlands Institute for Advanced Study for giving me hospitality during the academic year 1979–80 when I first started work on this book. I have also to thank the Leverhulme Trust for awarding me in the same year a grant to visit divided societies on the continent of Europe—The Netherlands, Belgium, Switzerland, and the South Tyrol. As it happened, I made little use in this book of what I found during those visits, but it has been valuable as background information; and I have also been able to use the material while teaching successive cohorts of students, first at the Queen's University of Belfast and now at University College Dublin. Finally, my deepest thanks go to my wife and children for their support and forbearance during the life of a project which has taken much too long.

University College Dublin
October 1989   J.W.

Contents

Tables

Illustrations

I
The Nature of the
Community Divide

The purpose of Part I of this book is to explore the nature of the community divide in Northern Ireland. At the outset, there are four preliminary topics which require discussion: (1) what kind of literature is available on the subject?; (2) how far is it true to say that Northern Ireland is divided into two communities?; (3) in so far as it is divided into two communities, what labels are best used to describe them?; and (4) what are their relative proportions? These four topics will be covered in Chapter 1. The remaining chapters in Part I will be devoted to particular facets of the divide. Chapter 2 will treat some of the religious aspects. Chapter 3 will examine economic aspects. Chapter 4 will treat political aspects (including attitudes to law and order). Chapter 5 will cover psychological aspects, and will also provide a review.

1

Some Preliminary Issues

A SURVEY OF THE LITERATURE

When the troubles broke out in 1968, there was very little literature available on the community divide in Northern Ireland. Back in 1947, John M. Mogey had published a book for the Northern Ireland Council of Social Service entitled *Rural Life in Northern Ireland: Five Regional Studies*. Intended as 'an attempt to describe the way of life of the country people of Northern Ireland' (p. 1), it contains much fascinating detail; but it focuses mainly on standards of living and patterns of work, and contains only incidental information on community relations. In 1960 a geographer then lecturing at Queen's University, Emrys Jones, published *A Social Geography of Belfast*, which contains much relevant information, including a chapter on religion; but it covered only one city in Northern Ireland, albeit much the largest. Some other books contained apposite information—for instance, *Ulster under Home Rule*, edited by Thomas Wilson (1956), and R. J. Lawrence's *The Government of Northern Ireland* (1965). There were propagandist works, like Frank Gallagher's *The Indivisible Island* (1957) from the nationalist side, and W. A. Carson's *Ulster and the Irish Republic* (1957) from the unionist. But there was practically no study directly on community relations.

The one exception was Barritt and Carter's *The Northern Ireland Problem: A Study in Group Relation* (1962). The authors were two Quakers—Carter, an Englishman, who was Professor of Economics at the Queen's University of Belfast for eight years; Barritt, a leading figure in the field of social welfare, who has lived in Northern Ireland for most of his life. Their little book, of hardly more than 150 pages, discussed the relations between Protestant and Catholic in various settings—politics, employment, education, and so on. Based largely on interviews, and buttressed by field-work in Newry and Porta-down, it has still not lost its value—indeed, it remains one of the best books to put into the hands of an outsider beginning to study Northern Ireland. Though much has happened since it came out, many of its conclusions have stood the test of later research. Society in Northern Ireland changes in some ways so slowly that observations made at the beginning of the 1960s can still be valid today. A second edition was published in 1972, with a new preface and postscript, but the core of the text remained unchanged.

Since 1968, the research done on community relations in Northern Ireland has expanded enormously. With the expansion has come a division of labour, as different researchers employ different techniques. Two of the most popular ways of studying a society are the attitude survey and the participant-observation study. Each method has its strength and weaknesses. Both have been employed in Northern Ireland, and I shall discuss each in turn.

Attitude Surveys

Attitude surveys entail putting a set of questions to a sample of the population, scientifically selected so as to be representative of the population as a whole. The strength of such surveys is that they represent all sections of the population being studied, and form a far more reliable means of getting at the opinions of that population than impressions based on a small and untypical sample—which is all that most individual observers have to go on. Among their disadvantages is that they are expensive—to interview a sample of 1,000 people, and then code and analyse the replies, can cost tens of thousands of pounds. Another weakness is that surveys secure replies only to the questions put: if the questions are badly phrased, or ignore important issues, the results will be correspondingly devalued. This disadvantage can be mitigated by running pilot studies with small samples, but even these cost time and money and cannot be repeated indefinitely.

A particular weakness in the case of Northern Ireland is that surveys may not give accurate results because not all respondents tell the truth. There is some ground for thinking that, in reply to questionnaires, Northern Ireland people express more moderate views than they really hold. For instance, the middle-of-the-road Alliance Party consistently gets more support in opinion polls than it does in elections, while an extreme party like Sinn Féin gets less. Figure 1.1. shows the difference in Alliance support as measured by polls and by elections. The fluctuations are sharper in elections than in surveys. This is because voters are constrained in elections by the

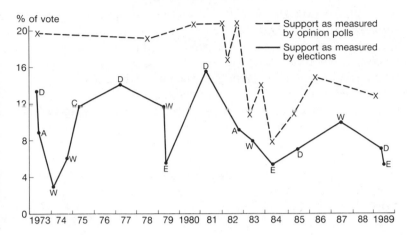

Fig. 1.1. Alliance Party support

choices available: for instance, Alliance's worst result (the Westminster election of February 1974) is partly explained by the fact that it fought only three seats out of twelve. Nevertheless, the generalization emerges clearly that Alliance does better in surveys than in actual elections. On the other hand, the gap is usually only a few per cent, and the surveys did pick up the Alliance decline in the early 1980s, together with the fluctuations in its fortunes since then. The surveys may exaggerate moderate opinion, but not so much as to bear no relation to reality.

There are two kinds of sample used in attitude surveys—the probability sample, and the quota sample. The former entails asking the interviewers to go to specific individuals, whose names and addresses have been obtained, probably, from electoral registers. The latter requires asking the interviewers only to look for specific types of respondent—50 per cent male, 50 per cent female, so many under/over 40, so many middle/working class, and so on. The former is more accurate, because the sample is more precisely representative of the population as a whole, but it is also more expensive, because the interviewer may have to make repeated calls at a given address before he or she finds the respondent in. Academics prefer to use probability samples, while newspapers and television stations usually commission the cheaper quota samples.

The classic attitude survey in Northern Ireland was directed by Professor Richard Rose of the University of Strathclyde in the spring and summer of 1968, and reported on in his book *Governing without Consensus* (1971). The survey was a massive affair: an attempt was made to interview 1,500 people, and 1,291 were actually interviewed, which was by international standards an unusually high success rate (Rose 1971, 183–5). The questionnaire was long, and the median interview lasted 75 minutes (p. 187). The amount of information gathered made it an exceptionally rewarding survey. As a bonus, Rose was extraordinarily lucky in his timing. The interviews took place in the last few months before the troubles began. They thus embalm for us a permanent record of attitudes in Northern Ireland at the last moment when the region was still at peace.

There have been two major academic surveys published since Rose completed his work. In 1978 Edward Moxon-Browne, a political scientist at the Queen's University of Belfast, directed a survey which he reported on in his book *Nation, Class and Creed in Northern Ireland* (1983). The number of interviews attempted was higher than for Rose's work—1,998—but the response rate was lower, 1,277 satisfactory interviews being obtained. This was not surprising, given the years of turmoil that had intervened. Moxon-Browne's detailed figures (Moxon-Browne 1983, 181) show, when compared with Rose's (1971, 186), that the higher failure rate was partly due to a greater inability to contact respondents, because they had moved or because their premises were demolished, and partly due to a greater reluctance on the part of those selected to be interviewed. The questionnaire was shorter, too, than it had been in Rose's survey. None the less, a great deal of useful information was collected. Moxon-Browne's work is given added value by the fact that it replicated many of the questions in Rose's survey, thus enabling us to measure changes in attitude over the decade. It was also designed to coincide with a survey in the Republic which asked many of the same questions, thus making it possible to compare attitudes north and south of the border. The southern survey was reported on by Davis and Sinnott (1979).

The third major academic survey was conducted in 1986 by David J. Smith of the Policy Studies Institute in London. The results were published by the Policy Studies Institute in the following year (Smith, 1987*b*). Smith's survey was more sharply focused than

Rose's or Moxon-Browne's. It was one of a group of research reports commissioned by the Standing Advisory Commission on Human Rights with the object of reviewing 'the coverage and effectiveness of existing laws and institutions in securing freedom from discrimination and furthering equality of opportunity in Northern Ireland' (Smith 1987*b*, 1). However, the survey was more wide-ranging than one might expect from that brief, and provides much interesting information about the general nature of the community divide. Smith's sample was the largest of the three academic surveys. He sought interviews with 2,528 people, and obtained them with 1,672 (p. 155).

Apart from academic surveys, there have been a number commissioned by newspapers and television companies. The first region-wide survey was undertaken for the *Belfast Telegraph* in November 1967. Many more have been conducted since. Those down to 1978 have been anthologized in a publication by Rose, McAllister, and Mair: *Is There a Concurring Majority about Northern Ireland?* (1978)—a work which also reports survey data on attitudes to Northern Ireland in Britain and the Republic of Ireland. Unfortunately no one has yet summarized the data published since 1978— though Harvey Cox (1987) has analysed surveys in the fifteen months or so after the Anglo-Irish Agreement of November 1985. However, I have myself made a collection of surveys since 1978, which is I believe comprehensive, and I shall refer to it in a subsequent chapter. It confirms to a remarkable extent the patterns revealed by Rose, McAllister, and Mair (1978). The intervening years of trauma have done little to alter underlying attitudes.

Surveys do not have to cover Northern Ireland as a whole. A number have been conducted of subsets of the Northern Ireland population. They are of course authoritative only for the populations in which they were carried out, but they can at least provide suggestions about the state of opinion in the wider society. The earliest carried out anywhere in Northern Ireland was a small-scale study of Portadown, Armagh, Newry, Kilkeel, and Dungannon, undertaken for Lancaster University in 1966 and reported on by MacRae (1966). Among other local surveys have been one of Belfast carried out in 1966 and reported on by Budge and O'Leary (1973); one of a small town in the northern part of Northern Ireland reported on by Hickey (1984, 127–40); and two surveys of school leavers, one in Belfast and the other in Derry and Strabane, carried out for the Fair Employment Agency and reported on by Cormack, Osborne, and Thompson (1980) and by Murray and Darby (1980). One of the most interesting was of church-going Protestants in Belfast, reported on by Boal and Livingstone (1986). Social psychologists have used surveys of students and schoolchildren a good deal—many of their findings have been summarized by Cairns (1987). One social psychologist, E. E. O'Donnell (1977), based a study of stereotyping on a quota sample drawn from three towns— Belfast, Derry, and Enniskillen.

One of the largest of these partial surveys (2,416 respondents) was conducted by John Jackson, then at the Queen's University of Belfast and now at Trinity College Dublin, in 1973–4. It formed part of a study of occupational mobility, and was confined to males aged between 18 and 64. It cannot be assumed, therefore, that its results would precisely reflect the opinions of the population as a whole. However, the findings from Rose's and Moxon-Browne's surveys suggest that the opinions of men do not diverge strikingly from those of women, so Jackson's data can probably be taken as a rough indication of attitudes in the Northern Ireland population as a whole at the time the survey was carried out. Its results have never been written up in book form, but some have been used in academic papers (e.g. McAllister 1982, 1983; Robert Miller 1978, 1983), and the main findings were made available in the form of duplicated reports.

Another very large survey, of 3,000 women, was conducted by Paul Compton of the Queen's University of Belfast and John Coward of the University of Ulster in 1983, and the results published in their book *Fertility and Family Planning in Northern Ireland* (1989). While this was planned as a demographic study, it throws considerable indirect light on community differences, by examining such topics as denominational differences in fertility and in attitudes to family planning, and the incidence of mixed marriages.

Participant-Observation Studies

Participant-observation studies are investigations of a particular group or community by an observer who, in most cases, lives among the people being studied, who observes their behaviour, and will probably carry out extended interviews with individuals. They are sometimes called community studies, or ethnographic studies. This kind of research is particularly associated with anthropology, and most of those who have applied it in Northern Ireland would classify themselves as anthropologists; some, however, come from sociology, and one (Sarah Nelson) from political science.

The strengths and weaknesses of participant-observation studies are almost the opposite of those of attitude surveys. One limitation is that any observer can study only one community, or at most a small group of communities, and there is no proof that the findings can be generalized to any area larger than the one studied. Another drawback is that participant-observation is relatively subjective: two observers of the same community may come to different conclusions, while two trained interviewers administering the same questionnaire ought to obtain similar results from similar interviewees. On the other hand, participant-observation studies can be subtler in their findings than attitude surveys. Survey analysts have the completed questionnaires to work on, and no more: they cannot (save at prohibitive expense) go back to the respondents and ask further questions. Participant-observers, on the other hand, can probe more deeply. If they are not certain of the meaning of some activity, they can observe it repeatedly until they are confident of its significance. Participant-observers, also, can raise new questions as they go along: they are not constrained by the initial design of their project as the attitude-surveyor is. Some of the most interesting findings in participant-observation studies have been on matters which the researchers had not thought to include in their initial research design.

The classic participant-observation study in Northern Ireland is Rosemary Harris's examination of a rural area near the border which she labels 'Ballybeg'. The research was conducted in the early 1950s, though the results were not published in book form till her work *Prejudice and Tolerance in Ulster* came out in 1972. The area under scrutiny was one where Catholic and Protestant farmers lived intermingled. Based on observation and interview, the study brings out how two communities could live side by side, maintain superficially courteous relations with each other, and still preserve deep suspicions and extraordinary stereotypes. The book is unfailingly lucid and perceptive, and remains one of the best ever published on Northern Ireland. Most subsequent participant-observers in Northern Ireland have sought to compare Harris's findings with their own.

Since Harris conducted her field-work there have been a number

Table 1.1. Participant-observation studies in Northern Ireland

Reference	Area studied	Nature	Denominational balance
Harris (1972)	'Ballybeg'	Rural, near border	50:50
Leyton (1974, 1975)	'Aughnaboy'	Ditto	P, surrounded by C territory
Larsen (1982a)	'Kilbroney'	Small town near border	P majority
Burton (1978)	'Anro'	Part of Belfast	C, surrounded by P territory
Glassie (1982)	'Ballymenone'	Rural, Fermanagh	Mainly C
Jenkins (1982, 1983)	'Ballyhightown'	Part of Belfast	P
Nelson (1975, 1984)	P activists	Belfast	P
McAnallen (1977)	'Drumness'	Village, Down	C majority
Campbell (1978)	Glenarm	Village, Antrim	50:50
Galway (1978)	'Glenlevan'	Village, Fermanagh	C majority
McFarlane (1978, 1989)	'Ballycuan'	Village, Down	P majority
Buckley (1982)	'Upper Tullagh'	Rural, 30 miles from Belfast	C majority
Bufwack (1982)	'Naghera'	Village	C majority
Murray (1985)	Two schools		One P, one C
Lennon (1984)	'London Park'	Urban	C estate in a mainly P town
Buckley (1983, 1984)	'Listymore'	Rural	Mainly P
Taylor (1986, 1988b)	Queen's University		Mixed
Bell (1987)	Waterside: youth study	Derry	P
Darby (1986)	Three locations: 'Kileen/Banduff',	Belfast	P and C
	'Upper Ashbourne',	Ditto	P and C
	'Dunville'	Town, mid-NI	Mixed
Cecil et al. (1987)	'Glengow'	Small town	P majority

Shanks (1988)	N. Antrim	Rural	Mainly P
Crozier (1989)	'Ballintully'	Rural, Down	Mainly P
Howe (1989*a,b*)	'Mallon Park' and 'Eastlough'	Belfast	Two areas: one C, one P
Byron and Dilley (1989); Dilley (1989)	Kilkeel, Down	Fishing port	Mainly P

Notes: Not all these studies focus on the community divide; e.g. Glassie's interest is in folklore, Cecil *et al.*'s is in welfare provision, Shanks's is in a group of rural gentry, Crozier's is in rural hospitality, Howe's is in the black economy, and Byron and Dilley are primarily concerned with the economics of fishing. However, all throw light, directly or indirectly, on community relations.

C = Catholic; P = Protestant.

of other participant-observation studies in Northern Ireland. They are listed in Table 1.1. Many of the places studied have been given fictitious names by the investigators, in order to disguise their location. This device is much used by anthropologists, so as to avoid embarrassment to their informants. The disguise is often transparent, and in any case the location of their work can generally be discovered through the academic grapevine: I know the real location of practically all those studies disguised under fictitious names. However, I shall respect the authors' wishes and not reveal these locations. Of those listed, Harris did her field-work in the 1950s, Leyton in the 1960s, and all the others in the 1970s and 1980s. I have listed their work in the table, not in order of publication, but roughly in order of date of field-work. In the table (though not in the rest of the text), I have indicated which names are fictitious by putting them in inverted commas.

Most of the works listed in the table are studies of particular communities—villages, small towns, or parts of a city. However, this is not a necessary feature of participant-observation. The technique can be used to study institutions—as Dominic Murray studied two primary schools and Rupert Taylor studied Queen's University. Nelson moved back and forth over the Belfast area, getting to know a kind of person (loyalists) rather than a particular community. Darby's work on three distinct areas has been listed here with the participant-observation studies, but in fact it lies on the fringe between participant-observation and attitude surveys, because his work is largely based on interviews with community leaders in his chosen locations. Desmond Bell's study of youth in the Protestant Waterside area of Derry also combined survey and participant-observation techniques.

Table 1.1 reveals some imbalances in the distribution of participant-observation studies around Northern Ireland. Villages and rural areas are over-represented, with more than half the total number of studies. Greater Belfast, which contains two-fifths of the population of Northern Ireland, is under-represented, with six studies out of a total of twenty-six. Northern Ireland's second largest city, Derry, would be missing from the table if it were not for Bell's study of Protestant youth in Waterside. Market towns are represented only by John Darby's study of Dunville, and by Brian Lennon's brief though interesting açcount of London Park. There is a tendency, for understandable reasons, for researchers to prefer the more peaceful areas of Northern Ireland to the more disturbed ones. I know of a projected study of one of the more strife-torn market towns which had to be abandoned because no one could be found to act as research assistant to the principal investigator and go to live in the town. All the same, the studies of hard-line populations in Belfast by Burton, Nelson, Jenkins, and Darby show that participant-observation is not impossible even in the most embittered areas. If all the participant-observation studies are taken together, they provide quite a comprehensive coverage of the different types of community in Northern Ireland: urban and rural, peaceful and violent, Protestant, Catholic, and mixed.

Other Methods of Research

Attitude surveys and participant-observation studies are not the only ways of studying a region in conflict. Other scholars have fruitfully used other methods, and a word must be said about their work.

A mass of material can be found in statistics collected by government, and important results can be obtained by reanalysing official data. A good example would be Aunger's article on 'Religion and Occupational Class in Northern Ireland', which appeared in the *Economic and Social Review* for October 1975, and which, simply by its interpretation of data collected in the 1971 census, revealed for the first time the extent of the economic gap between the Protestant and Catholic communities. Indeed most studies of economic conditions in Northern Ireland depend on data collected by government. A particularly valuable series is the Continuous Household Survey, which has been running since 1983. Administered by the government's Policy Planning and Research Unit, this survey is based on interviews with thousands of people annually, chosen by probability sampling, and provides a great deal of information on social and economic conditions. It also contains some data on social and political attitudes.

Social psychologists have used a variety of instruments. Their two most favoured methods are the attitude survey and the laboratory experiment, but others have been employed. Morris Fraser, in his book *Children in Conflict* (1973) drew on his case notes as a child psychiatrist in Belfast to present interesting hypotheses about the nature of the conflict. Two psychologists from Yale University employed the technique of an experimental workshop in order to explore Protestant–Catholic interaction (Doob and Foltz 1973)—an experiment which provoked some fierce controversy (Alevy *et al.* 1974; Boehringer *et al.* 1974; Doob and Foltz 1974).

Documentary research is not easy for a contemporary subject such as the community divide in Northern Ireland. The archives in Northern Ireland operate under a thirty-year rule, so that it will be some time before they have anything to contribute to a study of the current situation—and a number of important files are closed for even longer. However, occasionally a researcher has his own cache of information, which he can use with effect. Charles Brett's study of the Northern Ireland Housing Executive, *Housing a Divided Community* (1986), is based largely on documentation available to the author during his term as chairman of the Executive. Belfast and local newspapers, also, repay examination.

The books published by journalists and travel writers can provide valuable material. The more austere academics might reject such work as insufficiently scientific: it does not test hypotheses or explore an academic theme. But such writers can be just as acute as academic participant-observers. As a bonus, these authors are sometimes readier to investigate hard-line territory than are academics. Two particularly valuable works are Sally Belfrage's *The Crack: A Belfast Year* (1987), in which she ranged widely over republican and loyalist areas of Belfast, and John Conroy's more concentrated *War as a*

Way of Life (1988), in which he described life in part of Catholic west Belfast. Other works in this genre include Dervla Murphy's *A Place Apart* (1978), in which the author reported from many parts of Northern Ireland, and Colin Tóibín's *Walking Along the Border* (1987), in which, as the title indicates, the author covered the border areas of Northern Ireland.

Finally, one should not neglect the memoirs of participants. Some may feel that these should not be dignified by the title 'research', but they contain a great deal of information, sometimes painfully gathered. Two retired permanent secretaries in the Northern Ireland Civil Service have written their memoirs—one Protestant (Oliver 1978*b*), and one Catholic (Shea 1981). So have two prime ministers of Northern Ireland—Terence O'Neill (1972) and Brian Faulkner (1978)—and some British ministers with responsibility for Northern Ireland (Callaghan 1973, 1987; Rees 1985; Prior 1986). On the other side of the fence, nationalists of varying hues have written their memoirs (e.g. Adams 1982; McClean 1983; Curran 1986; McKeown 1986; Farrell 1988; McCluskey 1989). Perhaps the most readable of these is Bernadette Devlin's autobiography *The Price of my Soul* (1969). Eamonn McCann's *War and an Irish Town* (1974, 1980), while primarily a Marxist analysis of the Northern Ireland problem, contains much autobiographical material. Ciaran McKeown, one of the founders of the Peace People of 1976, has written an autobiography, *The Passion of Peace* (1984). Most of these books deal mainly with political and security issues; but they all throw light on community relations.

HOW FAR TWO COMMUNITIES?

The next question to be discussed is: how completely is Northern Ireland divided into two communities? There is a spectrum of opinion in the literature. At one extreme are authors who imply that the separation is almost unqualified. A psychologist, Geoffrey W. Beattie (1979, 250), has written that 'segregation was, and is, almost total'. At the other extreme we can find authors who stress the common bonds between the communities. One participant-observer, Henry W. Glassie (1982, 645), has written that 'Ireland appears remarkably homogeneous from an American perspective.' An Eng-

lish anthropologist working at the Ulster Folk Museum has pointed
out all the ways in which Catholic and Protestant are *not* divided:

With only very limited and specific exceptions, the cultural heritage for the
Catholic is likely to be much the same as that of a Protestant of the same
social class living in the same geographical area. There are no distinctively
Protestant or Catholic dialects, nor agricultural practices, nor housetypes,
nor pottery techniques, nor styles for cooking. Family life is much the same
on both sides, as indeed is the broader social morality. (Buckley 1988, 54.)

The emphasis may vary according to the question which
researchers set themselves. Most authors have asked, explicitly or
implicitly, 'why is there a conflict in Northern Ireland?', but it is also
possible to ask the question 'why is the conflict not worse?', and at
least two writers have done just that—Leyton (1974) and Darby
(1986, p. viii). A social psychologist, Ken Heskin, has asked the
question 'is society in Northern Ireland disintegrating?', and has
answered in the negative (Heskin 1981, 1985). His evidence comes
from comparative crime statistics. He shows that Belfast's crime rate
is only slightly higher than Dublin's and considerably lower than
that of England and Wales, and, moreover, that all three rates have
been increasing over the last twenty years to an almost identical
degree. Another psychologist, Karen Trew, has pointed to a body of
research into peaceful inter-group contact in Northern Ireland
(Trew 1986).

The emphasis may also vary according to discipline. Darby (1986,
5–7) notes that historians and political scientists have tended to
stress dissension, violence, and dysfunction, while the authors of
community studies (mostly anthropologists) have put more stress on
the relatively low influence of the conflict on day-to-day living.
Indeed, there can be considerable differences even within disciplines.
The various participant-observation studies give widely different
impressions of the degree of conflict. At one extreme is Buckley's
(1982) study of a quiet rural area in the east of Northern Ireland
which he has entitled *A Gentle People: A Study of a Peaceful
Community in Ulster*. At the other extreme are the studies by Burton
(1978), Jenkins (1982, 1983) and Nelson (1984) of bitterly antagonistic groups in Belfast. The remaining participant-observation studies
fall somewhere in between. The differences reflect the fact that there
are substantial objective differences between one part of Northern
Ireland and another; but they may also be in part due to differences
in standpoint between one observer and another.

However, on the whole there is a fair degree of consensus on how distinct the communities are from each other: greater here than on many topics connected with the Northern Ireland problem. It can be summed up in the phrase that the communities are seen as deeply but not totally divided. This perception goes back to before the beginning of the troubles. Barritt and Carter (1962, 154) found at the beginning of the 1960s that 'there is more of separation than of unity in Northern Ireland society', but they also noted 'at a number of points how a common interest or enthusiasm, or some uniting influence of the local social structure, can transcend the general religious influences'. The anthropologist Rosemary Harris (1972), reporting on her field-work in the 1950s, provides three chapters on the common culture of her area of study, before following them with five chapters on the differences between Protestant and Catholic. Another anthropologist, Elliott Leyton, working in the 1960s, found unity as well as discord, summed up in the phrase 'we're all the one blood if you go back far enough' (Leyton 1975, 13).

The relative extent of division and unity was explored by Rose (1971), in his attitude survey undertaken in 1968. Rose presents his findings in clearly laid-out tables, one feature of which is that the degree of divergence between Protestant and Catholic attitudes is quantified in the form of a 'difference index', so calculated that if every Protestant gave one response to a particular question and every Catholic gave a different response, the difference index would be 100, while if Catholics and Protestants gave identical responses, the difference index would be 0. A striking feature of Rose's findings is how small the difference index is on many issues. Protestants and Catholics found much the same reasons for liking and disliking Northern Ireland. They had much the same reactions to the thought of emigration, similar views on the role of trade unions and big business, similar attitudes to authority and to social class. When asked what their most serious family problem was, the pattern of replies was almost identical, and few mentioned worries about religion or politics. They felt, more surprisingly, similar degrees of difference from or closeness to the English and the southern Irish. It was only on strictly political issues, and on a cluster of questions relating to ecumenism, that Protestant and Catholic attitudes differed widely. Rose noted this, and suggested that 'the existence of much similarity about so many aspects of Ulster life' explained 'the persistence of civil society simultaneously with political discord and disorder' (p. 324).

All the writers just cited collected their evidence before the troubles began; but even in some of the work conducted more recently, similar results have been reported. Sidsel Larsen, the Norwegian anthropologist who surveyed a small town in County Down at the beginning of the 1970s, remarked (1982*a*, 135) that 'while stressing the differences, we should not overlook the very striking similarity in life style and values which is also a characteristic of the two groups'. Moxon-Browne (1983), reporting his survey of 1978, devotes a chapter to the question 'two communities or one?' His answer is that there are undoubtedly two (p. 135), but the differences are not absolute. He explores the extent to which respondents had friends, neighbours, relatives, or workmates from the other community, and found that, after ten years of disorder, the figures were not greatly different from those discovered by Rose in the peaceful spring and summer of 1968 (p. 128). Hickey (1984), reporting on a small-scale survey of a town in the northern part of Northern Ireland, found that 'there is a hard core of people within the Protestants who wish to retain the boundaries between them and the Catholics', and that the same was true to a lesser extent among Catholics. But he also found that 'among large proportions of both groups strict boundaries in a large area of social relationships are not being maintained, either in theory or in practice' (p. 139).

An interesting set of research findings is reported on by a social psychologist, Karen Trew (1983). Trew found that when a group of 278 first-year university students and final-year school pupils were asked for biographical details of themselves, 93 per cent were prepared to describe themselves as either Protestant or Catholic. But when they were asked, at an earlier stage of the questionnaire, the open-ended question 'write as much as possible in answer to the question, "what are you?"', only 8 per cent spontaneously referred to their religious denomination in describing themselves. She reports several other small-scale studies in which students or schoolchildren were asked to describe themselves, and in which only a minority, usually a small one, referred to their denominational labels. She concludes that 'although Northern Ireland is a divided society, the Protestant/Catholic dichotomy does not necessarily pervade the individual's self perceptions or social evaluations' (p. 119).

It is not surprising, then, that, as Liz McWhirter (1983*b*, 135) has pointed out, some of the writing on Northern Ireland has titles which include phrases such as 'prejudice and tolerance' (Harris 1972), or 'opposition and integration' (Leyton 1974), or 'integration and division' (Boal and Douglas 1982). Indeed the book edited by Boal and Douglas *Integration and Division: Geographical Perspectives on the Northern Ireland Problem* (1982) is an extended attempt to assess just where the balance between the two forces lies. The editors conclude (p. 5) that integration dominates within the communities, and that division is dominant between them, but that there are some divisions within the two communities, and some interaction between them. That squares quite well with the impression left by the literature as a whole.

In the rest of Part I of this book, then, we have throughout to consider, not just *why* the two communities are divided, but *how far* they are divided.

WHAT LABELS?

In so far as there are two communities in Northern Ireland, the question next arises: how should they be labelled? Several choices are possible. Many authors speak of Catholic (or Roman Catholic) and Protestant. Others speak of unionist and nationalist. T. J. Pickvance (1975, 8) has proposed Ulster British and Ulster Irish as the most appropriate names, and Desmond Fennell (1983, 105–6) has commended this choice with the amendment of 'six-county Irish' for 'Ulster Irish'. The labels are not wholly interchangeable. The political preferences of Protestants and Catholics will be explored in a later chapter; suffice it to say here that, while most Catholics are nationalists and describe themselves as Irish, not all do; and while most Protestants are unionist and would prefer to be called British rather than Irish, not all do. The choice of terminology, then, can affect our view of who is in conflict with whom, and why.

Practice in the choice of terminology has varied. The first-ever region-wide opinion poll, published in the *Belfast Telegraph* for 8–16 December 1967, did not use the Protestant/Catholic dichotomy, but reported separately on Presbyterians, Church of Ireland, Roman Catholics, and others. Budge and O'Leary (1973), reporting on a survey of Belfast residents taken in 1966, categorized them as

Presbyterians, other Protestants, Church of Ireland, non-believers, and Catholics. The nationalist writer Frank Gallagher (1957) wrote of nationalist and unionist, and the pro-unionist writer M. W. Heslinga (1962) wrote of Ulsterman and Irishman. Among early authorities, Barritt and Carter (1962) were perhaps exceptional in organizing their analysis around the Protestant/Catholic divide.

As time went on, however, religious labels were used with growing frequency. The examples of Rose (1971) and of Harris (1972) must have been influential here. As we saw earlier in this chapter, they respectively provided the classic attitude survey and the classic participant-observation study, and one or both have been used as reference points by much of scholarly writing since. The fact that they both used the Protestant/Catholic dichotomy meant that subsequent scholars had to use the same categories if they were to compare their results with Rose's and/or Harris's. I cannot think of a single subsequent attitude survey or participant-observation study which has not used the Catholic/Protestant classification.

The same evolution has, I think, been followed on the whole by the mass media and by politicians. In the absence of any research on this point I must rely on my memory: but, as I recall it, down to the 1960s it was usual to talk in terms of unionist and nationalist rather than of Protestant and Catholic. What made the old terminology unsatisfactory was the erosion of old-style nationalism, and its replacement by the civil rights movement. The civil rights movement of the late 1960s was certainly not unionist; but, since the point of its campaign was to secure British rights for British subjects, it could not fairly be described as nationalist either. There ensued a period when the simple terms 'majority' and 'minority' were often used. But these were uninformative, especially for outsiders with only a limited knowledge of the region. So from about 1969 it became normal for the media to use the terms Catholic and Protestant. There has been some swing back in recent years—for instance, the report of the New Ireland Forum (1984) preferred to use the terms unionist and nationalist—but not sufficient to obliterate the pattern set in the preceding fifteen years.

There are objections to using the religious dichotomy. To talk of unionist and nationalist, or of Ulster British and Ulster Irish, might seem more appropriate because these are political terms and the conflict is in the eyes of many political rather than religious (although as we shall see in Chapter 5, it is a matter of controversy how far the conflict is in fact religious). However, there are also difficulties in using political labels, because when it comes to politics the distinctions are not always clear-cut. On the unionist side, while all are agreed in opposing a united Ireland, there is a distinction between those whose primary loyalty is to Ulster and those whose first loyalty is to the United Kingdom as a whole. On the other side, there is a gradation from intransigent republicans, through constitutional nationalists who seek a united Ireland but only by consent and through peaceful means, to marginal nationalists who would settle for the British connection provided the conditions were right. Once one starts using political classifications, a dichotomy is not good enough: one needs more categories, or perhaps a scale of attitudes. The religious classification on the other hand has the merit of being all-inclusive. Virtually everyone in Northern Ireland can be identified with one community or the other. Even unbelievers are likely to have been brought up as Protestants or Catholics. Rose (1971, 248) reports about the respondents to his 1968 survey: '1,280 of the 1,291 persons interviewed promptly gave a denominational identification when asked their religion, and seven more readily stated a preference for Protestantism or Catholicism when asked to do so.' Smith (1978*b*, 13), reporting on his survey of 1986, found an almost equal readiness to accept confessional labels. Only eighteen out of his 1,672 respondents, or just over 1 per cent, could not be classified as either Protestant or Catholic.

The main advantage of using the Protestant/Catholic classification, however, is that it seems to correspond more precisely to the realities as perceived by individuals. An academic literature has grown up on how people distinguish Protestant from Catholic (Burton 1978, 37–67; Cairns 1980; Cairns 1987, 98–104; Jenkins 1982, 30–1; Darby 1986, 24–5). The fullest treatment is given by Burton, in his participant-observation study of Anro, a Catholic working-class area of Belfast. Burton, at first sceptical about the possibility of telling Protestant from Catholics, found himself using the rules:

One day, going back to Anro from the city centre, I stopped running for a bus. The significance of this trivial act lies in the meaning I had attached to the religious ascription of the people boarding the bus. The bus stop in question served two different buses. One would be bound for a homogeneous Protestant district and consequently only Protestants would be getting on. The other went through Protestant and Catholic areas and would have a mixed set of passengers. I determined, though not deliberately, that the bus at the stop was the 'Protestant' bus and not the one I wanted and so stopped running for it. This must either have been because I considered all the passengers getting on were all 'Protestant-looking' or that I thought there was an absence of 'Catholic-looking' people boarding the bus. Realizing why I stopped, I ran to see the number of the bus and its destination. As it happened my reading of the situation was confirmed. (Burton 1978, 52–3.)

This and similar episodes led him to reflect more deeply on how people distinguished one community from another. He concluded that a complex interplay of clues—name, face, dress, demeanour, residence, education, language, and iconography—provided the evidence. This corresponds quite closely with the list of cues which a group of university students stated that they used—area, school, name, appearance, and speech (Cairns 1980, 116).

There is no comparable literature on how people tell nationalist from unionist, or Ulster British from Ulster Irish. The problem, apparently, does not strike researchers into Northern Ireland society as equally meaningful.

A test of the relative importance of religious and political categories can be found by examining the Alliance Party. Alliance, which has gained an average of roughly 10 per cent of the vote at elections, is the only party in Northern Ireland to recruit in substantial numbers from both sides of the religious divide. According to Moxon-Browne's survey of 1978, its supporters divided five to four between Protestant and Catholic (Moxon-Browne 1983, 65). Smith's survey data from eight years later bring out almost identical proportions—56 to 44 (figures calculated from Smith 1987*b*, table 119). A postal survey of the 248 Alliance candidates in the 1973 local and regional elections found that, among the 162 responding, 33 per cent were Catholic (McAllister and Wilson 1978, 212). Of the ten Assembly members elected in 1982, six were Catholic (information from the then party leadership). Politically, however, Alliance came down firmly on one side of the fence. It is committed to support of the union with Britain, a commitment which binds its Catholic members as much as its Protestant ones. A study of Alliance supporters, then, should provide some indication of how far a common political commitment can transcend a religious division.

Two pieces of research are available on Alliance attitudes. The first is the survey undertaken by McAllister and Wilson (1978) of

Alliance candidates in local and regional elections. Though they found some differences between Catholics and Protestants, on the whole what struck them was the similarity of view across the religious boundary. The second study is by Moxon-Browne (1983, 64–80), who devoted a chapter of his report on the 1978 attitude survey to those who claimed to support the Alliance Party. He found that on a number of issues there were considerable differences between its Protestant and Catholic supporters, and concluded: 'Alliance followers tend to be more "moderate" than their coreligionists on nearly all issues but the religious divide continues to be a [*sic*] salient—even within a party dedicated to overcoming it' (p. 78). These two pieces of work, then, point in different directions. Their findings can perhaps be reconciled by saying that, while among party activists the religious division can be transcended, among the much larger number of people who simply cast a vote for Alliance, the religious division remains important.

There is a fair degree of consensus in the literature, then, that the most widely useful pair of categories for describing the two communities is the religious one—Catholic and Protestant. It is the classification I shall favour in Part I of this book. In Parts II and III, where I shall more often be discussing strictly political issues, I shall more often use the unionist/nationalist classification.

WHAT PROPORTIONS?

One last problem remains to be examined before leaving this chapter. If we are going to talk about Protestants and Catholics, how many are there of each? In recent decades, this has become a source of controversy within Northern Ireland.

A question about religious adherence was asked at each census of undivided Ireland between 1861 and 1911, and at most censuses of Northern Ireland since partition. The official returns, for the area which subsequently became Northern Ireland in the censuses of 1861–1911, and for Northern Ireland in the censuses of 1926–81, are presented in Table 1.2. They show that down to 1961 the vast majority—more than 98 per cent—of the population answered the religion question. The results were accepted on all sides as accurately representing the proportion of Catholics and Protestants in the population. As will be seen, the Catholic proportion, after reaching

Table 1.2. Denominational percentages in Northern Ireland

Census	Roman Catholics	All other denominations[a]	Not stated
1861	40.9	59.0	0.1
1871	39.3	60.7	0.0
1881	38.0	61.9	0.1
1891	36.3	63.5	0.2
1901	34.8	65.1	0.1
1911	34.4	65.4	0.2
1926	33.5	66.3	0.2
1937	33.5	66.3	0.2
1951	34.4	65.2	0.4
1961	34.9	63.2	1.9
1971	31.4	59.2	9.4
1981	28.0	53.5	18.5

[a] Includes a small number of adherents of non-Christian religions. In 1981 these came to 0.16% of the total; they were fewer in earlier censuses.
Source: Northern Ireland Census, 1981: Religion Report (1984), table 1.

its lowest level in the decades after partition, was beginning slowly to rise again.

The first real difficulty in interpreting the figures occurred with the census of 1971. This showed on the face of it a decline in the Catholic population from 34.9 to 31.4 per cent. However, the census was taken during a period of rising disturbance, and a number of Catholic families refused to answer the religion question as a gesture of civil disobedience. It is not surprising, then, to find that the non-response rate for this question jumped from 1.9 per cent in 1961 to 9.4 per cent in 1971. However, it cannot be assumed that all the non-respondents were Catholics. There was a fair degree of non-response in Protestant areas as well. The only scholarly attempt to adjust the official figures so as to make allowance for the non-respondents, so far as I am aware, has been made by Paul Compton, a demographer at the Queen's University of Belfast, in his *Northern Ireland: A Census Atlas* (1978, 80–1). Compton found a relationship between the rate of non-response and the percentage of Roman Catholics at the level of individual wards (of which there were 526 in Northern Ireland), and used a linear regression technique to assign the non-responders. He suggested that they should be divided 61:39 between Catholic and Protestant. If this is done, the true proportion of Catholics in 1971 rises to 36.8 per cent.

If the 1971 census caused difficulties, the 1981 census was a nightmare. It was taken in an extremely tense atmosphere, as Bobby Sands's hunger strike reached its climax. Many Catholics refused to answer the religion question, or to fill in the census forms at all. Two sets of corrections have then to be applied to the data:

1. An estimate has to be made of how the 18.5 per cent who failed to answer the religion question should be broken down between Protestant and Catholic.
2. An estimate has to be made of the number who failed to return a census questionnaire at all, and these in their turn have to be broken down between Protestant and Catholic, because they were not necessarily all Catholics.

Various authors have worked on these problems. The most comprehensive estimates come from Compton (1985), supplemented by Compton and Power (1986) on the one hand, and from Eversley and Herr (1985) on the other. Compton (1985, 213–15) uses a number of methods of calculation to produce for the Catholic population in 1981 three estimates, of 38.2 per cent, 38.6 per cent, and 37.6 per cent. In his later article, co-authored with Power (1986, 95) he proposes 38.5 per cent as the likeliest figure. Eversley and Herr, using a quite different set of calculations, concluded that the Catholic population in 1981 was at least 39.1 per cent, and might have been over 41 per cent (Eversley and Herr 1985, 10). The arguments on both sides are highly technical, and as a non-demographer I admit to being unable to choose between them. The gap between them, however, is not immense. In rough terms, one can assume that Catholics in 1981 formed two-fifths of the population or perhaps a little less.

On one other feature of the population there is less disagreement. The authorities concur in finding that the Catholic population is rising. In one of his latest publications Compton (1987, 246) suggests that by 1986 Catholics comprised 40 per cent of the population, and Eversley and Herr would presumably put the figure a little higher. This results from a higher Catholic birth-rate, and a consequently higher proportion of Catholics in the younger age groups—Eversley and Herr (1985, 11) calculate that Catholics in 1981 were 36.4 per cent of the population over 15, but 46.5 per cent of the population under 15. Whether this will ultimately produce a Catholic majority is more problematical. Compton and Coward (1989), in their exhaustive study of fertility in Northern Ireland, demonstrate that Catholic fertility has been rapidly falling towards Protestant levels, and that Catholic attitudes towards family planning have been moving towards those held by Protestants. Since Catholic emigration is higher than Protestant, they conclude that 'the attainment of a Catholic majority in Northern Ireland through demographic means seems an unlikely event' (p. 215). Demographic forecasts are of course hazardous: they can be upset by unanticipated changes in fertility or in emigration. But, to put it at its lowest, one cannot rely on population changes to solve the Northern Ireland problem. For the foreseeable future, the accommodation which has to be worked out is between a narrow majority of Protestants and a large minority of Catholics.

2

Some Religious Aspects

My purpose in this chapter is to examine how far Northern Ireland
is segregated by religion into two communities. I shall do this by
examining in turn a number of social institutions which have been
singled out—by some writers at least—as linked with religion. To
begin with, rather obviously, come the Churches themselves. Then
will come the Orange Order, residential segregation, segregation at
work, voluntary social activities, endogamy, and segregated education.

THE CHURCHES

The Christian Churches are so important in Northern Ireland
society that, paradoxically, there is little literature directly on them.
Perhaps the only book to survey their impact is the magisterial
survey by two Methodist authors, Eric Gallagher and Stanley
Worrall, *Christians in Ulster, 1968–1980* (1982). But generally the
Churches are so widely influential that it is difficult to disentangle
their role from that of the other institutions of society, and most of
the evidence for their importance comes from the general literature
on Northern Ireland.

One way of measuring the importance of the Churches is by
church attendance figures. By international standards these are high.
Rose's survey in 1968 found that 95 per cent of Catholics claimed to
go to church at least once a week. In 1978, Moxon-Browne found
the figure was 90 per cent. In 1986, Smith found that the figure was
still 90 per cent. Figures for Protestants were, as in most countries,
lower, but even among them Rose found that 66 per cent claimed to
go to church at least once a month, Moxon-Browne found that 59
per cent claimed to do so, and Smith found that 53 per cent made the
same claim (Rose 1971, 496; Moxon-Browne 1983, 125; Mr Smith's
figures are not included in the published report on his data (Smith
1987*b*), but he has kindly made them available to me).

Church affiliation is important, not just for itself, but because it
spills over into other activities. Barritt and Carter (1962, 75) drew

attention to the lively social life within the Protestant Churches: 'congregations are commonly of a considerable size, and can thus support a wide range of ancillary activities, such as women's guilds, youth groups, badminton clubs, and men's discussion fellowships'. On the other side of the divide, Darby (1976, 155) noted that 'Catholic associations like the St Vincent de Paul society, the Legion of Mary and parish youth clubs have received considerable support. The Catholic church has also been closely associated with parish socials, whist drives and bingo games, which has the double benefit of providing opportunities for social intercourse and supplementing parish funds.' The Norwegian anthropologist Larsen (1982*a*, 152) noted the following church-related activities in the small town which she studied: 'sermons, Sunday schools, missionary societies, youth clubs, young wives' groups, Mothers' Union, Senior Church Members' Club, Bible study groups, choirs, social evenings, outings during summer, Girl Guides and Boy Scouts, Girls' and Boys' Brigades, indoor sports like bowling, badminton and table tennis and—for some reason or other only on the Catholic side—bingo.' She added: 'it is possible to be occupied every evening of the week with some sort of church work, and very many people are'.

There are, however, factors which limit the responsibility of the Churches for maintaining the community cleavage. In the first place, their outreach over the population is uneven. It is probably weakest among working-class Protestants in Belfast: the studies of this group by Nelson (1975, 1984) and Jenkins (1982, 1983) contain rather few references to the Churches, which suggests that they meant little to many of Nelson's and Jenkins's informants. Indeed, even in working-class Catholic areas of Belfast the Church is probably less influential than it is in smaller towns and the countryside. Darby (1986, 36, 121) reports that church attendance was estimated by local clergy at 65 per cent in one Catholic area of Belfast, and at less than 33 per cent in another.

Secondly, some Church leaders and members have worked actively to assuage community divisions. This certainly does not apply to all: the Revd Ian Paisley, for instance, has done all he can to block closer relations between the Protestant and Roman Catholic Churches (Bruce 1986, especially 221–6). But a reading of Gallagher and Worrall's *Christians in Ulster, 1968–1980* (1982) will show that Church leaders have, on the whole, acted as bridge builders. Indeed the leaders of the four main Churches—Catholic, Presbyterian,

Church of Ireland, Methodist—meet regularly, and probably more often than their counterparts in most parts of Christendom.

Their example has been followed—or anticipated—lower down the ecclesiastical scale. Ian Ellis has published a directory of *Peace and Reconciliation Projects in Ireland* (1984). It lists eighty-three such projects. Thirty-six of them have an explicit religious basis; a number of others, I can state from personal knowledge, were founded by people whose motivation was religious. Perhaps the best known of these reconciliation groups is the Corrymeela Community, whose story has been told by Alf McCreary (1975) and by the founder, Ray Davey, in his autobiography *Take Away This Hate* (n.d.). Founded in 1965 by a group of Presbyterians, the community now consists of an interdenominational body of Protestants and Catholics. At its centre on the north Antrim coast it has hosted conferences, workshops, and holidays for all kinds of groups, often bringing together from across the divide those who would otherwise never meet.

A third reason for not overstating the contribution of the Churches to the community divide is that the Protestant community is in its turn subdivided. In the first place, there is the division between denominations. Nearly fifty were listed in the 1981 census. Most of these were very small, but several were large enough to account for a significant segment of the Protestant population. As was explained in the previous chapter, there are difficulties in the way of interpreting census data on religion in Northern Ireland, so no precise figures are available. The most careful estimate of denominational strengths has been made by Compton (1978, 81) who, extrapolating from the 1971 census, suggests that the proportionate strength of Protestant denominations in that year was as stated in Table 2.1

These denominational divisions are not trivial. In the distant past (the seventeenth, eighteenth, and part of the nineteenth centuries), there was much bitterness between different denominations, for the Church of Ireland was the Established Church, and all other Churches, Protestant as well as Catholic, were subject to various disabilities. Such tensions are muted today, yet several of the participant-observers have found continuing traces. Harris (1972, 156) found that, in the border area which she studied, 'to a degree surprising to the outsider, the different denominations displayed mutual hostility'. Presbyterians remembered past persecution by

Table 2.1. Protestant denominations, 1971

Denomination	% of total population	% of total Protestant population
Presbyterian	28.2	45.3
Church of Ireland (i.e. Anglican)	23.3	37.5
Methodist	5.0	8.0
Baptist	1.1	1.8
Brethren	1.1	1.8
Congregationalist	0.7	1.1
Free Presbyterian	0.5	0.8
Other denominations	2.3	3.7
Total	62.2	100.00

Sources: The figures in the first column are from Compton (1978, 81).
The figures in the final column are my calculation from Compton's data.

Anglicans (p. 159); both Presbyterians and members of the Church of Ireland resented the poaching of their members by smaller denominations (p. 158). Harris carried out her field-work in the 1950s, when the Churches may have been more important than they are today: but her finding is echoed by more recent studies. McFarlane (1978, 47) found tension between Presbyterian and Church of Ireland twenty-five years later in a village many miles away. Leyton (1975, 11), studying yet another area, found a cleavage between high-status Presbyterians and members of the Church of Ireland on the one hand and low-status Baptists and Brethren on the other.

The denominational division is only one of those in the Protestant community. There is also a division between liberal and fundamentalist Protestants. This cleavage has been explored most thoroughly in a survey of Belfast Protestants conducted by Boal, Campbell, and Livingstone, and reported on by Boal and Livingstone (1986). The researchers found that it cut across denominational boundaries. While the smaller denominations like Baptists and Brethren were overwhelmingly fundamentalist, and members of the Church of Ireland were mostly not, the Presbyterians and Methodists were quite evenly divided (Boal and Livingstone 1986, 170). The division had practical effects. Fundamentalists were more likely to be

Sabbatarians, to be distrustful of contact with Catholics, and to give a low priority to social problems like unemployment and the nuclear threat. In politics, while the Official Unionist Party drew support from both wings, the Democratic Unionists were more likely to find favour among fundamentalists and the Alliance Party among liberals (pp. 170–1).

The divisions between different kinds of Protestant are, to be sure, mild when compared to the overriding cleavage between Catholic and Protestant. Nevertheless, as social institutions the different Protestant denominations remain important, because each tends to generate its own network of ancillary organizations. If the Churches as such were the main source of division, one might expect to find, not two, but many more than two communities in Northern Ireland.

THE ORANGE ORDER

It might be argued that the inter-Protestant divisions just outlined are subsumed in the Orange Order, which acts as an umbrella organization open to Protestants of all kinds, regardless of denomination and regardless of their position on the fundamentalist–liberal spectrum. Many writers have been impressed by the importance of this society. Set-piece discussions of it have been provided in a book by Tony Gray, *The Orange Order* (1972), in a paper by the sociologist David Roberts (1971), and in an excellent article by the Norwegian anthropologist Sidsel Larsen (1982*b*). An insider's view is provided in the official history by M. W. Dewar, John Brown, and S. E. Long (1967). A number of other studies throw light on it in passing.

From such sources we can see that the Order plays a large part in the lives of many Protestants. Larsen (1982*b*) has described the excitement generated among the Protestants of one country town in preparing for, and then celebrating, the Orangemen's annual parade on the Twelfth of July. Wright (1973, 249–50) has described its similar role in a working-class district of Belfast. The child psychiatrist Morris Fraser (1973, 35, 111) has stressed the influence of the Junior Orange Association in socializing young Protestants into the beliefs of their community. Harris (1972, 162–7, 192–7) has described the multiple functions of Orangeism in a rural area: a bridge between denominations; an arena for friendly competition between lodges; an opportunity for celebration and display; a means of instilling discipline into the irresponsible; a forum where the low-status Protestant can make his voice heard.

Its influence has, especially in the past, extended considerably further than that. John Harbinson, in his study of *The Ulster Unionist Party, 1882–1973* (1973, 90–1), has shown how powerful its position was in the Unionist Party during the period that the latter ruled Northern Ireland. We have it on the word of an Orange historian that the membership of the Ulster Special Constabulary was always 'predominantly Orange' (Long 1967, 171). Gallagher and Worrall (1982, 15), who as leading Methodists had experience of the Order's power, state that 'it protected the employment of Protestants by its influence over employers, which is a polite way of saying that it contrived systematic discrimination against Catholics'. They also stress the pressures which the Order can bring to bear on Protestant clergy (p. 196).

Yet this Order, which is open to male Protestants of all denominations, formally excludes Roman Catholics. To Catholics indeed, as Larsen has pointed out (1982*b*, 288) an Orange parade can have very different meanings from those it possesses for Protestants. What Catholics observe are 'the massive demonstration of control of territory . . . a demonstration of Protestant power and a proof that nothing has changed in almost three hundred years since the Boyne.'

The importance of the Order can, however, be overstated. Membership figures are not published, but Rose (1971, 257) calculated from his survey data that its membership in 1968 comprised 32 per cent of Protestant men, or about 90,000 people: a figure which accords well with the 95–96,000 claimed by the Grand Secretary of the Order in an interview sixteen years later (*Irish Times*, 10 July 1984). Thus there are many more Protestants outside the Order than in it.

The impact of the Order varies widely from area to area. Harris (1972, 162) found that all but four Protestant men in the rural border area which she studied were Orangemen. Larsen (1982*b*, 284) was told that membership reached 90 per cent in the town, also not far from the border, where she did her field-work. But McFarlane (1978, 229), studying a village in a quiet area further from the border, found that only 92 out of 201 Protestant males belonged to the Order. Bufwack (1982, 98) and Buckley (1982, 139), describing Catholic-majority areas, found that few local Protestants joined the

Order. Jenkins's reports (1982, 1983) on a working-class suburb of Belfast suggest that the Order was of negligible importance there. Rose (1971, 258) estimated that only 15 per cent of Orangemen lived in Belfast, although the city contained about 28 per cent of the total Protestant population of Northern Ireland (figure calculated from data in Compton 1978, 80). It would seem that the Order is strongest near the border, is stronger where Protestants are in a majority, and is stronger in the countryside than in the cities, where other outlets for social life are more numerous. Even those generalizations, however, do not apply uniformly. Derry is near the border, but Desmond Bell (1987, 173) found in his study of Protestant youth in the city that their interest in Orangeism has declined over the last ten years.

Orangeism is also a mainly male phenomenon. Its female counterpart, the Association of Loyal Orangewomen, has, according to the Grand Secretary of the Order, only about 5,000 members (*Irish Times*, 10 July 1984). Harris (1972, 193) found that in her area, where male Orangeism was so strong, many women disapproved of it, as encouraging drunkenness, and as deflecting men's attention from their duty to their Churches.

Orangeism also seems to have had a differential impact on classes. Tony Gray (1972, 198) received conflicting information about the Order's class structure, but most observers have found that it is more popular among low-status Protestants than among high-status ones. McFarlane (1978) reported that, in the village which he studied, members were almost exclusively working-class (p. 229), and that the middle class scorned them as working-class bigots (p. 225). Wright (1973, 247) noted that 'Orangeism has been, particularly in the cities and towns of Ulster, a predominantly lower-class institution.' Barritt and Carter (1962, 62) observed that in general the Order received 'little support from the higher income groups, and practically none from professional men and intellectuals, who tend to look upon the order as an antiquated, intolerant and reactionary group'.

To conclude, the Orange Order certainly divides Protestant from Catholic. But the impression left by the literature is that it also divides Protestant from Protestant, along regional, class, gender, and (if Bell's findings in Derry apply generally) generational lines.

RESIDENTIAL SEGREGATION

Before the troubles began, little had been published on the extent of residential segregation in Northern Ireland. A geographer then at Queen's University, Emrys Jones, had published a paper (1956) showing that segregation was considerable in Belfast, particularly in working-class areas. Barritt and Carter (1962, 53) suggested that the phenomenon was widespread: 'in the towns, the two communities tend to live apart; . . . in the country (so far as it was affected by the Plantations) the Irish tended to be excluded from the good valley land and banished to the mountains'. However, this was only an impressionistic judgement: research has not yet been done on areas outside Belfast by which its validity could be tested.

During the 1970s, most research on segregation was concentrated in Belfast. Two geographers, Poole and Boal (1973), published a paper examining the situation on the eve of the riots of 1969. They discovered that, even then, Belfast was a highly segregated city. Sixty-nine per cent of Protestants lived in streets which were 91 per cent or more Protestant, and 56 per cent of Catholics lived in streets which were 91 per cent or more Catholic. Only 32 per cent of the population lived in streets which could be described as even in the loosest sense of the term 'mixed' (i.e. less than 91 per cent either Protestant or Catholic) (p. 14). In a later study Boal, Murray, and Poole (1976, 106) showed that by the end of 1972 the proportion of the population living in mixed streets, on the same definition of 'mixed', had dropped to 23 per cent, while the proportion of Catholics living in streets 91 per cent or more Catholic had risen to 70 per cent, and the proportion of Protestants living in streets 91 per cent or more Protestant had risen to 78 per cent. The increase in segregation was largely brought about by the widespread movement of population which took place in the wake of the disturbances of 1969–72: a movement which in the view of one pair of researchers may have affected 15,000 families (Darby and Morris 1974).

However, it should not be assumed that Belfast is typical of Northern Ireland as a whole. The differences became clear when, in the 1980s, research into segregation began to spread beyond Belfast. A pioneer study was Michael Poole's (1982) on twenty-six Northern Ireland towns. To facilitate comparison, Poole applied a 'dissimilarity index'. For the details of how this is constructed I must refer the reader to his article, but, in outline, a town would score 100 if every single Catholic lived in one part of the town, and every single Protestant lived in another part; and it would score 0 if Protestants and Catholics were distributed in exactly the same proportions in all parts of the town. What emerges from Poole's figures is the exceptional degree of segregation in Belfast. It comes top of his list, with a dissimilarity index of 76. The only other towns to score more than 50 are Armagh (74), Lurgan (73), and Derry (63). Most scored in the thirties and twenties, and a few went even lower—the bottom score was achieved by Randalstown, with 14. Poole has since extended his researches to all the towns in Northern Ireland, and, though he has not yet published his results, he informs me that the general picture—of most small towns being much less segregated than Belfast—is confirmed.

More recent data have enabled us to examine the situation, not just in the towns but across the whole of Northern Ireland, countryside included. Compton and Power (1986) were able to obtain data from the 1981 census for all the 2,800 enumeration districts in Northern Ireland. These enumeration districts are very small, averaging little more than 500 persons in each. To use them would be if anything to overestimate the degree of practical segregation in daily life. Compton and Power found that those living in homogeneous enumeration districts came to 38.8 per cent of the population (pp. 90–1). (Their definition of a homogeneous enumeration district is one in which either less than 5 per cent of the population was enumerated as Catholic, or less than 5 per cent was enumerated as belonging to the various Protestant denominations.) This figure squares remarkably with the subjective impressions of respondents to Smith's survey undertaken in 1986 (Smith 1987*b*, 56). In that survey 38 per cent of the sample stated that they lived in neighbourhoods which were either nearly all Protestant (23 per cent) or nearly all Catholic (15 per cent). One can sum up the discussion so far by suggesting that, in Northern Ireland as a whole, in round figures about 35 to 40 per cent of the population live in segregated neighbourhoods.

Where residential segregation exists, it can have powerful effects. A geographer at the Queen's University of Belfast, Frederick W. Boal (1976, 87–95), has described the functions which a residentially segregated area can have for its inhabitants. It gives them a base for self-defence. It enables them to avoid embarrassing contacts with unfriendly outsiders. It helps them to preserve their way of life. For the more aggressive members of the group, it provides a base from which they can attack their enemies. On the other hand, as Darby (1986, 29) has noted, lack of segregation can have benign effects. He points out that 'there has been a high correlation between integrated housing and the absence of overt community violence'.

A further effect of residential segregation is that it can reinforce other forms of segregation. This has been strikingly illustrated in another paper by Boal (1969), in which he studied two contiguous working-class areas of Belfast, one 98 per cent Catholic (Clonard), the other 99 per cent Protestant (Shankill). Boal found that the people of the two areas tended to read different newspapers, support different football teams, patronize different shops. They sent their children to different schools. Their kinship networks were totally distinct. When they made visits outside their immediate area, it was to quite different parts of the city. Some of his informants would even go to a bus stop further away from their home, but in their own religious territory, rather than use a bus stop nearer at hand but in the wrong territory (p. 41). In the weeks coming up to the Orangemen's festival on the Twelfth of July, streets in the Protestant area were profusely decorated while no decorations at all were to be seen in the Catholic area. Yet Boal did his field-work in 1967–8, when community relations were relatively good. Since the riots of August 1969, a high wall has physically separated the two areas which he studied.

Boal's study of the Shankill/Clonard divide in 1967–8 can be compared with a much more recent study by Darby (1986) of two other parts of Belfast where Protestant and Catholic areas adjoin each other. In one such area, Kileen/Banduff, a limited amount of contact took place across the community divide (pp. 100–1). In the more run-down Upper Ashbourne area, contacts were even fewer (p. 112). In both areas, the Housing Executive, Belfast Corporation, and social-welfare agencies had separate offices for the two communities, staffed by different workers. So, as Darby notes (p. 142), 'even the low-level contact offered by visiting the same office or dealing with the same social workers was not available'.

Residential segregation exists not just by religion. It exists also by class, and the results there can be quite as dramatic. Yet another study by Boal (1971) illustrates the point. Shortly after he completed the study, described above, of two working-class areas divided by religion, Boal carried out a study of two other contiguous areas of

Belfast, both predominantly Protestant, but divided by class—low-status Taughmonagh and high-status Upper Malone. He found that the degree of segregation was at least as striking. The two populations had visiting links with quite different parts of the city. They belonged to different clubs and societies. Their children attended different schools. Those who belonged to the same denomination attended different churches of that denomination.

Residential segregation by religion is most notable in working-class areas of Belfast (Boal *et al.* 1976, 99), in parts of Derry, in a few of the smaller towns, and some tracts of the countryside. Where it exists it may be the most potent factor in keeping the communities separated. But it affects only a minority of the population.

SEGREGATION AT WORK

If segregation by residence is incomplete, what about segregation at work? Barritt and Carter (1962, 100–4) in the earliest investigation of the problem came across a variety of patterns. Some firms employed only Protestants, and a smaller number only Catholics. Others recruited from both denominations, but kept Catholics in particular departments or in lower-grade posts. Others again mixed Protestant and Catholic workers on equal terms. Barritt and Carter did not, however, feel able to estimate what proportion of firms were in which category. Harris (1972, 139–43) noticed a tendency for Catholics to go to Catholic shops, and Protestants to Protestant ones, in the country area which she studied. Boal (1969, 41) noted the same phenomenon in a working-class area of Belfast. Aunger (1975, 5) pointed out that, in so far as a Catholic middle class existed, it existed largely to service its own community: he noted that teachers and clergy made up nearly twice as large a proportion of the Catholic middle class as they did of Protestants.

However, such patterns were not universal. For instance, if some participant-observers noted that each community preferred to buy from its own, others noticed a fair degree of mixing (Bufwack 1982, 82; Darby 1986, 50, referring to the market town of Dunville). Richard Rose found in 1968 that only 20 per cent of Protestants and 16 per cent of Catholics reported that all those they worked with were of the same religion as themselves (Rose 1971, 307). Ten years later, Moxon-Browne found the figures virtually unchanged: 20 per cent for Protestants and 15 per cent for Catholics (data provided by Mr Moxon-Browne). This was a lesser degree of segregation than respondents reported among their relations, friends, or neighbours.

The most thorough investigation of this subject has taken place quite recently. Gerald Chambers (1987), as part of a study of equality and inequality in Northern Ireland commissioned by the Standing Advisory Commission on Human Rights, conducted a large-scale investigation of workplace practices, involving interviews with the managers responsible for personnel matters at 260 establishments, stratified to control for size of workplace (p. 5). The interviewers found that employers were very conscious of the religious composition of their work-forces (p. 25), and indeed the great majority were, when pressed, prepared to estimate the religious composition to within 5 per cent (Chambers 1987, table 306).

The figures that emerged were as follows. Fifty-seven per cent of work-forces were described by the respondent as majority Protestant and 23 per cent as majority Catholic. Ten per cent were described as divided 50:50, and in the remaining 10 per cent of cases the respondent was unable or unwilling to reply (Chambers 1987, 101). Where there was a majority in one direction or another, it was often very large. Of the Catholic-majority workplaces, 43 per cent were 95 per cent or more Catholic. Of the Protestant-majority workplaces, 39 per cent were 95 per cent or more Protestant (p. 103). Though Chambers himself does not say so, one can deduce from these figures that about 32 per cent of respondents reported their work-forces as being virtually (i.e. 95 per cent or more) homogeneous. However, it does not follow that 32 per cent of employees worked in such establishments. Larger workplaces were less likely to be homogeneous than small ones.

On the whole, then, it would appear that segregation at work is one of the less acute forms of segregation in Northern Ireland. It does not of course follow that Protestant and Catholic are always employed at equal levels of responsibility. As we shall see in the next chapter, Protestants are more likely than Catholics to be in high-status occupations, and this has important consequences for community relations.

VOLUNTARY SOCIAL ACTIVITIES

A number of researchers have examined the extent to which voluntary activities in Northern Ireland are segregated by religion. The pioneer investigators in this field, as in so many others, were Barritt and Carter (1962, 144–52). Another writer who devotes some space to the subject is John Darby, in his book *Conflict in Northern Ireland: The Development of a Polarised Community* (1976, 140–61). Rosemary Harris (1972, 132–48) examines the patterns of segregation in her area of study, and a number of participant-observers have followed her example (e.g. Galway 1978, 124–34; Buckley 1982, 136–49; Larsen 1982*a*, 150–6).

These writers discovered some fairly startling instances of segregation. Barritt and Carter (1962, 145–6) found separate amateur-dramatics groups for Catholics and Protestants in several towns. They reported that among 42 youth clubs affiliated to the National Association of Boys' Clubs, 21 were Protestant, 14 Catholic, and only 7 fully mixed. Darby quotes a geographer who studied Lurgan in the peaceful 1960s and found that it contained a Protestant Mechanics' Institute and a Catholic Working Men's Club, segregated old people's homes, a Catholic Gardening and Crafts Club, a Catholic Young Men's Association, and an Orange Lodge (Darby 1976, 156, quoting Kirk 1967). Galway (1978, 124–33) noted how in the small Fermanagh village of Glenlevan, voluntary activities were largely segregated, and that, even when a group was set up with the intention of organizing across the community divide, one side or the other tended to fall away.

However, segregation is not complete. The participant-observation studies bring out that it can vary considerably with the area. In a peaceful district such as that studied by Buckley (1982, 141–4) non-sectarian organizations are quite strong. Another factor which affects the degree of division is class. Several observers note that middle-class groups are more likely to be integrated than working-class ones (Barritt and Carter 1962, 144–5; Darby 1976, 156; Larsen 1982*a*, 153).

Among sports and games, a complicated pattern exists. The highest degree of segregation applies to Gaelic games, which have an extensive following among Catholics but practically none among Protestants. On the other side, rugby and hockey have in practice been played largely by Protestants (Barritt and Carter 1962, 149;

Darby 1976, 153; Sugden and Bairner 1986). Association football is widely played in both communities, but Protestants and Catholics often support different teams. Boal (1969, 38), in his paper on contiguous Catholic and Protestant districts of Belfast, already referred to in the section on residential segregation, found that 73 per cent of respondents in Catholic Clonard supported Glasgow Celtic, and none supported Linfield, while 74 per cent of respondents in Protestant Shankill supported Linfield, and none supported Glasgow Celtic. Perhaps mixing is greatest in the high-status sport of golf (Barritt and Carter 1962, 151).

There is one exception to the apparent generalization that the working class is more segregated than the middle class. The trade-union movement is predominantly working-class, and yet it organizes both Catholic and Protestant workers. Catholic workers have not been organized into a distinct trade-union federation as has happened in a number of continental countries. However, a closer look at the operation of the trade-union movement suggests that it is less of an integrating force than might be supposed. A number of writers have pointed out that unity has been maintained only by avoiding issues which might separate Catholic workers from Protestant (Darby 1976, 150–1; Rolston 1980; Boyd 1984). The reluctance of the unions to take up contentious questions has been noted in a recent piece of research into workplace activities:

We asked all our union informants to tell us about their experiences of dealing with complaints of discrimination at the shop floor level. Very few shop stewards have experience of taking up complaints in a formal way and there is extreme reluctance to get involved in what are seen as sectarian issues. In general, when a shop steward says that he or she is there to represent all the members what is meant is that issues which draw attention to the sectarian divide but which might be crucial to *some* workers can't be taken up. (Chambers 1987, 50.)

No writer claims that segregation in voluntary activities is the most important factor in keeping the communities divided. But it forms part of the total pattern, and therefore deserves discussion.

ENDOGAMY

A further source of division between the communities is the lack of intermarriage between them. In the terminology of anthropologists, the two communities in Northern Ireland are highly endogamous—they marry within the tribe. The pioneer investigators of this topic are not, for once, Barritt and Carter. They mention the subject (1962, 26–7) but more as a consequence of the religious division than as a source of it. The first serious treatment of the issue came in Rosemary Harris's study of Ballybeg (1972, 143–6).

Harris found that, in the area which she studied, endogamy was the most powerful single factor in maintaining the community divide. The reason lay in the enormous importance of kinship ties. Normally it was only with their own kin that people got on to really close terms; if all one's kin came from one's own community, then the way was blocked to getting to know people from the other community intimately, and prejudice flourished. Harris found that this mechanism prevailed in her study-area. Intermarriage was rare, and when it happened it bridged no gaps because the husband dropped most of his former contacts.

Harris's research covered, of course, just one locality. Subsequent research, however, has shown that, in Northern Ireland as a whole, intermarriage is as rare as she found it to be in Ballybeg. Rose (1971, 329, 341) calculated from his survey data of 1968 that only 4 per cent of the population married across religious lines. The equivalent figure in Moxon-Browne's survey of 1978 was 4.5 per cent (Moxon-Browne 1983, 130). A special tabulation of the 1971 census undertaken for Lee (1979, 167) showed that Catholic–Protestant marriages accounted for something under 2 per cent of currently married couples in Northern Ireland—though as Lee points out, the census figures cannot take into account the extent of conversion, emigration, and underenumeration. Compton and Coward's large-scale survey of women, undertaken in 1983, indicated that 3.6 per cent of current marriages were mixed, but that 6 per cent had been mixed at the time of marriage, thus suggesting a substantial number of conversions by one spouse or the other (Compton and Coward 1989, 186). Somewhat more Catholics had converted to Protestantism than vice versa (p. 192). Smith's survey data from 1986 showed that 98 per cent of married Protestants and 95 per cent of married Catholics were married to someone from their own group (Smith 1987b, 64). One surprising finding reported by both Compton and Coward (1989, 186) and Smith (1987b, 64) is that the proportion of mixed marriages is higher in younger age groups. This suggests that, in one respect at least, Northern Ireland is not becoming increasingly polarized.

It does not follow that endogamy everywhere plays as important a role in keeping the communities separate as Harris found in Ballybeg. One would guess that in areas of high residential segregation, like the working-class districts of Belfast, sheer lack of contact with the other side is what matters most. In middle-class circles, kinship matters less, and friendships are frequently formed with non-kin: as a participant-observer in the Belfast middle class for eighteen years, I can report that cross-community friendships are not infrequent. In some areas, mixed-marriage rates are higher than in Northern Ireland as a whole. The geographer Michael Poole has done some research on this and, although he has not yet published his results, he tells me that the mixed-marriage rate reaches 10 per cent in some north-coast towns, and even 22 per cent in one north Londonderry village.

The community studies vary in their findings. Darby (1986, 49–50) found a number of mixed marriages in the country town of Dunville. Campbell (1978) found in Glenarm that though the level of intermarriage was low—there were five mixed households out of 181 (p. 43)—where kinship bonds existed across the religious divide they were maintained. Buckley (1982, 64) reported that in Upper Tullagh mixed marriages did not arouse disapproval, though he also notes that they occurred infrequently. Elsewhere, however, studies suggest that intermarriage is frowned upon every bit as much as Harris found in Ballybeg. McFarlane (1979) reports that in his area of study such marriages varied only in degree of unacceptability. Leyton (1975, 57) reported that in his border district only one mixed marriage occurred during his period of research, 'and a police escort was necessary at the wedding ceremony to protect the couple from the wrath of their families'.

One feature of endogamy is that on the whole it does not operate between Protestant denominations. True, some evangelical sects discountenance marriage even with members of other Protestant Churches; but they are small groups, accounting for only some 5 per cent of the population. Among the mainstream Protestant denominations, intermarriage appears to be common and relatively free from friction. Harris (1972, 48) reported that in her area, when two people from different Protestant denominations married, the wife almost invariably changed to her husband's Church. Cecil, Offer, and St Leger (1987, 33) noted the same custom in their study of a small town in a different part of Northern Ireland. My impression is that this rule applies generally over the region. It has the advantage that gains and losses made by each denomination are likely to cancel each other out, and so no Church is left feeling dissatisfied. However, this balancing mechanism has not applied to Protestant–Catholic marriages. The insistence of the Catholic Church, at least in the past, on the offspring of the children of all such marriages being brought up as Catholics ensured that it would not. Endogamy emerges from the literature as one of the more important mechanisms by which the communities are kept divided.

SEGREGATED EDUCATION

A striking feature of Northern Ireland society has been the existence of two parallel sets of schools. The 'controlled' schools are in theory non-denominational, but in practice they can be described as Protestant, partly because most Catholic children have been hived off into their own system, and partly because Protestant (but not Catholic) clergy are included on their boards of management (Murray 1985, 22–3). The 'maintained' schools, which attract a slightly lower level of State funding and are less directly controlled by the State, are also in theory open to pupils of all denominations, but in practice they have been set up by the Catholic Church and are avowedly Catholic. Apart from a few individual schools, the only non-segregated sections of the education system are the universities, the colleges of further education, and special schools for handicapped children.

The schools system has attracted more study than any of the other institutions of division. Here again, the pioneer researchers were Barritt and Carter (1962, 77–92), who devoted a chapter to the subject. Among the more important recent studies is a survey of the extent and nature of segregation by a team at what was then the New University of Ulster (Darby *et al.* 1977); a summary by a social psychologist of research on the effects of segregation (Cairns 1987, 118–43); and a survey of the general research findings by Darby and Dunn (1987). The most fascinating single piece of research has been Dominic Murray's book *Worlds Apart* (1985), which is a participant-observation study of two neighbouring primary schools, one Protestant and one Catholic.

I shall not spend time discussing the historical origins of the system, which is outlined in some of these books (Barritt and Carter

1962, 77–87; Murray 1985, 14–30). I shall pass immediately to some of the current problems. First there is the factual question: how far is the education system actually segregated? It is surprisingly hard to obtain statistics. For a period in the 1950s and 1960s the Northern Ireland Ministry of Education used to publish in its annual reports a denominational breakdown of pupils in different types of primary school: from the last of the reports to contain this information, that for 1964, it appears that less than 2 per cent of Catholic pupils were in County schools (as *de facto* Protestant schools were then called), and about 1 per cent of Protestant pupils were in Voluntary schools (as Catholic schools were then termed). Nothing has happened since to make one suppose that the situation has greatly changed. A sample survey of schools carried out in 1976 found that, taking primary and second-level schools together, 71 per cent of schools were either totally Catholic or totally Protestant, and only 3 per cent of schools had more than 5 per cent of their pupils from the 'wrong' religious group (Darby *et al.* 1977, 75). (I am using the term 'second-level' rather than 'secondary' for schools catering for the age-group above 11, because in Northern Ireland the term 'secondary' applies to only one kind of second-level school.) A survey in 1980 indicated that of those leaving Catholic primary schools only about 2 per cent transferred to Protestant second-level schools (Osborne *et al.* 1984, 125). In recent years a small network of integrated schools has developed, both primary and second-level, but in the academic year 1986–7 they still had between them only 900 pupils—out of a total school population of well over 300,000 (Darby and Dunn 1987, 86, 93). When all these fragments of evidence are put together, they suggest that an enormous majority of pupils are educated in schools of their own kind—the percentage must be in the high nineties.

A somewhat less extreme degree of segregation is suggested by Rose's survey data from 1968. Rose (1971, 501) found that 14 per cent of his sample claimed to have had part or all of their education in mixed schools. But one can reconcile this statistic with evidence from other sources if one supposes that most of these respondents had been at schools whose pupils were predominantly of their own kind, with just a sprinkling from the other community.

The next question to discuss is: why does it matter if education is segregated? The strongest defence of the current division has been made by the Catholic bishops in their submission to the New Ireland Forum (Irish Episcopal Conference 1984). The bishops make two main points. The first is that it is unfair to blame the schools for the community division when so many other factors are at work. They quote in support the findings of two researchers into the Northern Ireland education system, James Russell (1974), and John Salters (1970). One can largely accept this point, and indeed no writer that I know of thinks that segregated schooling is the *main* source of the community division. Their second point is more questionable. It is that the Catholic school system has a positively healing effect. They claim that 'the values which are the inspiration of the Catholic school system are incompatible with violence, hatred or intolerance' (p. 28), and they quote Salters's (1970) research as evidence that children in Catholic schools are somewhat more tolerant than those in Protestant schools. This is more dubious. There is other research, as we shall see shortly, which suggests that separate education does have negative effects' on children's attitudes. Moreover, even if it were true that children in *Catholic* schools were taught tolerance and flexibility, this ignores the possible effects on children in Protestant schools. Perhaps it is harder for *them* to learn such virtues, in the absence of Catholic schoolmates.

Certainly there are authors who find unfortunate side-effects in the divided school system. Three different issues can be detected in the literature. One is the claim that the mere fact that the two communities are educated separately allows prejudice and stereotyping to flourish. This point has been made by a psychiatrist, Morris Fraser (1973, 128–42), and a social psychologist, Ken Heskin (1980, 144–7). Their argument is supported by Dominic Murray's participant-observation study (1985, 91–105, 120–3), which uncovered much evidence of stereotyping in the two schools which he examined. The converse proposition—that integration will diminish prejudice—received support from a paper by Liz McWhirter (1983a), which summarizes four pieces of research done into the small number of integrated schools in Northern Ireland. McWhirter concludes that children in such schools readily make friends across the community divide, while the children retain highly positive attitudes to religion—which 'should allay the anxieties of those who fear that Catholic children's religious faith is under threat if they attend a non-Catholic school' (p. 22).

However, the research findings do not all point in the same direction. Rose (1971, 336–7) found that those respondents in his sample who had experienced mixed education were to only a limited degree more open-minded than those who had not. Harris (1972, 137) found that Protestants in her area of study who had been to a Catholic school achieved 'an ease of relationship with the Catholics of their district'; but she also observed that 'it would be idle to pretend that the ensuing contacts between Catholic and Protestant children spread only sweetness and light—boys everywhere gang up and what more natural than that at this school the gangs should be recruited on a sectarian basis'. A social psychologist at Queen's University, Karen Trew (1986, 102), reports a small-scale study which found that 'seven years' attendance at an integrated primary school had little impact on the intergroup perceptions of first-year secondary school pupils'.

So far the evidence for and against segregation is inconclusive. A second issue, however, needs to be considered—this is that the separate-school systems are divisive because they teach different curricula. Many observers, from Barritt and Carter (1962, 91–2) onwards, have noted that the two school systems differ not just in the religious instruction they provide but in other aspects of the curriculum: Catholic schools stress Irish history, Irish games, and the Irish language, while Protestant schools emphasize their Britishness. There is certainly anecdotal evidence in support of such claims. One of the raciest passages in Bernadette Devlin's autobiography, *The Price of my Soul* (1969, 62–70), is that in which she describes her encounters with the fanatically anti-British vice-principal of the Catholic School in Dungannon which she had attended. Another example can be cited from an article by a Catholic social worker: 'I remember my history teacher saying: "That is the answer that the (state) examiner will want to receive. Now I will tell you the truth"' (Cavanagh 1981, 33). Nor is the evidence merely anecdotal. Robinson (1971*a,b*), surveying 1,000 schoolchildren in Derry, found that Protestant and Catholic children differed widely in their perceptions of nationality and local history, and that the gap widened with the length of time in schooling.

However, the differences in curriculum can be overstated. Rose's survey (1971, 501) found that only 39 per cent of Catholics (as well as 4 per cent of Protestants) had been taught Irish at school. The most recent research on history teaching (Corken 1989) shows that Irish history is now widely taught in Northern Ireland schools: the difference between Protestant and Catholic schools is one only of degree. As far as games are concerned, the New University of Ulster survey found that, while it was true that Gaelic games were exclusive to Catholic schools, and rugby, cricket, and hockey were almost exclusive to Protestant ones, there was a considerable number of sports, such as soccer, tennis, netball, and basketball, which were common to both sets of schools (Darby *et al.* 1977, 43–4). Darby and Dunn (1987, 87) note that both sets of schools have in many ways a similar and rather conservative approach to curriculum and the organization of schools, and add that 'the two systems are more similar to each other than either is to the systems in, say, England or the Irish Republic' (p. 95). If there is a difference between the two systems, it is to be found most of all, not in the expected areas of history or the Irish language, but in science and mathematics, to which Catholic schools, particularly in the past, have given less weight than Protestant schools (Osborne and Cormack 1989, 52–3).

The overt curriculum of the two-school systems differs, then, less markedly than might have been expected. However, there is a third way in which the divided school system may have an impact—even if the overt curricula are largely similar, the hidden curricula may differ. As Cairns points out (1987, 128), not everything that is taught in schools is taught by teachers, and he quotes a study by a lecturer in education at the University of Ulster, Roger Austin (1986), which shows that Protestant and Catholic children differ considerably in their playground rhymes and games. More important, also, than what the teachers formally teach may be the values which they implicitly endorse. Here Dominic Murray's participant-observation study *Worlds Apart* (1985) provides some important information.

As Murray himself says, he concentrated more on the staff room than the classroom (p. 137). It is his conversations with teachers which provide the most interesting insights in his book. What comes through is that the two sets of teachers are putting across two sets of values. The differences are not primarily in the religious sphere: they are more to do with national identity and the legitimacy of the State. In the Protestant school the British identity of staff and pupils was stressed, while in the Catholic school the staff were actively hostile to British symbols (pp. 60–6). The Protestant school was on friendly terms with State bodies, while the Catholic school viewed them with suspicion (pp. 80–3).

On both sides, what seemed natural to one group could give offence to the other. Murray quotes a revealing pair of conversations. The Protestant school flew the Union Jack daily, a practice on

which a Catholic teacher commented: 'They fly the flag down there
to show that they are more British than the British themselves. It's
also to let us know that they are the lords and masters and we
(Catholics) should be continually aware of it' (p. 113). On the other
hand, the Catholic school was full of religious symbols, and a
Protestant teacher commented: 'It's hard to escape the view that a
special show is being put on for our benefit .... They must know
that these are the very things that we object to, yet still they are
flaunted everywhere' (p. 114).

Murray's study was of just two schools out of nearly 1,400 in
Northern Ireland. It may be that the contrasts between the two
schools he selected were unusually sharp, and were due to class as
well as religious differences—he notes that the Catholic school was
mainly working class in its pupil composition while the Protestant
one was mainly middle class (Murray 1985, 145). Another study, of
co-operation between schools in four areas of Northern Ireland
(Dunn *et al.* 1984), shows that, in some settings at least, relations
seem to have been more amicable than they were in Murray's pair of
schools. Nevertheless, even if Murray's schools are only partially
representative, then segregated education is divisive, not so much
because of what is formally taught, but because of the 'hidden
agenda', the values—political more than religious—which are in-
formally put across to the pupils.

Evidence from a recent survey lends support to this view (Smith
1987*b*, table 101). It shows, as other surveys have done (Darby and
Dunn 1987, 91), that Catholics are in principle well-disposed—much
better disposed than their bishops—to the idea of integrated education. In reply to the question 'should Area Education Boards do
more to encourage integrated schools?', 73 per cent of Catholics
replied 'yes'. But, within the Catholic population, easily the least
sympathetic group were supporters of Sinn Féin—only 53 per cent
of them replied 'yes'. This can hardly be because they particularly
value the religious ethos of the schools—Sinn Féin supports the
IRA, and the IRA has been repeatedly denounced by the Catholic
Church. It is presumably because they particularly value the schools
as a protection for the Catholic community's political identity.

Segregation by religion is not the only kind of segregation
practised in Northern Ireland schools. Many, particularly on
the Catholic side, segregated by sex. At primary level, a number of fee-paying schools exist, which are patronized chiefly by

middle-class Protestants. They are particularly prominent in the Belfast area: so much so that one writer on Belfast education has found it appropriate to speak of three education systems in the city, not two (Fee 1980, 1983). At second level, there is segregation by ability. Comprehensive schools, now normal in Britain, exist in only a few areas of Northern Ireland: in most places a minority of able pupils go on to a grammar school (whether Protestant or Catholic), while the rest go on to a secondary school (whether Protestant or Catholic). However, these further forms of segregation take place within the overriding Protestant/Catholic dichotomy.

RELIGION AND SOCIAL STRUCTURE: A SURVEY

In this chapter I have examined a number of institutions, religious and social, to ascertain what contribution they make to the community divide. Some are less important than others. Segregation at work affects only a minority of workers. Differing patterns of voluntary activities complement and strengthen the other divisions, but are not by themselves claimed by any author to be of primary importance. Residential segregation is important in some areas: indeed it may be the most important factor of all in keeping the communities divided for the 35–40 per cent who are affected by it. But that leaves 60–5 per cent of the population who are not. The Churches themselves, and the Orange Order, certainly divide Protestant from Catholic, but they also divide Protestants from each other.

The two factors which do most to divide Protestants as a whole from Catholics as a whole are endogamy and separate education. These are maintained with most emphasis by the Roman Catholic Church. It is the Catholic authorities which have most consistently maintained the right to develop their own school system and to enfold within it the children of their own community (Akenson 1973; Gallagher and Worrall 1982, 164–6). It is they too who have helped to make mixed marriages a divisive issue by insisting, in the past at least, that all children of such marriages be brought up as Catholics (Barritt and Carter 1962, 26). This is not to say that all the pressures come from one side. Survey evidence suggests that more Protestants dislike the idea of integrated schooling than do Catholics (Moxon-Browne 1983, 134–5; Darby and Dunn 1987, 91). At the level of Church leadership, the Presbyterian Church has welcomed the principle of integration but the Church of Ireland and the Methodists have been more cautious (Gallagher and Worrall 1982, 167). As far as mixed marriages are concerned, McFarlane (1979, 193) in a study of the subject reports that, in both religious groups, such a marriage is seen as lowering the standing of a family in the eyes of the community. None the less, the irony remains that the Catholic Church has, by the strictness of its rules on marriage and education, provided some of the mechanisms whereby the Catholic minority can be identified as an outgroup by the Protestant majority.

A point which emerges from the preceding discussion is that the two communities are not mirror images of each other. The Protestant community is more fragmented than the Catholic. It is divided by denomination—a phenomenon which has no counterpart on the Catholic side. It is divided by theological preference: while among Catholics there are differences of emphasis between conservatives and progressives, there is nothing so sharp as the fundamentalist/liberal division in Protestantism. It is divided more than it is united by the Orange Order, because Protestant attitudes to Orangeism are spread out along a spectrum from enthusiastic support to outright hostility. The Protestant community is more deeply divided by class than the Catholic community, perhaps because the Protestant middle class is larger, richer, and longer established. We have seen the class division weakening Protestant unity in residence, in education, and in attitudes to the Orange Order. The Catholic community on the other hand shares certain institutions. All the Catholics in a given area, regardless of class or political preference, are likely to attend the same churches and send their children to the same primary schools (though at second level, the same dichotomy between grammar and secondary schools prevails as among Protestants).

This has an implication for community relations. As Barritt and Carter noted (1962, 25), 'the fragmentation of the Protestant community tends, we suggest, to make Protestants overestimate the unity of the Church of Rome'. The point has been echoed by other writers. Heskin (1980, 42) claims that 'in terms of religion, at least, Northern Ireland's Catholics are very much more homogenous [*sic*] and cohesive than their Protestant counterparts'. The Grand Master of the Orange Order, Revd Martin Smyth, explaining to a mainly

Catholic conference how northern Protestants see the Republic, had this to say:

Among the people described as Protestants, there is vast variety. Not only is there great variety in temperament, teachings, attitudes and atmosphere as between Presbyterians, Anglicans, Methodists, Congregationalists, Unitarians and so on, but there is also great variety within each of those churches or groupings. . . . Such unity as we have among Protestants in Ulster arises not just from their thinking the same about everything. It is not monolithic. It is based on mutual recognition and acceptance among people who differ widely from one another. . . .

The one substantial religious body which seems unable as yet to enter at all into this spirit is the Roman Catholic church. Roman Catholics figure in many Ulster Protestants [*sic*] minds as a very idiosyncratic sect of 'exclusive brethren'. They are so peculiar that they do not even allow their children to learn sums or spelling in the same classroom as our children! (Smyth 1975, 27–8.)

Those who know the Catholic community from inside will argue that it is less monolithic than Protestants imagine. Particularly in politics, as we shall see in Chapter 4, it contains some sharp differences. But, even if this is conceded, it remains less fragmented than the Protestant community. We have here one reason for Protestant suspicions of the Catholic community. It is not the most important reason—we still have to explore several others—but it is part of the total situation.

This chapter has been concerned with the extent to which, and manner in which, religion shapes the segregation of Northern Ireland into two communities. Segregation by itself does not necessarily make for conflict. Aunger (1981) has shown, in his comparative study of New Brunswick and Northern Ireland, that French- and English-speakers in New Brunswick are at least as segregated as are Protestant and Catholic in Northern Ireland. Studies of Dutch society show that, at any rate until the recent past, Catholic and Protestant were if anything even more segregated from each other than are their co-religionists in Northern Ireland (Goudsblom 1967; Lijphart 1975*a*; Bakvis 1981). Yet in neither New Brunswick nor The Netherlands is there remotely the same degree of bitterness as in Northern Ireland. What segregation can do is exacerbate conflict—by increasing mutual ignorance and fostering the growth of stereotypes—in a situation where other reasons for conflict exist.

TWO WAYS IN WHICH RELIGION IS SIGNIFICANT

Religion can be important in Northern Ireland in two distinct manners:

1. It can be a basis for segregating the population into two communities, largely ignorant of each other and susceptible therefore to prejudice and stereotyping.
2. It can be an actual cause of conflict, because of a clash of values and interests related to religion.

In this chapter we have explored the first of these sources of division. The second is equally important. However, I have found it best to defer consideration of it till the later part of Chapter 5, where I shall be offering a review of the community divide. There I shall examine the relative importance of religious and other factors in keeping Northern Ireland divided.

3

Economic Aspects

THE GENERAL ECONOMIC SITUATION

All recent writers on the Northern Ireland economy agree that it is in a bad state. On this point the spectrum of academic opinion is narrower than on almost any topic examined in this book. It ranges only from those who paint the picture as bleak (e.g. Kennedy *et al.* 1988, 95–116) through to those who paint it as catastrophic (e.g. Rowthorn and Wayne 1988, 70–104). Unemployment is high. Emigration is rife. A substantial minority of the population lives in poverty. Manufacturing jobs have declined by 40 per cent since 1973. Attempts to start up new industries to compensate for the decline of old ones have had limited success. The economy is unhealthily dependent on public-sector jobs. Public services are maintained only by enormous subsidies from the rest of the United Kingdom.

There is general agreement, too, that the troubles are only a subsidiary cause of the economic decline. True, the Cambridge economist Bob Rowthorn (1987, 132) has written that the conflict is 'easily the most important single factor preventing a sustained economic recovery in the province', but in a book which he co-authored the following year he backed away from this position, and listed the troubles as just one of five factors explaining the region's poor economic performance (Rowthorn and Wayne 1988, 82–3). Indeed another set of Cambridge economists (Canning *et al.* 1987, 211) argue that the troubles may actually have led to a net gain of jobs in Northern Ireland. Both they and the Northern Ireland-based economist Graham Gudgin see the essence of the problem as demographic: a fast-growing population needs more jobs than the economy can create (Canning *et al.* 1987, 212; Gudgin 1989, 69). Rowthorn and Wayne (1988, 82–3) do not stress population growth, but find four other reasons, besides the troubles, for the region's difficulties:

1. The prolonged slump in the world economy following 1973,

which particularly damaged an export-oriented economy like Northern Ireland's.

2. The dependence of the Northern Ireland economy on exports to Britain, which itself is one of the more sluggish of the world's economies.
3. The industrial structure of Northern Ireland, with its above-average share of problem industries such as artificial fibres and shipbuilding.
4. The 'branch plant' nature of the Northern Ireland economy, in which many of its largest employers are multinationals based elsewhere, with the result that Northern Ireland plants are particularly vulnerable to contraction or closure in a time of recession.

A different but overlapping analysis was offered in a report on Northern Ireland published by the then SDP/Liberal Alliance in Britain (Alliance 1985, 105–6). It pointed out that hardly any other region in Western Europe suffered from Northern Ireland's combination of *three* disadvantages: an unfavourable geographical position, the economic decline of its traditional industries, and the lack of significant energy resources. It noted that the last of these disadvantages might be counteracted by the recent discovery of lignite deposits, but five years further on these have still made no significant difference to the region's situation.

It has been worth dwelling on Northern Ireland's poor economic situation because it helps to explain the community division. If the region were prosperous, one might expect prosperity to alleviate community tensions. In the South Tyrol, for instance, an economic boom has done much—along with important institutional changes—to reconcile the German majority to Italian rule (Alcock 1982, 53). But in Northern Ireland, two communities are scrambling for inadequate resources. Catholics on average are worse off than Protestants on average, but it is not easy to improve the lot of Catholics without damaging that of Protestants.

In the rest of this chapter I shall examine the economic differential between the Protestant and Catholic communities: its extent, causes, and consequences.

THE BEGINNINGS OF RESEARCH

On the eve of the troubles, not much was known about the economic gap between Protestant and Catholic. The censuses had not, since the last all-Ireland census in 1911, contained any cross-tabulation by occupation and religion. All that was available was some limited information from particular localities. J. M. Mogey's study (1947) of six rural areas had given figures for the Catholic proportion of the population, and also a discussion of the degree of poverty, in each area. There was a considerable, though not total, relation between poverty and Catholicism. Nine years later Emrys Jones published his paper on 'the distribution and segregation of Roman Catholics in Belfast' (1956)—subsequently subsumed, with few alterations, into his *Social Geography of Belfast* (1960)—which showed that Catholics were disproportionately concentrated in the poorer parts of the city. However, Jones's work contained none of the statistical tests which the computer age was to make commonplace only a few years later, and it is not easy to ascertain from his work how close was the correlation between Catholicism and poverty. It was certainly not total: his carefully drawn maps, based on small-area data made available to him from the census returns of 1951, show pockets of poverty in Protestant as well as Catholic areas. Barritt and Carter (1962, 54–5) devoted a couple of pages to the topic. They stated that there was 'a marked difference in the economic status of the two communities'. However, their empirical evidence was quite limited, being based on their own survey of Portadown, and on Rosemary Harris's (then still unpublished) research in Ballybeg.

The first author to offer data covering Northern Ireland as a whole was Richard Rose (1971), whose 1968 survey included questions on income and occupation. He found that there was 'a limited tendency for Protestants to have a higher occupational class than Catholics' (p. 280), and that Catholics were proportionately more numerous in the lowest income groups (p. 289). But he also noted that the median weekly family income in both communities was between £16 and £20 a week, and concluded that, given the larger number of Protestants in the population as a whole, 'there are more poor Protestants than poor Catholics in Northern Ireland' (p. 289). It was not till much later that Covello and Ashby (1980), and more cautiously Kelley and McAllister (1984), reanalysing

Rose's data, suggested that it could be used to show a greater degree of Catholic disadvantage than Rose had recognized.

Aunger (1975, 1), surveying the literature available at the time he wrote, stated that the dominant view appeared to be that there was little relation between occupational class and religious persuasion. He quoted three authorities in support of this view—Rose (1971); Frank Gallagher's impressionistic picture in his book *The Indivisible Island* (1957); and Budge and O'Leary's survey data from their study of Belfast (1973). He accepted that Barritt and Carter (1962, 54) took a different view. That makes three authorities on one side, and one on the other. So far as a dominant view can be detected at that date, it does seem to have been as Aunger stated. But it might be more accurate to say that there was little scholarly discussion of any kind, in the years before 1975, of the economic disparity between Protestant and Catholic.

The path-breaking study was published by Aunger himself (1975). Edmund Aunger is a political scientist teaching at a Canadian university who has subsequently published (1981) a comparative study of Northern Ireland and New Brunswick. In 1975 he published in the Dublin-based *Economic and Social Review* a paper entitled 'Religion and Occupational Class in Northern Ireland'. It was derived from then still unpublished data from the census of 1971, which had been made available to him. The 1971 census was the first since 1911 to cross-tabulate by religion and occupation: it therefore provided a far more extensive body of data than any which had been available since before partition. Aunger found three main ways in which Catholics were disadvantaged. First, they were somewhat more likely than Protestants to be low in the socio-economic scale. As Table 3.1 shows, Protestants were over-represented in the three highest classes, while Catholics were over-represented in the two lowest. Secondly, within each class there was a tendency for Catholics to cluster in the lower reaches, Protestants in the higher ones. 'While a clerk may be a Catholic, it is more likely that the office manager will be a Protestant; while a skilled craftsman may be a Catholic, it is more likely that the supervisor will be a Protestant; and while a nurse may be a Catholic, it is more likely that the doctor will be a Protestant' (p. 8). Thirdly, Catholics were more likely to be found in industries with lower status and more unem-ployment, like construction, while Protestants tended to be found in

Table 3.1.   Religion and occupational class, 1971 (%)

Occupational class	Catholic	Protestant	Total
Professional, managerial	12	15	14
Lower-grade non-manual	19	26	24
Skilled manual	17	19	18
Semi-skilled manual	27	25	26
Unskilled, unemployed	25	15	18
TOTAL	100	100	100

Note: Base = economically active men and women.
Source: Aunger (1975, 4).

industries such as engineering, which ranked higher in pay and
prestige (pp. 12–14). The cumulative effect of these differences was
to produce 'a noteworthy congruence between the class cleavage and
the religious cleavage in Northern Ireland' (p. 17).

Aunger's article was important for two reasons. First, it opened
up the study of an area to which scholars had previously devoted
little attention. Secondly, it established an orthodoxy in that area.
Since Aunger wrote, there has been little disagreement among
scholars that the economic gap between the Protestant and Catholic
communities is substantial. Argument has revolved round, not the
fact of the difference, but its nature and causes.

RESEARCH SINCE 1975

Since 1975, research in this area has burgeoned. The main agency
responsible has been the Fair Employment Agency for Northern
Ireland (FEA), which was set up in 1976 to promote equality of
employment in the region. The Agency has received more criticism
than almost any other statutory body in Northern Ireland. On the
one hand it has been criticized, with varying degrees of sharpness,
for toothlessness and ineffectiveness (Schmitt 1980; McCrudden
1983; Rolston 1983; Graham 1984). On the other hand it has been
criticized for an anti-Protestant bias and for finding inequities where
no inequities truthfully existed (Northern Ireland Assembly 1984;
Campbell, n.d.; Institute for Representative Government 1989). I

shall not attempt to assess these criticisms here, because I am not concerned with its overall performance. I am, however, concerned with its record as an initiator of research. Here its performance has been much less open to controversy. It has, to December 1989, published eleven research reports and thirty-one reports of investigations into particular industries, occupations, or enterprises. These reports have attracted much less criticism, and indeed have been used by writers of a wide range of views to provide ammunition for their arguments. The research reports in particular are by named academics, and present the evidence for their findings in such a way that readers can check the arguments for themselves. Several of the earlier research reports of the Agency, as well as some other material, have been collected in a volume of essays: *Religion, Education and Employment: Aspects of Equal Opportunity in Northern Ireland* (Cormack and Osborne 1983).

Not all the work in this area has been sparked off by the Fair Employment Agency. A number of participant-observation studies provide information on particular localities. The most prolific writers in the general area of stratification have been Robert Osborne, a specialist in social policy at the University of Ulster, Robert Cormack, a sociologist at Queen's University, and Paul Compton, a demographer at Queen's University. Some of their publications will be found in the bibliography. (Both Osborne and Cormack have also worked for the FEA; but their FEA work does not exhaust their contribution in this area.) The most substantial publication in the area has been a three-volume study, commissioned by the Standing Advisory Commission for Human Rights and undertaken by the Policy Studies Institute in London. The first of these volumes is a study of employment and unemployment in the two communities (Smith 1987*a*); the second is a survey of workplaces (Chambers 1987); and the third is a survey of attitudes in the Northern Ireland population as a whole (Smith 1987*b*).

There are still serious gaps in the literature on social stratification in Northern Ireland. No data yet exist on the ownership of land or capital. The work that has been done has been entirely in the fields of occupation, income level, employment, and unemployment. But in these areas, the amount of material now available, as compared with the mid-1970s—let alone the late 1960s, when the troubles began—is remarkable. There is perhaps no aspect of Northern Ireland on which research has grown so rapidly.

This material can best be analysed under two headings: the extent of Catholic disadvantage, and the reasons for that disadvantage. I shall discuss each in turn.

The Extent of Catholic Disadvantage

The first question to raise is how far Aunger's picture, of a 'noteworthy congruence between the class cleavage and the religious cleavage in Northern Ireland', still stands. It is unfortunately not possible to give a straightforward comparison between the 1971 and 1981 censuses, because there are many differences between the two censuses in their classification of occupations (Osborne and Cormack 1987, 15). However, by reanalysing the 1981 data, and using other sources such as Fair Employment Agency reports and the Continuous Household Survey which has been operating since 1983, it is possible to build up a picture of how much change has occurred, and a number of authors have sought to do so. Robert Miller, a sociologist at Queen's University, has contributed a discussion of the subject to the volume *Ireland: A Sociological Profile* (Clancy *et al.* 1986). Gafikin and Morrissey (1987, 149–51), two specialists in social policy at the University of Ulster, include a section on the issue in a study of poverty in Northern Ireland, as do Rowthorn and Wayne in their book *Northern Ireland: The Political Economy of Conflict* (1988, 105–19). The Fair Employment Agency includes a survey of the subject in its eleventh annual report (Fair Employment Agency 1988, 21–3). A survey of the research to date has been included in a report of the Standing Advisory Commission on Human Rights (1987, 14–20). The most comprehensive examinations of the subject so far published have been carried out by Robert Osborne and Robert Cormack (Cormack and Osborne 1987; Osborne and Cormack 1987) and by David J. Smith of the Policy Studies Institute (Smith 1987*a*). Osborne and Cormack base their findings largely on the 1981 census; Smith relies largely on the Continuous Household Survey.

There are some differences of emphasis between the various authors. Miller (1988, 227) is the most pessimistic. He sees no lessening of the gap. The Fair Employment Agency (1988, 21–2) is marginally the most optimistic. It sees little change in the manufacturing sector, but some improvement in the private service sector, and significant improvement in the public sector. In between are Osborne and Cormack (1987) and Smith (1987*a*). This is interesting because, as will be shown in the next section, Osborne and Cormack on the one hand, and Smith on the other, disagree sharply on the reasons for Catholic disadvantage; they are substantially in accord, however, on its extent. They agree that Catholics are not uniformly at a disadvantage. Osborne and Cormack (1987) note evidence of gains in sections of the middle class—most notably the legal profession (p. 53) and the civil service (p. 62). Overall, they see 'a slow and uneven improvement in Catholic employment profiles' (p. 69). Smith (1987*a*, 62) finds that, while Protestant men tend to have jobs at a higher level than Catholic men, the tendency is not very strong, and there are some non-manual jobs where Catholics are actually ahead. They are also proportionately more numerous in skilled manual occupations. However, one point noted by both Osborne and Cormack (1987, 29–30) and by Smith (1987*a*, 63) is that there is no sign of disparities decreasing to any significant extent in the younger age groups.

There is agreement that Catholic women are relatively better off than Catholic men (Osborne and Cormack 1987, 29; Smith 1987*a*, 62). This fact had already been noted by Aunger (1975, 9). However, it is of limited advantage to the Catholic community. Women of both communities earn less than men, and are considerably less likely to be in work (Smith 1987*a*, 60).

There is universal agreement as to where the gap between Protestant and Catholic is at its worst. It is in unemployment. The 1971 census revealed that Catholic males were 2.62 times more likely than Protestant males to be unemployed. Since then, the Northern Ireland economy has undergone great changes. Many long-established industries have gone to the wall. Overall unemployment has rocketed, and hit hitherto prosperous Protestant areas. Yet, when figures for the 1980s became available, they revealed that there had been little improvement in the unemployment differential. The census of 1981 showed that Catholic males were now 2.44 times more likely than Protestant males to be unemployed (figures for 1971 and 1981 from Smith 1987*a*, 16–17). During the 1980s figures derived from the newly established Continuous Household Survey, and based on large samples of the population, show that the gap has if anything worsened. In 1983–4 the ratio was 2.33. In 1984–5 it was

2.38. In 1985–7 it was 2.57 (figures for 1983–4 and 1984–5 from Department of Economic Development 1986, 47; the figure for 1985–7 is my calculation from PPRU 1989, 11).

Another way of looking at the unemployment differential has been provided by Rowthorn and Wayne, in their book *Northern Ireland: The Political Economy of Conflict* (1985, 115). They show that, while the Northern Ireland male-unemployment rate as a whole was in 1981 on a par with that of the worst-off regions in Great Britain (the figure was around 19 per cent in Merseyside, Northern Ireland, and Clydeside), the Northern Ireland Catholic male-unemployment rate, at 30 per cent, far outstripped the figure anywhere else, while the Northern Ireland Protestant male-unemployment rate, at 12 per cent, was only a little above the British average of 11 per cent.

The generalizations made in the preceding paragraphs mask, of course, local differences. This is brought out by the participant-observation literature. The pioneer participant-observation study, Rosemary Harris's of Ballybeg in the 1950s, found a substantial economic gap in that neighbourhood at that time. The poorer upland area was 72 per cent Catholic; the richer infield area was 65 per cent Protestant (Harris 1972, 21). However, more recent local studies have shown considerable variations. Henry Glassie (1982, 796), in his study of Ballymenone, County Fermanagh, specifically states that the association of Protestants with wealth was less marked in his area than it was in Harris's. Two observers who found little or no economic difference between Protestant and Catholic were Galway in Glenlevan (1978) and Buckley in Upper Tullagh (1982). On the other hand Leyton (1984, 187) found a considerable gap in Aughnaboy. Studies of Catholic areas in Belfast (Burton 1978; Darby 1986; Conroy 1988; Rolston and Tomlinson 1988; Blackman *et al.* 1989) found horrifying examples of multiple deprivation—though it must be added that studies of Protestant working-class areas in Belfast (Jenkins 1982, 1983; Darby 1986) suggest a level of deprivation not greatly less than in neighbouring Catholic areas. These local examples do not disprove the region-wide generalizations, but they do remind us that every figure is an average, which masks considerable differences between one part of Northern Ireland and another.

Reasons for Catholic Disadvantage

Most writers on this subject have concentrated on attempting to explain the most glaring gap between Protestant and Catholic—namely their different unemployment rates. A number of contrasting points of view have been expressed, and the discussion at times has been acrimonious. I shall take the reader through the more important contributions to the controversy.

Controversy on the subject began with the early reports of the Fair Employment Agency. The Agency came to believe that an important mechanism distinguishing Protestant recruitment practices from Catholic was the existence of informal networks of recruitment. In Northern Ireland many job vacancies were filled by word of mouth, through family or friends. Since more Protestants than Catholics were employed, and since among the employed population more Protestants were in high-status jobs, this meant that young Protestants entering the labour-market were considerably likelier than young Catholics to hear about good job opportunities. As the chairman of the FEA put it in his foreword to one of the Agency's research reports:

The informal networks which are still so powerful in Northern Ireland and through which so much employment is found, operate to maintain and reinforce employment patterns already established. Once these patterns have been established such a method of filling jobs means that, even if there were never in Northern Ireland a single instance of individual discrimination in the future, the patterns laid down will remain much the same. (Murray and Darby 1980, 5.)

This argument was challenged by the Queen's University demographer Paul Compton (1976, 1980, 1981). He argued that much of the inequality in unemployment was 'generated by factors specific to the Roman Catholic community' (1981, 140). He stressed three such factors: (1) that Catholics were more likely to live in peripheral areas of Northern Ireland, where employment was harder to obtain; (2) that Catholics were more likely to be unskilled—the unskilled everywhere are more likely to be unemployed; and (3) that they were more likely to have large families, a characteristic which for a variety of reasons is associated with unemployment. Drawing his figures from the 1971 census, he concluded that these three factors were together responsible for 56 per cent of the gap between the Protestant and Catholic unemployment levels (p. 137).

Compton's views were in their turn challenged by other scholars (Osborne 1978, 1980; Miller and Osborne 1980; Osborne and Cormack 1983, 232, 240; 1986). While it was not denied that Compton's points explained some of the Catholic disadvantage, it was argued that they were certainly not sufficient to account for most of it. For instance, while it was true that Catholics were more heavily concentrated in peripheral regions, even within those areas they had a higher unemployment rate than Protestants (Osborne and Cormack 1986, 222). Again, while it is true that Catholics have larger families, the economic differential between Protestants and Catholics can be traced back to a time before the gap between Protestant and Catholic birth-rates had opened up (Cormack and Rooney 1984). Osborne and Cormack (1986, 224) conclude that 'discrimination, particularly indirect discrimination, would appear to continue to contribute to unemployment differentials'.

There, for the moment, the controversy rested. It was reopened when David J. Smith of the Policy Studies Institute published his study of employment and unemployment in Northern Ireland, commissioned by the Standing Advisory Commission on Human Rights (Smith 1987a, 8–58). Smith used data from the Continuous Household Survey to examine the reasons for unemployment in Northern Ireland. He controlled for a number of factors which had previously been suggested in the literature—location, class, and family size (which it will be remembered had been Compton's original trio of factors); differential labour-markets, differential education qualifications, and different age structure (which had been suggested by other scholars). He concluded that even when all these factors are taken into consideration, a large residual is left, for which no adequate explanation has emerged 'apart from discrimination or unequal opportunities' (p. 39).

Smith's conclusions produced sharp disagreement. The controversy ran in the Belfast periodical *Fortnight* from December 1987 to March 1988. Compton, Cormack, and Osborne, who had previously been on opposing sides, joined forces to criticize Smith for underplaying the importance of structural variables (Compton *et al.* 1988). Smith (1988a) replied to their points, and his three critics, now writing separately, responded to him (Compton 1988; Cormack and Osborne 1988). Smith (1988b) fired the final shot in the *Fortnight* controversy, but it then flared again in the periodical *Policy Studies*. Smith (1988c) attacked his critics in the July 1988 issue, and Cormack and Osborne (1989) responded in the issue for Spring 1989.

It is not possible at this time to give a final judgement on this controversy. Neither side could deploy the full range of argument in short journal articles. Both Smith on the one hand and Osborne and Cormack on the other are planning further publications, where presumably they will put their points more extensively. But I shall make a few provisional comments on the controversy as it has developed so far.

Smith seems to me to win much of the detailed argumentation. The attempts by his critics to show that area of residence, or type of educational qualifications, or family size, are substantially more important than Smith admitted are not successful.

On the other hand, Smith's claim (1988b) that the six factors he has controlled for are the only relevant ones is excessive. In fact the Standing Advisory Commission on Human Rights, in its review of discrimination and equality of opportunity in Northern Ireland (SACHR 1987), which drew heavily on Smith's work, found three other factors worth discussion. One is the black economy. This will have the effect of making unemployment seem higher than it really is. The commission accepts that there is no way of measuring this factor, but suggests that it may be more important in Catholic than Protestant areas (para. 3.47). The commission's hunch is supported by the one, admittedly small-scale, study of the black economy that has so far been published (Howe 1989b, 165).

A second factor is the differential impact of service in security occupations. The security forces themselves are eager to recruit more Catholics, but Catholics have a number of good reasons for being reluctant to join. They may suffer ostracism in their own community or reprisal from paramilitaries; they may have to move to a new area and cut off ties with family and friends; they may feel that they would be unwelcome, and may be reluctant to give full legitimacy to the State (para. 3.46). None of these reasons can fairly be described as 'discrimination', yet they result in this area of employment, which accounts for more than 5 per cent of jobs in Northern Ireland (para. 3.45), being dominated by Protestants.

The most important factor identified by the Standing Advisory Commission is what they describe as 'the chill factor', which is the impact of intercommunal hostility and fear. Members of one community are often reluctant to take up work in a workplace dominated by the other community, or to travel to work through territory dominated by the other community. Employers may be reluctant to take on workers from areas known to be associated with paramilitary activity. The Standing Advisory Commission cites data from Smith's own attitude survey to show that such considerations apply, especially in Belfast (paras. 3.41–3.44).

Since the controversy began, another publication on the subject has appeared: David Eversley's *Religion and Employment in Northern Ireland* (1989). Eversley, like Smith, looks at structural variables such as differences in educational qualifications, differences in the location of population, and differences in age structure, and finds that these are inadequate to explain the gap between Protestant and Catholic unemployment levels. He adds two further structural variables to the factors examined by Smith—availability of housing, and availability of transport—and finds that these are of slight importance. Unlike Smith, he puts considerable stress on the reluctance of Catholics to take jobs which are located in, or which entail travelling through, what to them are unsafe areas. Having done that, however, he considers that there is still an unexplained residual which can be accounted for only by postulating that discrimination is at work. He does not consider that the Catholic disadvantage is 'solely or even mainly due to discrimination' (p. 16), but he does consider that discrimination is 'an important component part of the total labour market situation' (p. 235).

There is, then, a range of opinions to be found in the literature. Smith evidently considers the amount of anti-Catholic discrimination to be massive. Osborne and Cormack might prefer some more measured word, such as 'significant'. Eversley would appear to be in between—his view might be summed up in the word 'substantial'. But, wherever the balance of the argument ultimately comes to rest, one thing is clear—the argument has been, not about the existence of discrimination, but about its extent. All authorities are agreed that discrimination still goes on. That fact alone is sufficient to embitter relations between the two communities.

DIFFERENTIAL EMIGRATION

The controversy over differential unemployment rates has overshadowed another form of inequality between Protestant and Catholic—their differential emigration rates. The first authors to draw attention to this gap, so far as I know, were Barritt and Carter (1962, 107–8). They presented figures to show that in the intercensal periods 1937–51 and 1951–61 Catholics, with one-third of the population, provided 55–8 per cent of the emigrants. They concluded that this was 'a rough measure of the difference in the economic opportunities available at home to members of the two communities'. Mr Barritt has told me that these calculations, which were easily derived from the census returns, and which he made before starting any field-work, caused more stir than almost anything else in their book.

Since Barritt and Carter wrote, the gap in migration rates has remained. Compton (1985, 209, 215) has provided figures to suggest that in the intercensal periods 1961–71 and 1971–81 Catholics accounted for 60 per cent of net migration. Authors like Eversley and Herr (1985) who put the proportion of Catholics in the population in 1981 at a slightly higher figure than Compton would presumably put the proportion of Catholics among emigrants as slightly less: but the difference would not be more than a percentage point or so. The reality remains that differential migration rates are a further source of inequality between the communities. If they did not exist, the unemployment differential would presumably be even greater.

EFFECTS OF THE ECONOMIC GAP BETWEEN PROTESTANT AND CATHOLIC

In one way, the economic gap can be seen as one of the less important dividing lines between Protestant and Catholic. While Protestants tend to be better off than Catholics, there are enough well-to-do Catholics, and enough poor Protestants, to ensure that the fit between religion and social class is very far from perfect. Some other factors, as we saw in the last chapter and shall see again in the next, mark off one community from the other far more precisely than the economic differential does.

In another way, however, the economic gap is important. It is a thing of which Catholics are sharply aware, and with which they are much concerned. This is shown by the publicity given in nationalist news media to every report from the Fair Employment Agency which shows up some new instance of inequality of opportunity, and by the frequency with which the Irish side in the Anglo-Irish Conference established under the Hillsborough agreement of 1985 brings up issues of fair employment. On the other side, many Protestants have difficulty in facing the possibility that they may be treating Catholics unfairly. As Sarah Nelson (1975) reported, in a study of Protestant attitudes to discrimination, the self-image of many Protestants made it peculiarly difficult for them to acknowledge that they might have behaved unfairly: they believed themselves to be a just people, who did not do things like that.

The extent of the gap between Protestant and Catholic perceptions has been explored in attitude surveys. Rose, back in the peaceful days of 1968, found that on no item in his questionnaire did Protestants and Catholics differ so sharply as in response to the question: 'People sometimes say that in part of Northern Ireland Catholics are treated unfairly. Do you think this is true or not?' Seventy-four per cent of Catholics said it was true; 74 per cent of Protestants that it was not (Rose 1971, 272). Eighteen years later, the gap had scarcely lessened. Smith (1987b, table 74) asked in his 1986 survey: 'do Protestants and Catholics have the same chance of a job?' Sixty-eight per cent of Protestants said that they had; 67 per cent of Catholics said that they had not.

To sum up: as a factor objectively differentiating the two communities, the economic gap is substantial, but it does not distinguish between them so sharply as some of the differences linked with politics and religion. As a source of perceptions differentiating the two communities, it is one of the most important in Northern Ireland.

4

Political Aspects

The purpose of this chapter is to examine four areas where marked political differences exist between the communities:

1. Choice of national identity
2. Party preference
3. Reaction to proposals for a political settlement in Northern Ireland
4. Reaction to issues of law, order, and security

A final section will examine local variations in attitudes between one part of Northern Ireland and another.

NATIONAL IDENTITY

It was for long a matter of folk wisdom that national identity and religious allegiance coincided in Northern Ireland. The nationalist writer Frank Gallagher (1957), for instance, systematically used 'nationalist' when he appeared to mean 'Catholic'. The first scholar to research the correlation between religion and national identity was Richard Rose, in his survey of 1968. In response to the question 'which of these terms best describes the way you usually think of yourself?', he obtained the results to be found in Table 4.1. It will be seen that most Protestants thought of themselves as 'British' or

Table 4.1. National identities, 1968 (%)

	Protestant	Catholic
Irish	20	76
British	39	15
Ulster	32	5
Sometimes British; sometimes Irish	6	3
Anglo-Irish	2	1
Don't know	1	—

Source: Rose (1971, 208).

'Ulster', and most Catholics as 'Irish'. But the number of exceptions was large enough to be significant. The 20 per cent of Protestants who chose the label 'Irish' were not necessarily repudiating the title of 'British'—there was a long tradition among unionists that they were British and Irish at the same time, just as many Scots looked on themselves as British and Scots, or Welsh as British and Welsh. The 15 per cent of Catholics who thought of themselves as British were more of a surprise.

In 1978 Moxon-Browne replicated the question, and obtained the figures shown in Table 4.2. The greatest change was among Protestants, who swung sharply from 'Ulster' and 'Irish' towards 'British'. Indeed of all the results reported by Moxon-Browne where a comparison is possible with Rose's figures of ten years earlier, the change is greatest here. One can only speculate as to the reasons. By 1978 the IRA campaign to force the unionists into a united Ireland had been going on for seven years, and perhaps its effect had been to reinforce in them a non-Irish identity. On the Catholic side, the results were much more stable. The term 'Irish' remained much the most popular; but the term 'British' was still preferred by 15 per cent.

In 1986 Smith again asked the question 'which of these terms best describes the way you usually think of yourself?', offering a slightly different choice of labels, and obtained the answers to be seen in Table 4.3. The addition of the choice 'Northern Irish' makes Smith's data not totally comparable with Rose's or Moxon-Browne's. The availability of this choice seems to have drawn off some support for other labels among both Protestants and Catholics. (Mr Smith tells

Table 4.2.   National identities, 1978 (%)

	Protestant	Catholic
Irish	8	69
British	67	15
Ulster	20	6
Sometimes British; sometimes Irish	3	8
Anglo-Irish	2	2
Other	0.2	0.5

Source: Moxon-Browne (1983, 6), supplemented by figures provided by Mr Moxon-Browne.

Table 4.3. National identities, 1986 (%)

	Protestant	Catholic
Irish	3	61
British	65	9
Ulster	14	1
Northern Irish	11	20
Sometimes British, sometimes Irish	4	7
Other answers	2	2

Source: The data on this question do not appear in the published report of the survey (Smith 1987*b*), but Mr Smith has kindly supplied me with them.

me that the term 'Northern Irish' was included because support for it showed up in the pilot survey, and indeed his results make one regret that it had not been tested for in earlier research.) On the whole, though, Smith's findings show a high degree of continuity from Moxon-Browne's. 'British' remains much the most popular label among Protestants, and 'Irish' among Catholics.

One further exploration of national identities can be reported. It came midway in time between Rose's survey and Moxon-Browne's, being part of the occupational-mobility study directed by John Jackson in 1973–4. The results are not directly comparable with those of Rose and Moxon-Browne, partly because, as explained in Chapter 1, Jackson's sample was confined to males aged between 18 and 64, and partly because the questions asked were different. All the same, the results are worth recording. Jackson and his team presented respondents with pairs of identities, and asked 'which of these terms best describes the way you think of yourself?' The first pair was 'British or Irish', the second was 'Ulsterman or British', and the third was 'Ulsterman or Irish'. So far, Jackson was testing the relative popularity of the three most widely favoured labels in Rose's data. As a final question in this part of the survey, he threw in a new term, 'English', and tested attitudes to that label as compared with 'Irish'. The results are to be found in Table 4.4.

These results show similarities with, and differences from, the findings made by Rose, Moxon-Browne, and Smith. The similarities are strongest on the Catholic side, where the label 'Irish' proved by far the most popular, no matter what alternative was proposed, but

Table 4.4. National identities among men, 1973–1974 (%)

	Protestant	Catholic
British	84	16
Irish	13	81
Neither	3	3
Ulsterman	72	57
British	26	15
Neither	2	28
Ulsterman	85	17
Irish	9	77
Neither	6	6
English	21	3
Irish	50	93
Neither	29	4

Note: Base = men aged 18–64.
Source: Boyle *et al.* 1976, 18.

where a significant minority (in this case 16 per cent) preferred the label 'British'. Indeed a small minority, 3 per cent, actually preferred the label 'English' to 'Irish'. This raises the possibility that a perceptible number of Catholics in Northern Ireland actually come from England, which would make it unlikely that national identity and religion will ever totally coincide. On the Protestant side, the greatest similarity with the other surveys is in the reluctance to use the label 'Irish': large majorities prefer 'British' (by 84 to 13) or 'Ulsterman' (by 85 to 9). The only way that even half the Protestants could be induced to choose the label 'Irish' was by giving 'English' as an alternative: even then, 29 per cent rejected both labels, and 21 per cent preferred 'English'—although in the sense of 'coming from England' this would certainly be false for most of them.

The greatest difference between this and the other surveys is found in the Protestants' choice of positive identity. In Rose's data from 1968, 'British' had a narrow lead over 'Ulster' (39 to 32); in Moxon-Browne's data from 1978, the lead had greatly widened (67 to 20). One might have expected then that Jackson's data from an intermediate date would have given an intermediate result. In fact, it showed a swing towards 'Ulster', which won by 72 to 26. One might deduce from this that, while Protestants are very sure what they are not, they are less certain about what they are.

A similar conclusion emerges from a recent paper, 'Situational Perspectives on Social Identity in Northern Ireland', by Neil Waddell and Ed Cairns of the University of Ulster at Coleraine (1987). Waddell and Cairns found, like previous researchers, that, when choosing between the labels 'Irish' and 'British', Catholics preferred 'Irish' (by 83 to 17 in this study), while Protestants preferred 'British' (by 97 to 3). However, they were not content to leave it at that. They explored *how far* people would feel British or Irish in different circumstances. They asked their respondents to rate themselves on a five-point scale from very British (5) through neutral (3) to very Irish (1), in response to a variety of situations. They discovered a difference between the two groups. While Catholics felt roughly similar degrees of Irishness in all situations (their average scores varying by only 0.52), Protestants' feelings differed more according to the circumstances (*their* average scores varying by 1.26). There were three items where the average score for Protestants actually crossed the neutral line and they felt more Irish than British. The three items were 'being amongst English people', 'injustice and discrimination against Irish people', and—with by far the largest margin—'watching Ireland play rugby'. Waddell and Cairns reasonably conclude that 'for Protestants social identity is somewhat more situationally determined' (p. 29).

Waddell and Cairns based their study on a small-scale sample of 181 respondents, mostly university students (p. 27). One cannot therefore generalize their conclusions to the Northern Ireland population as a whole: at most they can only be suggestive. None the less, when taken in conjunction with the variations between the findings of Rose, Moxon-Browne, and Jackson, they indicate that Protestants' choice of national identity is more complex than that of Catholics. The great majority of Catholics have a preference for one identity, 'Irish'; but Protestants are divided between 'British', 'Ulster', and even 'Irish', and tack uncertainly between them. Overall, the picture given by the study of national identity replicates that given by the study of social structure in Chapter 2: namely, that the situation among Protestants is more complicated than the situation among Catholics. It remains to be seen whether the same complexity is shown in party allegiances.

PARTY SUPPORT

In most countries with a mixed Protestant–Catholic population, there is some difference in the voting behaviour of the two groups. Political scientists have devised an instrument for measuring this difference, called the index of religious voting (Alford 1964, 91; Lijphart 1971, 6). Details of how the index is constructed will be found in the references just cited, but in outline one can say that, in a country where every single Catholic votes for one group of parties, while every single Protestant votes for an entirely separate group of parties, then the index of religious voting will be at its maximum of 100; while, in a country where every party wins Protestant and Catholic support in exactly the same proportions, the index of religious voting will be 0. Lijphart (1971, 8–9), using survey evidence from various dates in the late 1950s and early 1960s, calculated indices of religious voting for a number of countries of mixed religion (see Table 4.5). The figures ranged from a high of 59 for Switzerland to a low of 7 for Great Britain. On the same index Northern Ireland, according to calculations derived from Rose's survey data of 1968 (Lijphart 1975*b*, 87), attained the uniquely high figure of 81. In most countries, the influence of religion on party allegiance is declining (Bakvis 1981, 5, for data on The Netherlands, Switzerland, Belgium, and Italy; Whyte 1981*a*, 100–1, 111, for data on seven European countries). In Northern Ireland, however, it remains stable. I have calculated the index of religious voting for 1978 and 1986, using data from Moxon-Browne (1983) and Smith (1987*b*). The figures resulting are 78 for 1978, and 84 for 1986.

These figures compare well with those obtained by McAllister (1975), using another technique known to political scientists as

Table 4.5.   Indices of religious voting

Switzerland	59
The Netherlands	50
West Germany	29
Canada	21
United States	16
Australia	14
Great Britain	7

Source: Lijphart (1971, 8–9).

ecological analysis. This entails noting the proportion of votes gained by different parties in the various constituencies, and then correlating them with the social and economic characteristics of those constituencies, as obtained from the census. Applying this technique to the Convention elections of 1975, McAllister found that there was a correlation of 0.8 between the proportion of Protestants and the proportion voting for the United Ulster Unionist Coalition, and a correlation of 0.88 between the proportion of Catholics and the proportion voting for the Social Democratic and Labour Party (p. 22). On a world scale, such high correlations between party vote and a social characteristic are extraordinary.

However, though the relationship between religion and vote in Northern Ireland is uniquely close, it still does not reach the maximum possible figures—of 100 according to the index of religious voting, and 1.00 in ecological analysis. There are two sources of 'slippage'. One is that small numbers of Protestants and Catholics vote differently from the bulk of their community, as nationalists and unionists respectively. The second is that there is a centrist tradition in Northern Ireland, of parties which gain substantial support from both sides of the community divide. Down to the beginning of the 1970s this tradition was mainly represented by the Northern Ireland Labour Party (NILP), which upheld the union with Britain but opposed the Unionist Party on economic issues. Since the early 1970s it has been mainly represented by the Alliance Party, which also upholds the union with Britain, but which works for equality between Protestant and Catholic.

There is another complication in correlating religion with party support. This is that neither the unionist nor the nationalist camps are united. The Ulster Unionist Party, even in its heyday from the 1920s to the 1960s, always suffered a seepage to independent unionists of one kind or another. After the current troubles began, the seepage became a torrent, and a high point was reached in the local elections of 1977, which were contested by five parties including the name 'unionist' in their title (Ulster Unionist Party; Democratic Unionist Party; United Ulster Unionist Party; Vanguard Unionist Party; and Unionist Party of Northern Ireland), together with a number of independent unionists. Since then some of the smaller groups have disappeared, and, from the late 1970s, two groups have dominated all others: the Ulster Unionist Party (often referred to as the Official Unionists) and the Democratic Unionist

Party. Although these parties co-operate on some issues, particularly following the Anglo-Irish Agreement of 1985, and although in PR elections unionists of all kinds usually give their lower preferences to each other, they remain distinct and often competing entities. The Official Unionists are generally seen as somewhat more moderate—but also as more internally divided—than the Democratic Unionists.

On the nationalist side, divisions run deeper, and are of longer standing. At the very beginning of the Northern Ireland State, nationalists were divided between Republicans, who advocated physical force, and the Nationalist Party, which advocated reuniting Ireland by constitutional means, and the division has continued ever since. (The most thorough study of nationalist/republican politics in the Stormont period is to be found in Michael Farrell's *Northern Ireland: The Orange State* (1976).) In the 1970s, the Nationalist Party was replaced as the vehicle of moderate, constitutional nationalism by the Social Democratic and Labour Party or SDLP. For a time the SDLP appeared to have almost a monopoly of the nationalist vote. But in 1981, following the success of the hunger-striker Bobby Sands in the Fermanagh and South Tyrone by-election, Sinn Féin—the political wing of the IRA—decided to contest elections. The hostility between it and the SDLP is much greater than that between the various unionist parties, as is shown by the fact that in PR elections there is much less transfer of lower-preference votes between SDLP and Sinn Féin than there is between unionists of various kinds: indeed many SDLP supporters give their preference to the pro-union Alliance Party sooner than to Sinn Féin. (For the Assembly elections of 1982 see Elliott and Wilford 1983, 59; for the local elections of 1985 see Elliott and Smith 1986, 36.)

For completeness's sake, two smaller parties should be mentioned. The first is the Irish Independence Party, which contested elections for a time in the late 1970s and early 1980s. It was more nationalist than the SDLP; it became squeezed out when Sinn Féin began to contest elections. The second is the Workers Party (formerly Republican Clubs). Though this party sprang from the republican tradition, it now seeks to mobilize Catholic and Protestant workers on class issues.

A good deal of evidence on the distribution of support between political parties is available from attitude surveys. In citing this material, the caveat made in Chapter 1 must be borne in mind—that surveys in Northern Ireland appear to over-represent moderate opinion and under-represent extremism. None the less, it was also shown there that the distortion appears to be only of a few percentage points, so the survey evidence will still provide a rough guide to the distribution of opinion.

I shall confine myself to citing the three major academic surveys, by Rose in 1968, Moxon-Browne in 1978, and Smith in 1986. Their findings are shown in Tables 4.6, 4.7, and 4.8.

Table 4.6. Party preference 1968 (%)
Question: 'generally speaking, what party do you usually think of yourself as supporting?'

	Protestant	Catholic
Unionist	79	5
Nationalist	0.5	51
Northern Ireland Labour Party	11	27
Liberals and others	1	5
None; don't know	8	11

Source: Rose (1971, 235).

Table 4.7. Party preference, 1978 (%)
Question: 'could you tell us which of these political parties you feel closest to?'

	Protestant	Catholic
Official Unionist	47	*
Democratic Unionist	14	*
Vanguard Unionist	1	0
Unionist Party of Northern Ireland	3	0
Northern Ireland Labour Party	4	6
Alliance	13	21
Social Democratic and Labour Party	*	41
Irish Independence Party	0	2
Republican clubs	*	5
Other, none, or refused to reply	18	24

* Less than 0.5% of respondents fell into the category.

Source: These figures are not contained in the published report of the survey (Moxon-Browne 1983), but can be derived from the raw data. I have to thank Professor Ian McAllister for providing me with them.

Table 4.8. Party preference, 1986 (%)
          Question: 'which political party do you feel closest to?'

	Protestant	Catholic
Official Unionist	48	1
Democratic Unionist	22	*
Other Unionist	4	0
Alliance	10	14
Social Democratic and Labour Party	*	41
Sinn Féin	0	10
Irish Independence Party	0	2
Workers Party	1	4
Labour/Socialist	2	3
None or not stated	13	25

* Less than 0.5% of respondents fell into the category.
Source: Smith (1987*b*, table 119).

From these data we can draw the following conclusions.

1. The proportion of Catholics supporting unionist parties, or of Protestants supporting nationalist parties, is tiny.
2. There is, however a centrist stream, represented by NILP and Alliance, which accepts the union while rejecting Unionist domination. This draws support from both communities, but the proportion is higher among Catholics.
3. In general, Protestants are more cohesive than Catholics in their voting behaviour. All the parties they support, centrist or unionist, favour the link with Great Britain. The various pro-union parties exchange lower preferences to a greater extent than do SDLP and Sinn Féin. This is the first area we have found in which Protestants are less fragmented than Catholics.

ATTITUDES TO PARTICULAR CONSTITUTIONAL ARRANGEMENTS

The survey material goes far beyond measuring party support. It also contains a great deal of information on attitudes to particular settlements of the Northern Ireland problem. I shall divide this material into two chronological periods. First, there are a couple of surveys from 1967–8, before the troubles had begun. Secondly, there is a whole series of reports from 1973 onwards.

The Surveys of 1967–8

During this period, the main issue in Northern Ireland politics was the civil rights movement, and the demands it generated for better treatment of the minority on specific issues, such as housing, jobs, and electoral arrangements. No serious discussion was going on about a fundamental restructuring of Northern Ireland. Survey questions, therefore, are correspondingly vague. None the less, they are worth reporting because of the continuity and contrast which they display with subsequent attitudes.

The first region-wide survey ever undertaken in Northern Ireland was carried out for the *Belfast Telegraph* by National Opinion Polls in 1967. It did not aggregate respondents into Protestant and Catholic, but reported the different Protestant denominations separately, which makes precise comparison with later surveys difficult. Nevertheless, the responses to one question are worth reporting: see Table 4.9. They show a large measure of support—half the Catholics, approaching half the Protestants—for the compromise constitutional arrangement of a 'united Ireland linked to Britain'. It may be that, if respondents had been asked what they meant by 'a united Ireland linked to Britain', differences between Protestant and Catholic would have become more obvious. But the figures do suggest that, in those closing years of peace, Northern Ireland was not polarized into two fundamentally divided communities. Another feature of the figures is that they suggest Catholics had moved further from the traditional goal of their community than had

Table 4.9. Attitudes to constitutional change, 1967 (%)
Question: 'which of these arrangements do you think would be best for Ireland?'

Arrangement	Catholic	Church of Ireland	Presby- terian	Others
Situation as it exists today	20	52	53	62
An independent united Ireland	30	1	3	4
United Ireland linked to Britain	50	45	41	32

Source: *Belfast Telegraph*, 8 Dec. 1967.

Protestants. Only 30 per cent preferred an independent united Ireland; 70 per cent were prepared to accept a continued British link in one form or another. On the other side, the vast majority of Protestants wished to maintain that link; but nearly a half were prepared to combine it with some form of Irish unity.

One other survey of attitudes took place before the troubles began: Richard Rose's monumental one of 1968. He asked questions about the border, and about the constitutional position of Northern Ireland, the results of which are shown in Tables 4.10 and 4.11. On the border, the expected differences are there: Protestants were much likelier to advocate the status quo, or even closer integration with Britain; Catholics were much likelier to advocate an end to the border. But the polarization was not total. Among Protestants, 23

Table 4.10.   Attitudes to the border, 1968 (%)
Question: 'what changes, if any, would you like to see concerning the Border?'

Change	Protestant	Catholic
Merge with Britain	10	2
No change	45	21
More co-operation across the Border	12	9
Abolish: alternative vague	19	42
Abolish and unite Ireland	4	14
Don't know	11	12

Source: Rose (1971, 213).

Table 4.11.   Attitudes to constitutional change, 1968 (%)
Question: 'there has always been a lot of controversy about the Constitutional position of Northern Ireland. On balance, do you approve or disapprove of it?'

	Protestant	Catholic
Approve	68	33
Disapprove	10	34
Don't know	22	32

Source: Rose (1971, 477).

per cent were prepared to envisage the abolition of the border in some form; among Catholics, 23 per cent were prepared to accept the status quo or even to merge with Britain. On the constitutional position, some respondents evidently had difficulty in deciding what the question meant, as is suggested by the large number of 'don't knows'. None the less, it is interesting to find that, once again, polarization was far from total. While most Protestants, predictably, supported the constitution, only one-third of Catholics disapproved of it, and another one-third actually approved.

These early polls suggest a fair degree of flexibility existed in the 1960s, particularly on the Catholic side.

The Surveys of 1973–1989

When surveys revived, after the height of the troubles in the early 1970s, the situation had been transformed. The Northern Ireland Parliament had been suspended; constitutional change was in the air. From now on, it was possible to refer to much more precise options when polling the people, because a number of such options—a united Ireland in various forms, integration with the rest of the United Kingdom, an independent Northern Ireland, joint sovereignty—were being floated. Most of all, 'power-sharing' became a concept with content and meaning when the power-sharing executive took office at the beginning of 1974, comprising ministers drawn from both the Protestant and Catholic communities. Even though the executive fell within a few months, the fact that it had existed meant that people had an image of a power-sharing system to which to refer when they were asked their opinions. It is not surprising, then, to find that the survey data from now on are much more precise in their questions than the surveys of 1967–8.

Between 1973 and 1989 at least twenty-five polls have been taken in Northern Ireland which have sought to elucidate attitudes to various constitutional arrangements. I have listed them in Appendix B. Responses vary according to the precise question asked, so that it is not easy to sustain comparisons. None the less, if one is careful to allow for variations in the questions asked, there is a considerable degree of consistency between the different polls. Even events which are supposed to have traumatized one community or the other, like the hunger-strikes of 1981 or the Anglo-Irish Agreement of 1985, made little difference to underlying preferences. I shall outline the salient findings, discussing the level of support to be found for eight different solutions that have been explored at one time or other in the polls.

1. There is little support among Protestants for any form of a united Ireland. When asked what solution they would prefer, the proportion of Protestants choosing a united Ireland varied between 1 and 4 per cent. When asked what solution would be acceptable to them personally, the results were usually in single figures. The best result from a nationalist point of view came in a poll of February 1982, when 15 per cent of Protestants said they could accept a federal united Ireland, and 6 per cent said they would even accept a unitary State. Most Protestants are reluctant to see a united Ireland, even as something for the distant future. Two polls have probed on this issue. The first, in June 1974, asked if a united Ireland sometime in the future would be best for Northern Ireland. Eighteen per cent of Protestants said 'yes'; 81 per cent said 'no'. The second, in February 1982, asked if respondents would like to see a united Ireland sometime in the future. Eight per cent of Protestants said 'yes'; 85 per cent said 'no'.

   There is far from complete support among Catholics for a united Ireland. True, as a long-term objective it receives widespread acceptance. In 1974 77 per cent and in 1982 82 per cent of Catholics favoured a united Ireland sometime in the future. But, when asked about it as an immediate objective, the proportions are much lower. In only one poll (February 1982) did a majority of Catholics give any kind of a united Ireland as their preferred solution (38 per cent for integration with the Republic plus 13 per cent for a federal Ireland). Usually a united Ireland was a less popular preference than power-sharing within a devolved parliament.

2. There is more Catholic support for integration with Britain than there is Protestant support for a united Ireland. Though it is not often mentioned by Catholics as their first choice—the percentages have varied between 6 in April 1974 and 19 in March 1976—it is much more frequently mentioned as an acceptable outcome—by 55 per cent in March 1976, by 39 per cent in June 1981, by 45 per cent in February 1982, and by 36 per cent in February 1989. Protestants, naturally enough, are

prepared to accept it by massive majorities—80, 91, 88, and 83 per cent in the four polls just cited. It is the first preference of a sizeable minority of Protestants—the percentage usually being in the thirties or forties.

3. One option popular with Protestants is a return to majority rule within Northern Ireland. When asked if this is acceptable to them, a majority of Protestants have always said 'yes'. However, in view of the consistent opposition of the London government to such a settlement, it has hardly been a realistic option, and the polls indicate that this has been appreciated. When asked for their preferred option, only a minority of Protestants have chosen it. The highest figure occurs in Moxon-Browne's poll of 1978, in which 38 per cent of Protestants described it as the solution in their view 'most workable and acceptable' (Moxon-Browne 1983, 85). Catholics, with memories of fifty years of majority rule, usually find it the most distasteful of all courses. When asked which settlement they prefer, the proportion of Catholics choosing majority rule has generally been 1 or 2 per cent. When asked if it is acceptable, most will say 'no'. The best that this option has done among Catholics was in March 1976, when 25 per cent said it would be acceptable to them personally.

4. There is little support in either community for an independent Northern Ireland. The percentages choosing it as their first preference have consistently been in single figures for both Protestants and Catholics. The only circumstance in which it becomes popular is among Protestants, when proposed as the only alternative to a united Ireland. In February 1982, in reply to the question 'if the future of Northern Ireland had to take one of two forms—a United Ireland of 32 counties, or an Independent Ulster, which would you prefer?', 71 per cent of Protestants preferred an independent Ulster, as against 12 per cent for a united Ireland. (The equivalent figures for Catholics were 75 for a united Ireland, and 9 per cent for an independent Ulster.) Moxon-Browne's data (1983, 25) also showed that Protestants found an independent Northern Ireland less unpalatable than a united Ireland, but by a much narrower margin. When asked which solution they would *least* like to see, 50 per cent of Protestants chose a united Ireland, but 31 per cent chose independence. (Among Catholics, independence was the

most unpopular, with 47 per cent choosing it; devolution, whether power-sharing or by majority rule, came second, with 32 per cent.)

5. Another option with limited support is repartition. This has been asked about only twice, in June 1981 and February 1982. The percentage of Protestants finding it acceptable was 9 and 8; of Catholics, 22 and 24. One can see that to those Catholics in border areas who desire union with the Republic it might be acceptable as meeting their personal preferences; but it would do nothing for Catholics living in the unionist heartland.

6. The option which attracts most widespread support in both communities is power-sharing. Among Catholics, it has normally been the most popular first preference, with percentages selecting it usually in the thirties or forties. If asked whether it is acceptable, percentages rise much higher—to 88 in April 1974, 83 in January 1978, 75 in May 1982, 78 in January 1986, 78 again in February 1989. Among Protestants, positive support has been considerably lower—normally in the tens or twenties. But the percentage finding it acceptable has been larger—52, 51, 45, 61, and 57 in the five polls just cited.

7. Joint authority has occasionally been asked about, particularly since the New Ireland Forum of 1984 broached it as a possible form of settlement. It is few people's first choice, but is less unpalatable to Catholics than to Protestants. For instance, in April 1988 28 per cent of Catholics but only 4 per cent of Protestants were prepared to accept it.

8. Direct rule has seldom been a popular option. The high point of favour was shown in a poll of March 1976, when 72 per cent of Protestants and 79 per cent of Catholics stated that it would be acceptable to them; but, even in that poll, only 14 per cent of Protestants and 26 per cent of Catholics made it their first choice. Direct rule is, after all, only intended as a temporary device. It is not surprising, therefore, that few people make it their preferred form of settlement.

In assessing the evidence just summarized, the reader must remember the warnings given in Chapter 1 about the use of survey evidence. There is reason to believe that in Northern Ireland people tend to sound more moderate than they really feel when replying to interviewers. I would suspect, then, that the proportion of Protestants who hanker after majority rule, and of Catholics who want a united Ireland, is higher than the survey evidence indicates, and that the proportion of Catholics who would accept integration with Britain, or of both communities who would settle for power-sharing, is lower than the data suggest. Nevertheless, even when these provisos are made, one conclusion from the evidence seems inescapable: that Catholics are less determinedly in favour of a united Ireland than Protestants are against it. In this section as in the section on party support, we find that Protestants are more cohesive than Catholics.

LAW AND ORDER

So far in this chapter we have been discussing political differences without reference to the violence which Northern Ireland has endured since 1969. But the violence is there, as a constant backdrop to political contention. According to British official figures there were, between 1969 and the end of 1988, over 30,000 shooting incidents, nearly 9,000 explosions, nearly 14,000 armed robberies, and over 8,000 malicious fires (Irish Information Partnership 1989). The number of deaths was 2,710, and the number of injuries 31,046. The violence comes from several quarters. Taking deaths as an index, the most detailed statistics have been worked out by Michael McKeown in his pamphlet bleakly entitled *Two Seven Six Three* (1989), to commemorate the 2,763 fatalities which occurred in the twenty years between the first death on 13 July 1969 and 12 July 1989. He calculates that 57.6 per cent of the deaths had been caused by the IRA and other republican paramilitaries; 25.8 per cent by loyalist paramilitaries; 11.8 per cent by the security forces; and 4.7 per cent by mob violence or unidentified sources (p. 4). The violence of republican and to a lesser extent loyalist paramilitaries has provoked an array of countermeasures: internment without trial (from 1971 to 1975), trials without jury, a vast expansion of the police force (Royal Ulster Constabulary, or RUC), the raising of a local regiment of the British Army (the Ulster Defence Regiment, or UDR), house searches, road-blocks, police interrogations, the use of supergrasses, the employment of plastic bullets, and many more. The violence of the paramilitaries, and the counter-violence of the State, are likely to have marked different people in different ways, according to where they perceive the main threat as coming from. Reactions to the violence can be traced in the survey data. The data on such issues are less satisfactory than on constitutional matters—partly because fewer relevant surveys have been conducted, partly because the evidence is bunched towards the end of the period. All the more illuminating surveys date from 1978 or later, as if pollsters only slowly woke up to the fact that the violence itself was part of the problem, not a by-product that would disappear once the right constitutional formula was found. The warning must be repeated that surveys are likely to under-report extreme views and over-report moderate ones: we may suspect, for instance, that support for republican and loyalist paramilitaries is stronger, and support for State forces is weaker, in reality than the surveys show. None the less, the material available is sufficient in quantity and variety to make its examination worth while. The two most illuminating surveys are the academic ones by Moxon-Browne in 1978 and by Smith in 1986. (Moxon-Browne's results on this issue are to be found, not in his book *Nation, Class and Creed in Northern Ireland* (1983), but in a separate article (Moxon-Browne 1981).) I shall also cite polls commissioned by newspapers and television companies, where these are relevant.

The survey data show that the two communities' experience of violence were not identical. Smith (1987*b*, 21–34) is the most important source on this matter. He found that a considerably higher proportion of Catholics than of Protestants reported violent incidents as having occurred in their neighbourhood (p. 21). The gap was widest in Belfast, where, for instance, 72 per cent of Catholics as against 49 per cent of Protestants reported that there had been a shooting incident in their neighbourhood (p. 22). The sources of violence, however, were surprisingly similar for both communities. Republican violence had been experienced by Catholics as well as Protestants; loyalist violence by Protestants as well as Catholics. Smith concludes that, while there is some tendency for each community to see members of its own community as victims and the other community as attackers, 'what is most striking is that this tendency is not particularly strong' (p. 25).

In view of the violence which both communities have experienced from both groups of paramilitaries, it is not surprising to find that paramilitaries are widely disliked in both communities. The IRA draws virtually unanimous hostility from Protestants, but also extensive hostility from Catholics. In Moxon-Browne's survey (Moxon-Browne 1981, 58) 92 per cent of Protestants agreed with the statement that 'the IRA are basically a bunch of criminals and murderers'—but then so did 66 per cent of Catholics. True, perhaps inconsistently, 46 per cent of Catholics also agreed with the statement that 'the IRA are basically patriots and idealists'—but then so did 35 per cent of Protestants. On the other side, the statement that 'the actions of loyalist paramilitaries are a justified reaction to what has happened in Northern Ireland' was agreed to by only 25 per cent of Catholics—but it was also agreed to by only a minority (44 per cent) of Protestants (Moxon-Browne 1981, 59). A poll in February 1982 showed that the formation of a Third Force by the Revd Ian Paisley was disapproved of by 98 per cent of Catholics—but it was also disapproved of by 58 per cent of Protestants.

It does not follow, however, that the security forces are invariably popular. Moxon-Browne found in 1978, as Table 4.12 shows, that they received almost unanimous approval from Protestants and considerable support from Catholics. But, eight years later, Smith found, as Table 4.13 shows, that approval had fallen off sharply among Catholics and to some extent even among Protestants. Smith's data show also a growing difference in perceptions of the three security forces. The regular Army comes off best from the comparison: both Catholics and Protestants are likelier to see it as impartial than they are the police or UDR. The UDR comes off worst. Even in 1978 the gap was noticeable; by 1986 it was massive. Not only most Catholics, but even a substantial minority of Protestants, saw it as being biased against Catholics. A survey conducted for the BBC in May 1985 which asked whether the UDR should be given a greater role found that 76 per cent of Protestants but only

Table 4.12. Attitudes towards the security forces, 1978 (%)

Statement	Proportion agreeing	
	Protestant	Catholic
The RUC is doing its job well	94	73
The UDR is doing its job well	94	64
The British Army is doing its job well	92	71

Source: Moxon-Browne (1981, 65).

Table 4.13. Attitudes towards the security forces, 1986 (%)

Statement	Proportion agreeing	
	Protestant	Catholic
The police treat both groups equally	75	42
The British Army treat both groups equally	85	68
The UDR treat both groups equally	68	27
The police treat Protestants better	11	56
The British Army treat Protestants better	9	28
The UDR treat Protestants better	27	68
The police treat Catholics better	12	1
The British Army treat Catholics better	3	*
The UDR treat Catholics better	1	—

* Less than 0.5% of respondents fell into the category.
Source: Adapted from Smith (1987*b*, 125).

11 per cent of Catholics agreed. The RUC occupied an intermediate position. Smith's data, shown in Table 4.13, indicate this. The BBC poll of May 1985 showed Catholics as being somewhat more willing to accept a stronger role for the RUC than the UDR. In reply to a question on whether the RUC should be strengthened, 38 per cent of Catholics, as well as 90 per cent of Protestants, said they would approve. A poll taken for the *Belfast Telegraph* in January 1985 which asked 'how fair do you think the RUC is in the discharge of its duties in Northern Ireland?' found Catholic opinion almost equally divided. Forty-seven per cent thought it fair or very fair; 53 per cent thought it unfair or very unfair. Protestants, needless to say, were almost unanimous in its support: 96 per cent of them thought it fair or very fair.

These variations are explicable. The regular Army units which serve in Northern Ireland are recruited overwhelmingly from mainland Britain. They serve on limited tours, and remain relatively detached from both communities. The UDR is locally recruited and overwhelmingly Protestant in composition. There have been many Press reports over the years of Catholics complaining of harassment by UDR patrols. The RUC is also locally recruited and predominantly Protestant, but it has sought to distance itself from the tensions of a divided society 'through emphasis on professionalism and autonomy' (Brewer *et al.* 1988, 81).

Behind the security forces lie the courts. Attitudes to the courts have been less extensively tested than attitudes to the Army and police. However, there are a couple of relevant polls. A survey in February 1985 found that 89 per cent of Protestants, and only 36 per cent of Catholics, thought that the legal system in Northern Ireland dispensed justice fairly. On the other side, 57 per cent of Catholics, and only 9 per cent of Protestants, thought that it dispensed justice unfairly. Smith's survey of 1986 provides further data. Smith asked respondents if they thought the courts were fair when dealing with Protestants, and the great majority, both Protestant and Catholic, thought that they were. He then asked if they thought the courts were fair when dealing with Catholics, and here he got a split reaction. Seventy-eight per cent of Protestants, as against 45 per cent of Catholics, thought that they were fair; 36 per cent of Catholics, as against 7 per cent of Protestants, thought that they were unfair (Smith 1987*b*, 120).

Opinions in the two communities differed most widely in respect of specific security measures. In the late 1970s there were reports, subsequently sustained in part by a government inquiry (Bennett 1979, paras. 158–64), that suspects were being maltreated while in RUC custody. Moxon-Browne (1981, 65) found that 64 per cent of Protestants, but only 22 per cent of Catholics, dismissed these reports as propaganda. During the 1980s there has been a sharp controversy on whether the RUC operates a 'shoot-to-kill' policy against terrorist suspects. A poll in May 1985 asked whether there ought to be a shoot-to-kill policy. Sixty-one per cent of Protestants, but only 7 per cent of Catholics, said there should. A poll in September 1988 asked if internment should be reintroduced. Sixty-seven per cent of Protestants, but only 10 per cent of Catholics, agreed. The sharpest division of all was revealed by a question about plastic bullets. A poll in February 1985, at a time when several Catholic children had been killed by plastic bullets, asked 'do you approve or disapprove of the use of plastic bullets by the security forces as a weapon during riots?' Eighty-six per cent of Protestants, but only 9 per cent of Catholics, approved. Eighty-seven per cent of Catholics, but only 8 per cent of Protestants, disapproved. This is the sharpest division that I have found on any question in any opinion poll held in Northern Ireland. Given the fact that surveys in Northern Ireland appear to overstate moderate opinion, then one may presume that in reality the polarization between Protestant and

Catholics on issues such as shoot-to-kill, internment, or the use of plastic bullets is even greater than the polls indicate.

On security matters, polarization between the communities is not total in all respects. The IRA has killed Catholics as well as Protestants, so some Catholics have as good reason as many Protestants to approve of strong measures against it. The security measures used against the IRA have also been used against Protestant paramilitaries, and so have provoked hostility among some Protestants as well as many Catholics. However, it seems true to say that there is an even greater degree of disagreement between Protestant and Catholics on security policy than there is on constitutional questions. Security issues remain as an unhealed sore. Even if, by some miracle, leaders from the two communities could agree on a political settlement, it might still be jeopardized by disagreement over the security measures needed to combat the extremists, who, on one side or both, could be expected to keep alive the conflict.

THE EVIDENCE FROM PARTICIPANT-OBSERVATION STUDIES

So far in this chapter I have used survey evidence. This is natural, because the great bulk of the evidence on mass political attitudes comes in survey form. But survey questions do often force respondents into a spurious precision about their opinions. A question which asks for a yes/no answer, or even an answer in terms of 'strongly agree/mildly agree/mildly disagree/strongly disagree', squeezes out nuance and ambiguity. To explore the full range of popular attitudes we need some more sensitive instrument of research. Fortunately the participant-observation studies can sometimes meet the need. Not all of them examine the overt political attitudes of the communities under study, but those that do are in a better position than a survey to portray the less easily articulated emotions, such as ambivalence or frustration. I shall take two examples, one from each side of the community divide.

Father Brian Lennon, SJ, describes the attitudes of Catholics in London Park, a seriously deprived housing estate in an unnamed town. After describing the intensely felt grievances against the security forces and the judicial system, he goes on:

Despite all this the attitude of Nationalists in this estate towards continued unity with Britain remains ambiguous. There is a mixture of bitterness, dependance [*sic*] and interest. Bitterness because it is realised that Britain does have enormous military, economic, and legal power in the conflict and has used this more often than not to support Unionists; dependence, because Nationalists realise the Republic of Ireland could not support the Northern welfare system; interest, in aspects of British life such as football and royalty.

The attitude to Dublin is similarly ambiguous. On the one hand the desire for a United Ireland is vociferously expressed and Nationalists identify with the flag of the Republic of Ireland. Yet . . . the Republic is seen as a country with bad roads, bad telephones, high prices and a place where the Northern Nationalist receives little understanding or sympathy. (Lennon 1984, 311.)

On the other side of the divide, John Darby brings out the splits and feuds in two working-class Protestant areas of Belfast that lie behind their apparently monolithic loyalism:

What sort of activities, then, constituted the organised community life of Everton/Vestry? A Glasgow Rangers Supporters' Club was sufficiently popular to be able to restrict its membership to 150. Separate community associations had been formed at different times in Vestry and Everton and both had collapsed as a result of internal feuding. Vestry Community Association was formed in 1976, but was largely the creation of one family and supported by 'Peace People types'; the UDA tried to take it over, the original founders left and the association folded. In Everton a community association had been formed in the mid-1970s and played a part in the campaign to build Everton Community Centre. But shortly afterwards strong splits developed between individual members, Belfast Corporation took over the running of the Centre and the association dissolved. As in Vestry there was a paramilitary dimension to the feuds. (Darby 1986, 115.)

Darby notes the territorial antagonisms between and within both estates (p. 119), and the weakness of the Protestant Churches (p. 114). His conclusion is that 'the predominant impression of the communities in Everton and Vestry was one of social fragmentation' (p. 119).

Another way in which participant-observation studies are valuable is that they tap differences between one area and another. Survey data, as usually reported, give only average figures for Protestant and Catholic in Northern Ireland as a whole. These can conceal great local variations. It is only when local studies are consulted that the full range of such variations becomes apparent. For instance, at one extreme is a district such as Upper Tullagh, examined by Buckley in his book aptly entitled *A Gentle People: A Study of a Peaceful Community in Ulster* (1982). This district, about three-quarters Catholic and one-quarter Protestant, is portrayed as existing in harmony. 'It is, in general, rare to hear anyone in the Upper Tullagh express strong unionist or republican sentiments' (p. 163). The only violence in the area was attributed to strangers, and, 'it was under the auspices of the local protestant and Catholic clergy that "vigilante" patrols of all denominations were set up to patrol the streets. These quickly disappeared as they were found to be unnecessary' (p. 141). Friendships crossed the sectarian divide. When, a few years previously, the local Protestant band had been in danger of dissolving, it was a Catholic who organized the fund-raising function which put it back on its feet (p. 140).

There is no way of knowing how typical of other parts of Northern Ireland Upper Tullagh might be. Campbell's study of Glenarm (1978) and Bufwack's of Naghera (1982) suggest that it is not unique. Darby's study (1986) of Dunville, a market town which had suffered from a bout of communal intimidation in 1981, showed that even in such a context peaceful relations could be restored and a fair degree of cross-community integration maintained. Indeed Upper Tullagh may not even be at the extreme end of the scale of harmony. In Upper Tullagh Catholics remain nationalist and Protestants remain unionist, albeit mildly so. No researcher has yet studied the north Down coast, from Holywood through Bangor to Donaghadee. This is the richest part of Northern Ireland (see the map in Compton 1978, 135). I have been told that some of its small Catholic minority are so well integrated with their neighbours that they are active in the Official Unionist Party. It may be significant that the All Children Together movement for integrated education originated in this area. However, I would suspect that an Upper Tullagh-like degree of harmony, or more, is experienced by only a small minority of the population of Northern Ireland.

At the other extreme, even though only thirty miles away from Upper Tullagh, lies Catholic west Belfast. It has been studied by a number of authors: most notably Burton (1978), Darby (1986), Belfrage (1987), and Conroy (1988). A composite picture can be drawn from these sources. Social conditions are deplorable: high unemployment, bad housing, lack of amenities, dirt, vandalism (e.g. Darby 1986, 40–2). There is virtually no contact with Protestants: the only outsiders whom the people regularly meet are the Army and the RUC. The Army is hated or ignored (Darby 1986, 36, 123; Burton, 1978, 86). The RUC is also disliked, but the people sometimes need its services—for instance, to authenticate a claim for insurance (Darby 1986, 123; Belfrage 1987, 249). Sinn Féin and the IRA enjoy substantial support. Burton (1978, 81–110), who did his field-work in 1971–2, portrays the IRA as having solid backing from about one-third of the people of Anro, while the other two-thirds tacked back and forth, depending on whether the latest atrocity had come from the Army or the IRA. The other authors, who did their field-work in the 1980s, give the impression of a more settled stratum of support for Sinn Féin. Conroy (1988, 8–9) draws a vivid picture of the republican counter-culture which has grown up in west Belfast:

No child in west Belfast knows the words to the national anthem; not a school in the district sings 'God Save the Queen.' The Union Jack flies only above the police barracks and the army forts, while Irish tricolors—the flag of the Republic of Ireland—fly everywhere else. Families proudly advertise that their kin have done time in prison, decorating their walls and window sills with prison crafts. ... IRA veterans drink in a club called the Felons Association and proudly march in parades behind signs identifying them as ex-cons, banners identifying the Lower Falls Former Prisoners of War, the Andersonstown Ex-Prisoners Association, or any of a half dozen similar groups.

That does not mean that everyone backs the IRA. Belfrage (1987, 115–34) interviewed members of the Workers Party who had plenty of reason to be anti-British but who did not draw the same conclusions as Sinn Féin. Darby (1986, 109) portrays the Catholic Church as making a determined attempt to win back influence in 'a strong campaign against the Provisionals, which was conducted with the style and vigour of the counter-reformation'. Perhaps the most stubborn obstacle to IRA hegemony were the 'hoods'—non-political young criminals—who were amazingly brazen and prepared to defy the law-enforcement efforts of the IRA as well as of the RUC (Darby 1986, 158–61; Belfrage 1987, 91; Conroy 1988, 80–92). But what we do not find in these studies of west Belfast is any support for the State or empathy with the Protestant majority. This is an embattled community, which feels oppressed and is divided only on how to express its defiance.

How far west Belfast is representative of other Catholic parts of Northern Ireland remains uncertain. Such areas elsewhere have not been extensively researched. But one would expect that some other solidly Catholic parts of Northern Ireland, such as Derry city west of the Foyle or south Armagh, would display similar attitudes. In such areas the British and the Protestants are met mainly in the guise of invading security forces. A visiting Dublin journalist reports a conversation with a Sinn Féin activist in south Armagh:

He wondered what the British were doing here. . . . . They weren't keeping the peace, as the place was perfectly peaceful, there was no trouble between Catholic and Protestant, neighbour and neighbour as there was elsewhere. The war was between the locals and the British army. So what would happen if the British army withdrew? Peace, quiet, harmony, that's what would happen. (Tóibín 1987, 143.)

Embittered attitudes are also to be found in loyalist areas. Jenkins (1982, 1983) studied the housing estate of Ballyhightown, north of Belfast. It was almost exclusively Protestant: the reason was that the Catholic minority had been intimidated out, or at least had left in fear, early in the troubles (Jenkins 1982, 12; 1983, 35). This did not mean that tolerance had returned: Jenkins records some bitterly anti-Catholic remarks (1982, 31, 38). Sarah Nelson in studying Belfast working-class loyalists found that though they were confused and bewildered about many things there was one issue on which they were rock-firm: they would not have a united Ireland on any terms:

There was least confusion about the Irish Republic. Like other loyalists, most people in the workers' wings saw that a [*sic*] society as alien and hostile. Few could think of anything they had in common with southerners, and [they] were convinced these would only use any proposed Council of Ireland as a base for extending their political power over the North. A favourite slogan of the time, 'Six into twenty-six won't go', was very revealing of the general outlook among loyalists. . . . They cannot visualise unity that does not involve annexation or suppression. (Nelson 1984, 113.)

One thing that seemed to arouse particular annoyance among Protestants was the assumption that they were better off than Catholics (Nelson 1984, 73–4; Belfrage 1987, 38–40, 52, 101, 269–70). They felt that they were just as impoverished, just as often discriminated against, and they resented the favour which world opinion seemed to bestow on the Catholics.

The participant-observation studies are important because they bring out these local variations. If we were to go by the survey data alone we might think that a compromise solution was practicable, on the lines of power-sharing in a United Kingdom context. The local studies bring home that the survey results are only averages. It is difficult to imagine such a compromise being acceptable to either the Catholics of west Belfast or the hard-line loyalists of some other areas. One of the difficulties built into the Northern Ireland problem is that Northern Ireland, small though it is, encompasses widely varying sub-regions, and a compromise that might be acceptable to the people of one such sub-region may be intolerable to the people of another.

5

Psychological Aspects, and a Review

PSYCHOLOGICAL FACTORS

Anyone who studies Northern Ireland must be struck by the intensity of feeling which the conflict evokes. It seems to go beyond what is required by a rational defence of the divergent interests which undoubtedly exist. There is an emotional element here, a welling-up of deep unconscious forces. It is worth examining what contribution psychology can make to an explanation of the conflict.

The first observer to stress such an approach was a journalist, Harold Jackson, whose pamphlet for the Minority Rights Group *The Two Irelands* (1971) was heavily psychological in its emphasis. Jackson described Northern Ireland as 'a society suffering from a deep psychosis in which rational thought and action are invariable [*sic*] overtaken by emotional spasms the moment it comes under stress' (p. 4). He added:

It is fatally easy for the detached observer to ask loftily why the two sides don't just do this or that to resolve their differences. There is always the calm assumption that reasonable men sitting round a table can come to terms with any problem. But it is vital to grasp that this sort of 'reason' is still far off in Ulster because of the enormous build-up in pressure created by the quite genuine fears on each side. The fact that these fears are often based on incorrect assumptions does not mean that they are any less strongly felt on that account.

He went on to give many examples of unreasonable conduct or beliefs, coming from both sides of the divide.

Jackson, however, was not a professional psychologist, and, apart from a couple of references to the work of Robert Ardrey and Konrad Lorenz, he provided no theoretical explanation for the patterns of behaviour he observed. One of the first writers with qualifications in any area of psychology to explore the Northern Ireland problem was the child psychiatrist Morris Fraser. In his book *Children in Conflict* (1973), Fraser, applying what is known as frustration-aggression theory, argued that every culture needs an out-group, particularly in a period of change. The out-group's function is to act as scapegoat for the majority's frustrations. It is defined by stereotypes which are surprisingly uniform from culture to culture: fecklessness, overbreeding, and so on. Doubts about the validity of these stereotypes are stilled by imposing social distance, and discontent is explained away as the work of agitators. Meanwhile, the out-group is obeying its own laws of development. As economic conditions improve, its expectations rise, and conditions previously acquiesced in become intolerable. The out-group's increasing self-assertion reinforces the majority's hostility, and conflict ensues. Fraser believed that the development of Northern Ireland fitted this pattern well (Fraser 1973, especially 87–104). He supported his argument with quotations from loyalist publications such as the *Protestant Telegraph*, and from the clinical notes which he had collected in his practice in Belfast.

Fraser provided a lucidly argued and testable explanation of the rising tension. If he was right, one would expect to find higher levels of prejudice and rigidity among Protestants, as the dominant group under threat, than among Catholics. Psychologists have developed tests for measuring prejudice, tolerance, and related characteristics, and researchers have applied these tests in Northern Ireland. Some of the results support Fraser's hypothesis. Salters (1970) tested over 900 children in Belfast grammar and secondary schools, and found that Catholics appeared more tolerant than Protestants on tests both of general and of religious tolerance. Jahoda and Harrison (1975, 17), testing a small sample of Belfast primary schoolboys, found a depressingly high level of ethnocentrism, but reported that such difference as there was showed a more charitable attitude among Catholics. Fairleigh (1975), using a small sample of further-education students, found that Protestants showed more social distance towards Catholics than vice versa. The same finding was reported by Arthur (1974), using a larger, though admittedly unsystematic, sample of children who had been away together on inter-faith holidays. Russell (1974, 7), who conducted extensive research on primary and second-level schoolboys in the early 1970s, found that Catholics were somewhat more likely to express friendliness towards Protestants than Protestants were to Catholics. Doob and Foltz, who brought Catholics and Protestants together in a psychological workshop, found that Catholics seemed to have a rather better understanding of Protestants than the other way round. 'This', they reported, 'was dramatically illustrated during a role-playing simulation when otherwise very capable Protestants taking Catholic roles performed ineptly, while Catholics playing Protestants drew cheers from real-life Protestant observers' (Doob and Foltz 1973, 504). Greer (1985) developed an 'openness scale' to test openness towards the other religion and administered it to 2,000 schoolchildren. He found that Catholics were significantly more open to Protestants than vice versa.

However, not all studies have supported Fraser's hypotheses. E. E. O'Donnell (1977), testing a large sample of Catholics and Protestants in three different locations, found that Catholics had more hostile stereotypes of Protestants than vice versa. Kremer, Barry, and McNally (1986), using two devices for measuring prejudice known as the misdirected letter and the quasi-questionnaire, found that in disturbed areas Catholics appeared more prejudiced than Protestants, though there was no difference in peaceful areas. Karen Trew attempted with her students to replicate the findings of Fairleigh and of Jahoda and Harrison, and was unable to do so (Trew 1980). Indeed Trew and McWhirter (1982, 200) conclude that the findings in this field are 'contradictory and sometimes incomprehensible'. Moreover, scholars from other disciplines who have listened carefully to what Protestants have to say do not always report hearing the racialist stereotypes that Fraser assumes. Harris (1972, 171) stated: 'I mixed a great deal with the poorer hill Protestants and they never gave me directly or indirectly the impression that they thought of their farmer neighbours as anything but their social equals.' Nelson (1975, 167–8), reporting on conversations with Protestant activists in Belfast, found that most did not consider Catholics as inherently work-shy, and that few used language that could be described as racialist. Leyton (1974, 194), reporting on two neighbouring areas, one Catholic and one Protestant, wrote: 'in contrast to many divided societies which deny the humanity of opposing groups or classes, the inhabitants of Aughnaboy and Blackrock regard each other as equally and fully human, only misguided and perverted by heretical doctrines and evil institutions'.

It is perhaps also worth mentioning that, in the general psychological literature, the frustration-aggression theory appears to be dated. As one authority puts it (Konečni 1979, 100): 'Almost all of the important original (1939) postulates of the frustration-aggression hypothesis have been shown to be wrong. ... For example, neither is frustration always followed by aggression, nor is aggression always preceded by frustration.'

The appeal made by Fraser to frustration-aggression theory has, then, had inconclusive results. In these circumstances, it is not surprising that psychologists researching the Northern Ireland conflict have looked elsewhere for a theoretical underpinning to their work. Since the early 1980s they seem to have lost interest in efforts to measure the relative levels of ethnocentrism, tolerance, and so on in the two communities. Instead many of them have turned for inspiration to a theory pioneered by Professor Henri Tajfel (1919–82) of the University of Bristol, which has achieved growing popularity among social psychologists. It is known as social identity theory (see e.g. Tajfel and Turner 1979, especially pp. 40–3).

In outline, it goes as follows. Individuals belong to social groups. They also strive to maintain or enhance their self-esteem. They do this largely by distinguishing their group from neighbouring groups along some dimension which makes them superior. That in itself is sufficient to generate competition. Tajfel and his colleagues found in laboratory experiments that the urge to evaluate one's group positively is very deep-seated: it can apply to groups which had no existence before the experiment began, and competition between groups holds even when it conflicts with self-interest.

Social identity theory can reasonably be applied to Northern Ireland. Ed Cairns, a social psychologist at the University of Ulster, has assembled evidence from a number of research studies which indicate that Northern Ireland data fit the theory (Cairns 1982; 1987, 95–117). If the theory is right, it has advantages. It can explain why in Northern Ireland the intensity of group conflict appears to go beyond what the real interests of the groups would seem to require. Furthermore, it can help explain the preoccupation with identity that many observers have noted in Northern Ireland.

THE NORTHERN IRELAND PROBLEM AS A CLASH OF IDENTITIES

In recent years a number of authorities, none of whom are psychologists and most of whom, one may safely guess, have never heard of Tajfel, have talked about the Northern Ireland conflict as being fundamentally a clash of identities. A British white paper saw the problem in this way:

The majority of the population in Northern Ireland think of themselves as British. They regard themselves as part of the social and cultural fabric of the United Kingdom and their loyalty lies to the Crown. . . . There is also a substantial minority within Northern Ireland who think of themselves as Irish, whether in terms of their identity, their social and cultural traditions, or their political aspirations. . . . This difference in identity and aspiration lies at the heart of the 'problem' of Northern Ireland; it cannot be ignored or wished away. (UK Government 1982, paras. 15–17.)

Similar analyses can be found on the nationalist side of the fence. Dr Garret FitzGerald, the then taoiseach, called his Dimbleby lecture of 1982 *Irish Identities*, and used it to explore the confusion of identities existing within Ireland. As he put it:

All of us human beings feel that we must *belong*, not just to a nuclear family, but to a larger community, which demands a loyalty to it, but gives in response a comforting sense of being part of a greater whole, a wider family of millions. It would be a defective statesmanship that ignored this reality.

It is when more than one focus of identity is to be found within a single geographical area—whether it is the identity of white or black in South Africa or the Southern States of America—or in Brixton—or of Greek or Turk in Cyprus, or of Christian or Arab in the Lebanon—that an explosive situation may be created. This is the nature of the problem of Northern Ireland. (FitzGerald 1982, 5–6.)

Much the same argument was developed in the report of the New Ireland Forum, which spoke at length of the two identities in Northern Ireland and the need to reconcile them (New Ireland Forum 1984, paras. 4.6–4.16).

Academic writers have written along similar lines. The historian A. T. Q. Stewart, in his discussion of the Northern Ireland problem *The Narrow Ground* (1977), does not use the word 'identity', but he is clearly aware of the concept. He speaks of two communities living in the same territory but with contradictory myths and aspirations. Desmond Rea of the University of Ulster at Jordanstown, editing a volume of papers on *Political Co-operation in Divided Societies* (1982), writes that 'the conflict in Northern Ireland is one between different traditions and identities and allegiances' (p. 1). The historian Charles Townshend (1988, 11–12), after noting that Protestants in many ways share a common culture with Catholics, argues that 'if it is not cultural distinctness, it must be some form of identity that accounts for the universally attested persistence of a feeling of apartness'. Another historian, Brian Girvin of University College Cork (1986*b*, 107), writes in a survey of the Northern Ireland problem that 'the question of identity is at the heart of any understanding of the conflict'.

Other writers, too, have seen the importance of identity. The travel writer Dervla Murphy, in her book on Northern Ireland, *A Place Apart* (1978, 162) reports a remark by one of those she interviewed: 'It's all about identity; who's what? If everybody in Northern Ireland could answer that question, *without* hesitation, we'd be more than halfway to a solution.' The American journalist Sally Belfrage (1987, 112, 162, 267, 294–5), who spent a year in Belfast, refers repeatedly to the preoccupation with identity shown by the people she met. The Irish author Desmond Fennell states in his latest book *The Revision of Irish Nationalism* (1989, 39) that he has been writing about the need to recognize both identities since 1971.

There is widespread agreement, not just that identity is important, but that of the two communities it is the Protestants who have more difficulty in deciding what their identity is. We have seen in Chapter 4 how Protestants, when asked to choose a national label for themselves, have tacked uncertainly between 'British', 'Irish', and 'Ulster'. Bruce (1986, 249–70) has, as we shall see later in this chapter, argued that the religious label was so important to Protestants because it was their only secure identity. Sarah Nelson (1985, 12), in her participant-observation study of Belfast Protestants, noted that 'most loyalists have complex and ambivalent feelings of identity, in different situations, a sense of "Ulsterness", "Britishness" or even "Irishness" may dominate'. Sally Belfrage (1987, 294), after referring to loyalists' constant celebrations of past events, concludes: 'those events are just about the sum of their past; without them they don't know who they are, but only who they aren't (or, more accurately, who they don't want to be)'.

It is reasonable to suppose that those who are insecure in their identity are precisely the ones who will feel most strongly about the issue. There is some empirical support for this hypothesis. In his 1968 survey Richard Rose, as was shown in Chapter 4, found that Protestants were much more divided in their choice of national label than Catholics. Whereas most Catholics labelled themselves 'Irish', Protestants were split three ways between 'British', 'Ulster', and

'Irish'. He then asked his respondents 'Would you say that you are a strong (Irishman/Ulsterman/British, etc.) or average?' Forty-five per cent of his Protestant respondents said they were a strong Ulsterman or whatever, while only 28 per cent of Catholics said that they held strongly to their chosen label (Rose 1971, 485). If Protestants on average seem to have stronger feelings than Catholics on average, uncertainty about identity may be part of the problem.

THE DOUBLE-MINORITY MODEL

One way of looking at the Northern Ireland conflict which is implicitly psychological is to see it as a double-minority situation. The implication of this model is that minorities are groups which feel threatened; that threatened groups are liable to be hypersensitive; and that in Northern Ireland both groups display these characteristics.

This model has, explicitly or implicitly, been in the air for many years. Michael Poole (1983, 180) has pointed out that the concept, if not the precise term, can be found in writings by Gallagher (1957), Shearman (1970), and Gibson (1971). However, the first explicit formulation, so far as I know, was provided by Harold Jackson (1971, 4), the journalist who as we have already seen pioneered the psychological approach to the study of the Northern Ireland problem. He saw the Protestants as 'a ruling establishment with the reins of power irremovably in its hands but acting under the stresses of a besieged minority', while on the other side 'fifty years of failing to get any real say in the government of the province ... left the Catholics with a burning sense of grievance'. This model has found favour with authors of diverse views and backgrounds, such as the constitutional lawyer Claire Palley (1972, 372), the historian A. T. Q. Stewart (1977, 162), the psychologist Rhona Fields (1977, 196), the political scientist Padraig O'Malley (1983, 7), and a specialist in housing policy, Dale Singleton (1985, 308).

More recently, a number of authors have re-examined the model. Cairns (1982, 286–95; 1989, 125–7) and Poole (1983, 160–1) have suggested that a double-*majority* model may also be appropriate: that on each side the perception that they are a majority (in Ireland for the Catholics, in Northern Ireland for the Protestants) gives them a self-confidence which they would not display if they were genuine minorities. Cairns finds that both sides, but particularly the Protestants, display a positive self-identity of a kind that is generally associated with majorities. The difficulty with this reinterpretation is that it drains the model of its explanatory value. One might expect majorities to be relatively relaxed. In that case it is hard to see why they should display such mutual fear and suspicion.

On the other hand, some authors have extended the model by suggesting that Northern Ireland can be seen as a *triple*-minority situation (Douglas and Boal 1982, 3; Moxon-Browne 1983, 82, 88; Poole 1983, 157–8; Kennedy 1988, 227). Northern Protestants are not just a minority in Ireland, but a minority in the United Kingdom as well. They thus feel vulnerable twice over, because, if they consider the Irish majority hostile, they also find the British majority to be unreliable friends. If this view is valid, one would expect Protestants to show the psychological characteristics of a minority even more sharply than Catholics do. This seems a more fruitful development of the model, and one which accords more with the realities.

The psychological approach to the Northern Ireland problem does not provide a complete explanation of that problem, and no psychologist makes any such claim for it. What it does is to offer an explanation of the intensity of feeling engendered by the cleavages in Northern Ireland. As to the nature of those cleavages, the psychologists as such cannot help us. It is left to those scholars who explore the religious, political, and economic aspects of the divide to provide an answer.

THE COMMUNITY DIVIDE: A SUMMARY SO FAR

It is time to sum up the findings of the last three chapters and of this one. We have uncovered the following sources of community division (I list them in the order in which they were mentioned, not in their order of importance):

1. Society in Northern Ireland is largely, though not entirely, segregated along religious lines. Segregation by itself does not entail conflict; but it helps intensify conflict if it breaks out for other reasons. (Chapter 2.)
2. Religion is important, not just as a basis for social cleavage,

but as in itself a matter for conflict. (Mentioned in Chapter 2; to be discussed more fully below.)

3. The Protestant community is in most ways more fragmented than the Catholic one. This helps to foster insecurity among Protestants. (Chapter 2.)

4. There is an economic differential between Protestant and Catholic, which is in part due to discrimination. Catholics are keenly aware of this, and it is a source of bitterness amongst them. Many Protestants have difficulty in accepting the existence of this factor. (Chapter 3.)

5. Protestant and Catholic have contrasting national identities. Most Catholics feel themselves to be Irish. The most popular identity among Protestants is 'British', but they are less certain about their identity than Catholics. (Chapter 4.)

6. Protestants and Catholics have differing political aspirations. Protestants are almost solidly against a united Ireland. Catholics are less solidly for a united Ireland, but many favour it. Protestants and Catholics also largely support different political parties. (Chapter 4.)

7. Protestants and Catholics have contrasting attitudes to the security forces, to the courts, and to particular security policies. The gap between them on security policy is even larger than on constitutional issues. (Chapter 4.)

8. There are variations in the strength of feeling in both communities. While the moderates in both might be induced to compromise, the intransigent elements are sufficiently strong to make compromise difficult. (Chapter 4.)

9. In both communities there are psychological forces at work which intensify the strength of feeling beyond what the real conflict of interests would appear to justify. These psychological forces display themselves in the form of an intense concern with identity. The concern seems to be even stronger among Protestants, perhaps because their identity is less certain. (Chapter 5.)

10. In the eyes of some authors at least, the double-minority model is appropriate. This means that both communities display the anxieties and sensitivities which go with being a minority. (Chapter 5.)

THE COMMUNITY DIVIDE: WHAT MATTERS MOST?

The next question that arises is: which of these factors matters most? Classifying the views of the experts seems at first sight a daunting task. Some authors emphasize economic factors, some political, some religious. Yet others favour implicitly psychological approaches such as stressing a clash of identities or the double-minority model. There are many more who favour a combination of these explanations. Indeed there are almost as many interpretations of the community divide as there are authors.

However, a thread through the maze of differing interpretations can be found. It is to be seen in the varying answers to the question 'how far is the Northern Ireland conflict religious?' This question seems to fascinate writers on Northern Ireland. In most parts of Europe religious wars went out in the seventeenth century, yet here we find Protestants and Catholics fighting each other in the late twentieth. The question of whether the conflict is really religious, or whether the religious labels simply mask a conflict over economic or political issues, has aroused endless discussion. A full spectrum of opinion can be found, ranging from those authors who accord religion a paramount importance through to those who almost wholly discount it.

At one extreme can be found those writers who pay scant attention to religious influences. A number of these are Marxists of one school or another (e.g. BICO 1971*a,b*; Farrell 1976; Bew *et al.* 1979; Pringle 1985), and are best dealt with in Chapter 7, where the Marxist approach is examined. However, they are not all Marxists. I shall select as an example for further consideration a book by an American political scientist, Michael MacDonald, *Children of Wrath: Political Violence in Northern Ireland* (1986).

To MacDonald, what matters most is that 'Protestants were colonizers, while Catholics were colonized' (p. 6). Religion is important chiefly as a badge to distinguish settler from native. He explains why it is so important that Northern Ireland is a settler society:

Whereas the elites of most societies would prefer full to partial legitimacy, Northern Ireland's Protestants are threatened by the mere prospect of extended legitimacy. The point is not that other societies achieve full legitimacy, or even that it is actively pursued, but only that most elites would want full legitimacy were it available at an affordable price. In contrast, Protestants in Northern Ireland justified their political power and social privileges on the grounds of their 'loyalty' and Catholic 'disloyalty' to the established social order. The catch is that Protestant 'loyalty' is meaningful only in contradistinction to the 'disloyalty' of Catholics. Thus Protestants, especially the more marginal ones, have developed an enduring stake in sustaining the disloyalty of Catholics, even at the cost of chronic instability and violence. (p. 8.)

MacDonald writes trenchantly. He has a gift for summing up a discussion with an epigrammatic phrase. There are, however, limitations to his argument. He overlooks a point made by Bruce (1986, 6), that if settler and native had been of the same religion, a common religious culture might have encouraged intermarriage and eroded the ethnic boundaries. He states that 'conflict between Protestants and Catholics is scarcely normal in Western Europe, and so must be explained in something other than religious terms when it does occur' (p. 4). But this ignores the fact that no other group of Protestants are under threat of absorption by an intensely Catholic State next door. Indeed nowhere does MacDonald consider the justifications offered by Protestants for their point of view. Their case may be exaggerated, but they do have one. I am not claiming that MacDonald's thesis is devoid of merit, but it cannot be made to bear the weight that he puts on it.

At the other extreme can be found writers who put great stress on the religious aspect. As an example I shall take a sociologist formerly working at the University of Ulster at Coleraine, John Hickey. In his book *Religion and the Northern Ireland Problem* (1984) he acknowledges that 'religious belief is not the only causal factor in the situation' (p. 89), but he places great weight on it, devoting a whole section (pp. 68–88) to showing that doctrinal differences do matter, at least on the Protestant side. Indeed he argues that religion has been increasing in importance, as economic modernization has taken place in Northern Ireland: 'While differences in the social structure between Protestants and Roman Catholics are being slowly eliminated, the importance of the other difference—religion—is being increasingly emphasised. Conflict now centres upon the distinction of religious belief and the world view based upon it' (p. 105). This, however, is perhaps to go too far in the opposite direction. One may question how far differences in social structure between Catholics and Protestants are really being eliminated. As was shown in Chapter 3, the economic differential between them has proved remarkably persistent.

In between these extreme positions are any number of intermediate ones. The pioneering study of the community divide by Barritt and Carter (1962) puts considerable stress on religion, though it takes account of political and economic factors. The classic participant-observation study by Rosemary Harris (1972) also stresses the importance of religious differences. The classic attitude survey by Richard Rose (1971) holds the balance more evenly between religious and political factors. Near the middle of the spectrum, but leaning somewhat to the side of those who say that religion is not decisive, is a judicious assessment of the question by the anthropologist Richard Jenkins (1986), in a paper entitled 'Northern Ireland: In What Sense "Religions" in Conflict?' Jenkins concludes that 'the situation may most accurately be described as a conflict with a religious dimension. Although the struggle in the six counties is not about religion, it is contributed to and coloured by religious themes' (p. 18).

One point that has been made by a number of authors is that the terms 'Catholic' and 'Protestant' do not have the same meaning in Northern Ireland as in most parts of the world. In most parts of the world they mark a purely religious difference, between two kinds of Christian. But in Northern Ireland, where religion is so closely linked to other differences, the terms have wider associations. As a psychologist, E. E. O'Donnell, has put it (1977, 5), in Northern Ireland these terms 'involve a combination of historic, national, tribal, social, economic and other differences, all subsumed under the heading of religious allegiance'. The same point has been put more fully by Conor Cruise O'Brien in his book *States of Ireland* (1972). O'Brien sees the quarrel as a religious one, but with 'religious' having a special meaning. After rejecting the ideas that it can be seen as primarily a conflict of nationalities or primarily one between settlers and natives, he goes on:

So we are brought back, inescapably, to what so many people seek to deny: that rather obvious fact of a conflict between groups defined by *religion*. This does not mean it is a theological war. It would not even be exact to say that it is a conflict between Catholics and Protestants. It is a conflict *between IRISH Catholics and ULSTER Protestants*. . . .

The actual *religions*—the systems of beliefs and of feelings about those beliefs—cherished by Ulster Protestants and by Irish Catholics are distinct, in reality though not formally, from the religions of the same name as practised elsewhere.

In both cases the actual, as distinct from the formal, religion is an amalgam of the strictly ecclesiastical body of doctrines and practices, and of other doctrines and practices derived from the past history of Irish Catholics and Ulster Protestants. (pp. 307–8.)

If we are to accept the analysis put forward by authors such as E. E. O'Donnell and Conor Cruise O'Brien then religion has an indirect influence on the situation which must be added to its direct influence.

Where the authorities vary so widely in their conclusions, how can we choose between them? Firstly, we must recognize that the answer to the question 'how far is the conflict religious?' may be different for different sections of the Northern Ireland population. To begin with, we can distinguish between Protestant and Catholic. Protestants are more worried about Catholicism as a religion than Catholics are about Protestantism. This has been pointed out by a number of authors—for instance, Richard Rose (1971, 256), Edward Moxon-Browne (1983, 3), and John Darby (1976, 120–2). An author who explores this aspect with particular clarity is the social psychologist Ken Heskin, in his book *Northern Ireland: A Psychological Analysis* (1980). Heskin marshals survey and other evidence to show that the two communities see each other differently. As he sums it up: 'Protestants object primarily to Catholics as Catholics but not as people. . . . Catholics object primarily to Protestants as people and not as Protestants' (p. 47). In other words, Protestants fear the Catholic religion and the consequences of living in a State dominated by the Catholic Church, while Catholics object not to the Protestants' religion but to their political outlook and their grip on power.

In particular, Heskin provides an interesting analysis—all the more authoritative because he himself is of Ulster Protestant background—of just where the Protestant fear of the Catholic Church lies (pp. 28–30). He sees three main components—a fear of the Catholic Church as an organization; a fear of the Church's power through its priests to impose its views on its members; and finally 'a vague, almost primitive uneasiness with a body which to the Protestants is so full of mysticism, symbolism, clandestine activity (the Vatican, convents, monasteries, retreats, separate schools) and unworldly practices such as clerical chastity, monastic silence and so forth'.

The most extreme views on Roman Catholicism are held by the Revd Ian Paisley and his supporters. After many years in which only two books on Paisley appeared (Ó Glaisne 1971; Marrinan 1973), he has suddenly become the subject of intense research. In the last few years four books have come out on him and/or his followers, covering a spectrum of opinion. There is a hostile biography by Moloney and Pollak (1986); a critical one by Paisley's former follower, Clifford Smyth (1987); a more friendly study by a specialist in the sociology of religion, Steve Bruce (1986); and a laudatory treatment by Dr Paisley's daughter Rhonda Paisley (1988). There have also been a number of shorter studies (Gallagher 1981; Taylor 1984; Smyth 1986; Wallis *et al.* 1986, 1987; MacIver, 1987). Ample evidence of his opposition to Rome can be found in these works. It will suffice to cite a couple of examples. MacIver (1987, 365) in a well-informed and non-judgemental account of Paisley's views, writes:

The Roman Catholic Church's rôle in Paisley's apocalyptic world view aligns her totally with the forces of tyranny, so that history necessarily involves for him a perpetual conflict between Romanism and Protestantism. The exhortations made by moderate Ulster leaders for Ulster to put her history behind her and move foreward to new cooperation between Protestants and Catholics represent Satanic lies for an adherent of Paisley's apocalyptic world view; Romanism will always be the enemy and Paisley seeks to prove this by drawing parallels between current events and past Protestant/Catholic conflicts.

Bruce (1986, 222) offers a similar picture of the Paisleyites' world-view: 'in their eyes Rome goes beyond simply offering false teaching; the Catholic Church is actively evil in that it has a history of both persecuting "true" Christians and suppressing the democracy which Protestants regard as something which was created by their faith'.

A corollary of this vision of history as a struggle between evil (Roman Catholicism) and good (evangelical Protestantism) is that good will ultimately prevail. In the words of Paisley's paper the *Protestant Telegraph*:

The Almighty does not make mistakes; He alone is infallible. Our presence in Ulster is no accident of history. ... We have an historic and a Divine Commission. We are the defenders of Truth in this Province and in this island. ... Ulster is the last bastion of Evangelical Protestantism in Western

Europe; we must not let drop the torch of Truth at this stage of the eternal conflict between Truth and Evil. ... We are a special people, not of ourselves, but of our Divine mission. Ulster arise and acknowledge your God. (Quoted in MacIver 1987, 368–9.)

To people who hold such beliefs, religion can truly be said to be the main source of the conflict. They see the Roman Catholic Church as Antichrist, and any compromise with it as a surrender to evil. At the same time they have the assurance that, no matter what tribulations they may have to suffer, in the end God will make sure that they prevail.

However, not all Protestants are extreme evangelicals of the Paisleyite stamp. As we saw in Chapter 1, many are liberals, and many are not even church-goers. So those who wish to stress religion as a primary force in the Northern Ireland conflict must find some way of arguing that its influence extends beyond the evangelical wing of Protestantism.

Ingenious attempts to do just this have been made in two recent works. The first is a trenchant pamphlet by Roy Wallis, Steve Bruce, and David Taylor, *"No Surrender!": Paisleyism and the Politics of Ethnic Identity in Northern Ireland* (1986). The second is Steve Bruce's book *God Save Ulster! The Religion and Politics of Paisleyism* (1986). The arguments of the two works are, while not identical, closely similar. For brevity's sake I shall confine my discussion to Bruce's book. Bruce states uncompromisingly the importance of the religious factor: 'The Northern Ireland conflict is a religious conflict. Economic and social differences are also crucial, but it was the fact that the competing populations in Ireland adhered and still adhere to competing religious traditions which has given the conflict its enduring and intractable quality' (p. 249). In reply to those who see a desire to maintain their social supremacy as the driving force among Protestants, Bruce does not dispute that Protestants are objectively better off than Catholics, but he argues that perceptions are what matter, and it is his conclusion, after talking to many Protestants, that they do not perceive themselves to be advantaged (pp. 255–7). For Bruce, what Protestants are most concerned about is not supremacy, but identity. They want above all to avoid being absorbed into a united Ireland. That leads them to stress an identity which expresses their difference from the rest of Ireland. A British identity might be thought to fulfil this function, but they 'are well aware that the British public is largely indifferent to their efforts to preserve themselves and entirely uncomprehending of their history, attitudes, and culture' (pp. 258–9). Socialism, ecumenism, and Terence O'Neill-type liberal unionism are unsatisfactory because they erode the difference between themselves and Catholics (pp. 259–61). The only secure identity they have is evangelical Protestantism. Thus evangelical Protestantism appeals even to those who are not personally religious.

There is much that is attractive in this theory. It is buttressed by more evidence than appears in the bald summary which I have just provided. A possible objection is that it uses the word 'religious' in a peculiar sense. Bruce calls the conflict religious, not because the antagonists are contending about religious doctrines or interests, but because those on the Protestant side need religion as a badge of identity. If the reader is content to accept the use of the word 'religion' in this wide sense, however, then Bruce may be said to have made out a good case.

A limitation to all the analyses we have discussed so far is that they assume that most Protestants are driven by much the same motivations. Perhaps we should distinguish more sharply between different kinds of Protestant. Certainly some commentators have felt it important to do so. Richard Rose (1971, 33) distinguished between the allegiant individual, who supports the government and complies with its laws, and the Ultra, 'who supports a particular definition of the existing regime so strongly that he is willing to break laws, or even take up arms, to recall it to its "true" way'. Frank Wright, in an article on 'Protestant ideology and politics in Ulster' (1973), explored the difference between two kinds of Protestant—those who believed it possible to achieve Catholic support, and those who believed it undesirable, impossible, or too conditional to depend on (p. 221). Bew, Gibbon, and Patterson, three Marxist historians whose work will be examined in Chapter 7, devote considerable space to exploring differences within the Protestant bloc (Bew *et al.* 1979). They distinguish an 'anti-populist' strand among the bourgeoisie, and a secular-labourist strand among the working class, from the admittedly preponderant Orange-populist ideology.

Intra-Protestant differences have recently been explored with particular perceptiveness by a political scientist of Northern Ireland background at University College Dublin, Jennifer Todd. Todd's article 'Two Traditions in Unionist Political Culture' (1987) is based on wide study of the literature on and by Ulster Protestants. She distinguishes between two ideologies—the Ulster loyalist and the Ulster British. Ulster loyalism is the framework of ideas to which Bruce's research primarily applies. Loyalism derives its power from evangelical Protestantism. In such a world-view there are no half measures, either in the religious or political sphere. 'Sin is thought of as a blot or a stain, passed on as if by contagion and requiring purification and removal of the source of the stain. . . . The concept of sin as stain is paralleled in the political realm so that, for example, the very presence of the Irish tricolour of Garret FitzGerald speaking Irish at Hillsborough, is seen as an insult to the purity of the Protestant state' (p. 5).

Todd, however, argues that a second ideology can also be found among northern Protestants. This is the Ulster British. Those who hold this ideology stress that 'their unionism is not a product of prejudice but a cherishing of British ideals' (p. 13)—British ideals being defined as progressive, liberal, and democratic. Ulster British patriotism is multi-levelled: it can include an identification with Ulster and to some extent with Ireland (p. 16). The Ulster British perceive themselves as tolerant, and among those they dislike are Protestant sectarians and aggressive loyalists (p. 19).

Ulster loyalists and Ulster British are not two sharply defined groups. 'Individuals' beliefs are often overdetermined products of several ideological traditions, lacking in coherence and constantly changing' (p. 2). However, Todd believes that there is a tendency to gravitate to one or other pole.

The preceding interpretations can perhaps be reconciled on something like the following lines. It seems that there is no single answer to the question 'how far do religious attitudes cause the Northern Ireland conflict?' To Catholics, on the whole, they do not. For Catholics, the issues are political and economic. To those whom Todd calls the Ulster British, the issues are also political rather than religious. To extreme evangelical Protestants, the conflict is primarily religious: they see the struggle as one between Christ and Antichrist. To a much wider spectrum of Protestants, the conflict is religious in the sense used by Bruce, of religion as being a badge of identity. MacDonald's thesis that Protestants are a privileged group seeking to preserve their advantages is also a part, though only a part, of the total picture.

VARIATIONS WITHIN NORTHERN IRELAND

However, to leave the discussion there would be to risk giving the impression that the Northern Ireland problem is simpler than it really is. A point that has emerged repeatedly so far in this book is the difference between one area and another. Northern Ireland has only one and a half million people, but it is astonishing how much variety it contains within it. On issue after issue in preceding chapters we have found great local differences—in the influence of the Churches, in the degree of residential segregation, in economic conditions, in the impact of violence, in political attitudes. These make the community divide much more complex than one might imagine from drawing on region-wide generalizations. The sharpness of the divide varies from one place to another. The mix of religious, economic, political, and psychological factors which underpins it varies from one place to another.

II
Interpretations of the Northern Ireland Conflict

In Part II of this book, I propose to survey the principal interpretations of the Northern Ireland conflict. In principle, there are almost as many interpretations as there are books, for virtually every author will differ in some detail from others. To make the differences intelligible, however, it is essential to simplify, by grouping authors together into schools of thought. One way of doing that is according to how authors define the principal antagonists in the conflict. Four different pairs of antagonists can be postulated, as follows:

1. Britain v. Ireland
2. Southern Ireland v. Northern Ireland
3. Capitalist v. worker
4. Protestant v. Catholic within Northern Ireland.

To say that authors can pick out one of four pairs of antagonists as primary is, of course, to oversimplify the complexity of scholars' views. Hardly anyone can be found who believes that one, and only one, of these conflicts exists in Northern Ireland. Virtually every author perceives at least two of them as being present; many would accept three; and it is quite possible to accept all four as being present in some degree.

However, human beings are too limited to hold the full complexity of a situation in their minds at once. They need a simplifying model, which stresses what they perceive as the most important element in a situation. In practice, I have found that virtually all the authors who have examined the Northern Ireland problem emphasize one or other of the four conflicts listed above, and organize their material accordingly. There are, then, four basic interpretations of the Northern Ireland problem.

The question next arises: what labels to give them. I shall adopt the following:

1. traditional nationalist
2. traditional unionist
3. Marxist
4. two-community, or internal-conflict.

The first two of these labels require explanation. Why *traditional* nationalist and *traditional* unionist? Why not just nationalist and unionist—which indeed were the terms I used in a previous paper on 'Interpretations of the Northern Ireland Problem' (Whyte 1988)? The reason is that the terms 'nationalist' and 'unionist' in common speech generally refer to political objectives. A nationalist is someone who aspires to a united, independent Ireland. A unionist is someone who wants to retain the link between Northern Ireland and Great Britain. Now it is true that, in the past, most nationalists were traditional nationalists in the sense in which I am using the term — that is, they saw the root conflict as being between Ireland and Britain. However, many nationalists today would accept that the core of the conflict is between the two communities within Northern Ireland, without abandoning their aspirations for a united Ireland. They would therefore fit into my fourth category rather than my second. The same, *mutatis mutandis*, is true of traditional and modern-day unionists.

I shall take the reader through these four interpretations in turn. One chapter will be devoted to each.

6

The Traditional Nationalist Interpretation

THE DEVELOPMENT OF THE TRADITIONAL NATIONALIST INTERPRETATION

The traditional nationalist view of Northern Ireland can be summed up in two propositions: (1) the people of Ireland form one nation; and (2) the fault for keeping Ireland divided lies with Britain.

This view can be traced back to the foundation of Northern Ireland itself. Among early statements of it are *The Handbook of the Ulster Question* (1923), published by the North-Eastern Boundary Bureau, which had been set up by the Irish Free State government, and Henry Harrison's *Ulster and the British Empire: Help or Hindrance?* (1939). In the late 1940s and early 1950s the pamphlets of the All-Party Anti-partition Conference gave a renewed ideological basis to the nationalist interpretation. A historical underpinning was provided by Denis Gwynn in his *History of Partition* (1950) and by P. S. O'Hegarty in his *History of Ireland under the Union* (1952). The most comprehensive statement of the case was presented in Frank Gallagher's *The Indivisible Island* (1957), which subsumed and amplified the publications of the Anti-partition Conference.

All these works took the view that unionist opposition to Irish unity was artificially worked up by the British. As the North-Eastern Boundary Bureau put it (1923, p. vi):

The problem of North-East Ulster is unique in only one respect—it is the only religious minority in the world which has, through the assistance of powerful outside influences, been able to frustrate the organic development of the nation for more than a century, and then to insist on cutting off from the nation not only its own adherents but a large minority whose traditional allegiance was to the nation as a whole.

P. S. O'Hegarty (1952, 2–3) saw a spirit hovering over Ireland which made its own of every race that came there. It affected even the Irish unionists who, if they did not want home rule, did not want partition either: partition was 'primarily an English Conservative Policy, designed as propaganda to dish the Liberals' (p. 563). Frank Gallagher (1957, 88) saw partition as a product of British malignancy:

Britain based her partition policy on divergences she herself created and fostered among the Irish people. Other democratic nations have had similar problems to those of Ireland. These have been solved, with justice to all concerned and within the framework of the national units in question, because no powerful neighbour set out to prevent a settlement by exploiting internal differences.

I shall explore Gallagher's argument in a little more detail, as the most fully worked out example of the traditional nationalist interpretation. His evidence is largely historical. Much of his book is a survey of the mischievous role played by British politicians in fomenting Irish differences during the nineteenth and early twentieth centuries. He argues that, on the rare occasions when British politicians did not stir the pot, Irishmen of different traditions proved capable of reaching agreement. He claims that partition was not wanted by either nationalist or unionist within Ireland, and that it would not have come about had not British politicians engineered it for party advantage. He maintains that Northern Ireland was viable only because Britain paid vast subsidies to Northern Ireland, and that despite partition the two parts of the island retained many characteristics in common.

The view encapsulated in Gallagher's book was for many years orthodoxy for Irish nationalists, north and south of the border. It was repeatedly expressed in the speeches of Éamon de Valera (which can now be conveniently studied in the anthology edited by Maurice Moynihan (1980)). It was formally placed on record in the Constitution of 1937, which declared in Article 2 that 'the national territory consists of the whole island of Ireland, its islands and the territorial seas'. It was proclaimed again in a unanimous declaration which Dáil Éireann passed in 1949, following a British Act of Parliament laying down that partition would not end without the consent of the parliament of Northern Ireland:

Dáil Éireann,

SOLEMNLY RE-ASSERTING the indefeasible right of the Irish nation to the unity and integrity of the national territory,

RE-AFFIRMING the sovereign right of the people of Ireland to choose its own form of Government and, through its democratic institutions, to decide all questions of national policy, free from outside interference . . .

CALLS UPON the British Government and people to end the present occupation of our six north-eastern counties, and thereby enable the unity of Ireland to be restored and the age-long differences between the two nations brought to an end. (Dáil Debates, vol. 115, col. 786: 10 May 1949.)

It will be noted that this resolution ignores any feelings which the majority in the six north-eastern counties might have about the situation, and takes for granted that the British presence is the only thing preventing the unification of Ireland.

To account for the hold which such an explanation had on Irish nationalists, it must be said that it was consistent with their historic experience. It was indeed true that Ireland had suffered a long series of injustices under English rule. When a new problem came up, in the form of Ulster unionist opposition to Irish unity, it was natural to see an English hand at the back of it. As Denis Gwynn put it in his *History of Partition* (1950, 23):

In Ireland the old suspicions of British imperialism still survive strongly. The conviction is deeply rooted that English policy is always inspired by the doctrine of 'Divide and Rule.' The enforced partition of Ireland appears so obviously as a direct application of that policy, that most people in Ireland take it for granted that Partition was deliberately devised by English politicians as a means of retaining a grip on Irish territory which could at any time be expanded.

THE BEGINNINGS OF REASSESSMENT

However, the difficulty remained that Ulster Protestants, by overwhelming majorities at election after election, rejected candidates who favoured a united Ireland. As the 1950s wore on, some nationalists were beginning to wonder if their traditional assumptions were adequate to account for so adamant a resistance. A veteran Irish nationalist, Ernest Blythe, published numerous articles in English and Irish, and a book in Irish, *Briseadh na Teorann* ('The Smashing of the Border', de Blaghd 1955), in which he argued that partition existed, not because of the British, but because of the northern Protestants, and that the only way to bring about a united Ireland was by enticing sufficient northern Protestants to vote for it. Blythe's voice carried weight because, while his own nationalist credentials were undeniable—he had been twice imprisoned by the British, and was subsequently a minister in the first government of the Irish Free State—he was of northern Protestant stock. (For

Blythe see Ó Gadhra 1976.) In 1955 a young Irish Catholic, Michael Sheehy, published a book entitled *Divided We Stand: A Study in Partition*, in which he argued that there were two distinct peoples in Ireland, that unionists had good reasons for not wishing to join with the south, and that there was no moral case for the ending of partition. In 1959 a young barrister (who has since become a distinguished judge), Donal Barrington, published a pamphlet on similar lines entitled *Uniting Ireland*. Since Barrington's pamphlet was designed as a direct response to Frank Gallagher's book, I shall select it as the example of reassessment to be considered here.

Barrington challenged the central tenets of traditional nationalism:

It is quite misleading to say that Partition was forced on Ireland by the British Government against the wishes of North and South. It would be more correct to say that Partition was forced on the British Government by the conflicting demands of the two parties of Irishmen. It is true that both North and South were dissatisfied with partition but that was because the North wanted all Ireland for the Act of Union and the South wanted all Ireland for Home Rule. Both demands could not be met, neither party was prepared to give way, and the inevitable result was Partition. (p. 3.)

With regard to the charge that British politicians had stirred up Irish animosities, he wrote:

It is true that Tory leaders came over to Ireland to wake up the Orangemen to the dangers of Home Rule, but the Orangemen did not need much waking up, and little is to be gained by counting all the Tory leaders who came to Ireland to speak to the Orangemen and ignoring all the Orange leaders who went to England to speak to the Tories. (p. 6.)

He considered that the religious fears of the unionists had far more reality than nationalists had traditionally been disposed to accept. His conclusion was that the only realistic policy for ending partition was to create conditions in which trust and understanding could grow.

Barrington was a nationalist, in the sense that he desired a united Ireland. But he was an innovator in that he put the root of the opposition to unity, not in Britain, but among the Protestants of the north. This entailed switching the thrust of nationalist policy from trying to induce the British to leave Ireland and trying to induce the Protestants to join in a united Ireland. Thus there were signs, even before the troubles erupted in Northern Ireland at the end of the

1960s, that traditional nationalist ideology was undergoing re-appraisal.

THE IMPACT OF THE TROUBLES

Once the troubles began, the process of reappraisal speeded up. It was simply not plausible to argue that Britain was stirring up the Protestants into displaying an intransigence which they would otherwise not have shown. The British government forced through the reform packages of 1968–9 against the wishes of a substantial proportion of the Protestant population. When British troops first intervened in 1969, they came—and were seen by both sides as coming—to rescue the Catholics from Protestant and RUC violence. True, the Army was operating in support of the civil power, which remained in Protestant hands until the introduction of direct rule in 1972, and the troops therefore slid during 1970–2 into operating openly on behalf of the unionist regime, as witness their part in the Falls Road curfew of 1970, the introduction of internment in 1971, and Bloody Sunday in January 1972. Many Catholics would feel that, ever since, British policy has been skewed in favour of the Protestants. But that is a long way short of maintaining that Britain has actually egged on the Protestants into taking up more extreme positions than they otherwise would have done. Certainly Protestants do not think so—they (or at least very large numbers of them) have protested many times since 1969 that British policy is unduly favourable to Catholics. The events of the last twenty years have been illuminating for nationalists. They have made it far more difficult to argue that Protestant opposition to Irish unity is essentially artificial, blown up out of proportion by British machinations.

The effect of such considerations on many who had been brought up in the nationalist tradition can be illustrated by two books published in 1972. The first, *Towards a New Ireland*, by the future taoiseach, Garret FitzGerald, maintained part of the traditional interpretation; the author argued that Ireland was 'one nation' (p. 175), despite the existence in it of different cultures. But he conceded that British interference in Ireland was no longer the crucial problem (p. 91). Instead, he argued that Protestant intransigence could largely be explained as the result of fears, by no means ill-founded, of what would happen to them in a united Ireland: 'the Irish problem is quite simply the fruit of Northern Protestant reluctance to become part of what they regard as an authoritarian Southern Catholic state' (p. 88).

The other book published in 1972, Conor Cruise O'Brien's *States of Ireland*, went further. In it the author argued, with copious evidence from recent Irish history and from his own family memories, that Irish nationalists had never fully believed their own dogma: by countless unguarded words and actions they showed that they did not consider the Protestants to be one nation with themselves. Recent events had brought the contradiction into the open. 'What has been coming across to ordinary people is that our problem is not "how to get unity" but how to share an island in conditions of peace and reasonable fairness, and that such conditions *preclude* unity as long as the Ulster Protestants reject that' (O'Brien 1972, 297).

'REVISIONIST' HISTORIOGRAPHY: THE UNION PERIOD (1801–1921)

While the march of events was weakening the credibility of the traditional nationalist view, the progress of historical scholarship was having a similar effect. This scholarship has sometimes been labelled 'revisionist'. The label is imperfectly accurate. It implies that a body of historical writing existed already, waiting to be revised. In fact scholarly historical writing on any scale is a recent phenomenon in Ireland. It is often dated to the founding of the journal *Irish Historical Studies* in 1938. The importance of this event has been brought out by one commentator (Lee 1968, 439): 'Irish Historical Studies (I.H.S.) took history out of politics. In its pages it is virtually impossible to identify authors as catholic or protestant, nationalist or unionist, southern or northern. In the context of the centuries-long polemical tradition, it would be difficult to exaggerate the significance of this achievement.' However, it took time for the new journal to make its influence felt. There were few Irish historians at the time of its foundation, and it was not till the 1950s or even the 1960s that serious scholarly works on Irish history began to appear in any number.

Work on any period of Irish history can throw light on the origins of the Ulster problem. Some authors (Adamson 1974, 1981; Hall

1986) have even written books tracing it back to the differences between Picts and Celts in the pre-Christian era. If that seems too fanciful, one can certainly trace it back to the settlements of the early seventeenth century. However, for the purposes of this chapter it is sufficient to confine ourselves to the historiography of the nineteenth and twentieth centuries. As late as the end of the eighteenth century, it was not inevitable that the peoples of Ireland should get into two antagonistic communities. Presbyterians as well as Catholics took part in the 1798 rising. True, there is scope for controversy about how secure their alliance was. But it did happen. It is only at some stage after 1798 that the Protestants of Ulster became dedicated to the British link.

When the troubles began in 1968, the only recent history of Ulster available was to be found in the two volumes entitled *Ulster since 1800* (1954, 1957), edited by T. W. Moody and J. C. Beckett. These had originated as two series of lectures broadcast on BBC Northern Ireland, and, although they were by reputable historians they contained no great weight of scholarship, being based on the meagre material then available. When reread thirty years later, the main impression left by them is one of blandness. For instance, the sectarian riots which repeatedly erupted in Belfast during the nineteenth century are barely mentioned—it was left for Andrew Boyd's book *Holy War in Belfast* (1969) to bring these riots back into the consciousness of historians. We now know, from Cathcart's history of the BBC in Northern Ireland (1984), that this blandness was not accidental. In the 1950s the BBC was following a policy of bringing both sides of society together. This meant that 'the positive aspects of community relations were emphasised and the negative underplayed' (Cathcart 1984, 263).

Since the early 1970s there has been an efflorescence of writing on Ulster history. In addition much of the writing on Ireland as a whole has included a more careful scrutiny of its Ulster aspects than had been customary earlier—a product, no doubt, of the heightened interest which the current troubles in Northern Ireland created in their historical roots. There is now an enormous historical litera-ture dealing with, or at least touching on, ulster during the union period. The question it raised for our current purposes is: which side does the weight of recent historiography favour—the interpre-tation of such as Frank Gallagher, who saw unionist opposition to a united Ireland as not intrinsically serious, and who put the main

responsibility for the partition of Ireland on to Britain; or the interpretation of those such as Donal Barrington, who saw the main
cause of partition as lying among the unionists of the north-east? I
shall not attempt to cover all the literature, but shall confine myself
to some of the more striking items on one side or the other.

Some recent scholarship will give comfort to those who favour
Frank Gallagher's view. An argument hostile to British politicians
was developed by an English historian living in the United States,
George Dangerfield, who examined the period 1912–23 in his book
The Damnable Question: A Study in Anglo-Irish Relations (1977). He
believed that the Ulster unionists could have been induced to accept
the Home Rule Bill of 1912, if the Liberal government had stood
firm, instead of colluding with the Conservatives to force a
compromise on the Irish nationalists. Another work implicitly
critical of British policy is Ian F. W. Beckett's (1986) authoritative
study of the Curragh mutiny of 1914. This provides further evidence
in support of the well-established fact that the British officer caste
was unashamedly biased in favour of the unionists, and could not
have been relied on to suppress the unionists' defiance of an Act of
Parliament. It is complemented by an article, 'The Royal Navy and
the Curragh Incident' (Beckett and Jeffery 1989), which brings out
the much less well-known fact that the Navy was as disaffected as
the Army. Catherine Shannon, in her *Arthur J. Balfour and Ireland*
(1988) stops well short of full-blooded traditional nationalism, but
she brings out the condescending attitudes, the racial stereotyping,
the concern for party advantage which warped the attitudes of
British Conservative statesmen in their dealings with Ireland.

If there is anyone left who believes that the British record at the
time of partition was beyond reproach, they will find enlightening
the comparative study by a historian at the University of Ulster,
T. G. Fraser, *Partition in Ireland, India and Palestine* (1986). Of the
three cases, the one from which the British emerge best is the Indian.
British officials tried hard to find some compromise which would
avoid the need for partition, and, when at last it came, its inevitab-
ility was accepted by Indian nationalist politicians as soon as by the
British administration. The original Muslim claim, like the unionist
one, was for an area larger than that to which they were entitled on a
strict head-count. But the Muslims were confronted, as the unionists
never were, with a choice. If they wanted the maximum area, then
they could have it only in a federal relationship with the majority. If

they wanted total separation, then they would get only the areas in which they were indisputably the local majority. In Ireland, on the other hand, the dissident minority was treated with indulgence. It was given a larger area than it was entitled to, and supported financially and militarily by the imperial power. This lack of even-handedness gave colour to the traditional nationalist argument that the unionists were encouraged to display an intransigence which they would not have shown if they had not been able to count on British support. (The third case, Palestine, was different—there it was the United Nations, not Britain, which decided on partition. The complaint against Britain is not that it divided the country but that, having handed over the problem to the United Nations, it then did nothing to help the United Nations implement its decision.)

A great weight of historical writing can, however, be put in the other side of the balance. On the whole, recent historians have been struck by the depth of Ulster unionist opposition to a united Ireland separate from Britain, and the independence of that opposition from British support. Some of the most important contributions to the literature—Peter Gibbon's *The Origins of Ulster Unionism* (1975), Henry Patterson's *Class Conflict and Sectarianism: The Protestant Working Class and the Belfast Labour Movement 1868–1920* (1980), and the publications of the British and Irish Communist Organisation (BICO)—will be discussed in the chapter on Marxist interpretations; but even among non-Marxist historians there is an impressive volume of writing on the same side. I shall take just some of the possible examples. F. S. L. Lyons, in his magisterial biography of Charles Stewart Parnell (1977, 350–5), criticizes Parnell for his failure to take seriously the problem posed by Ulster unionist opposition to home rule. Ruth Dudley Edwards, in her equally authoritative life of Patrick Pearse (1977, 214), considers him naïve for believing that the Orangemen could be won over to the nationalist cause. Patricia Jalland, author of the most exhaustive study of the crisis surrounding the third Home Rule Bill, *The Liberals and Ireland: The Ulster Question in British Politics to 1914* (1980), puts the main blame for the crisis on the Liberals for not appreciating the strength of unionist opposition until it was too late, rather than on the Conservatives for fomenting Ulster unionist opposition, which she considers genuine and deep-seated. A slightly later period is examined in George Boyce's *Englishmen and Irish Troubles: British Public Opinion and the Making of Irish Policy*

1918–22 (1972). He shows that by the post-war period Ulster unionists, far from basking in British support, aroused irritation even among Conservatives for their intransigence, and at times came under intense pressure to compromise. A somewhat similar interpretation has now been applied to an earlier period in Alvin Jackson's recent book *The Ulster Party: Irish Unionists in the House of Commons, 1884–1911* (1989). Jackson finds that the intransigence displayed by Ulster Unionists in 1911, on the eve of the third Home Rule Bill, arose precisely because they were *not* sure of how much support they would receive from British Conservatives. After all, it was only a few years since Conservatives had flirted with a watered-down version of home rule during the devolution crisis of 1905. It was not until Bonar Law became Conservative leader in 1912 that Ulster Unionists felt that the Conservative Party was in the hands of someone on whom they could rely. (See in particular the chapter on 'The Emergence of Ulster Unionist Militancy, 1905–1911' (Jackson 1989, 284–321).) Finally, it may be mentioned that two recent histories of Irish nationalist ideology, Robert Kee's *The Green Flag* (1972) and George Boyce's *Nationalism in Ireland* (1982), also criticize Irish nationalists for underestimating the strength of Ulster Protestant opposition.

I should like to deal at greater length with a few works which have particularly illuminating things to say about Ulster Protestant attitudes in the union period. An outstanding local study is Donald Akenson's *Between Two Revolutions: Islandmagee, County Antrim 1798–1920* (1979). Islandmagee, an almost purely Protestant and predominantly Presbyterian area, had in 1798 joined in the United Irish rebellion against English domination. By 1920, however, it was solidly in favour of the union with Britain. To examine the reasons for this change is to provide a kind of litmus test against which some theories of the growth of unionism—traditional nationalist, but also Marxist—can be tested. The change could not be ascribed to the creation of marginal advantages for Protestants as against Catholics—there were hardly any Catholics in the area to be discriminated against (Akenson 1979, 162, 176). It could not be ascribed to the influence of the Orange Order, which was weak in Islandmagee (pp. 152–3). It could not be ascribed to the growing economic differentiation between the industrial north-east of Ireland and the agricultural society in the rest of the island, because Islandmagee itself remained overwhelmingly rural (p. 177). The most plausible explanation of why the people of Islandmagee became such staunch defenders of the status quo, in Akenson's view, is that, under the union, and particularly from about 1850, their society had worked (p. 173). In addition, their culture was predominantly Scottish (p. 175). In these circumstances there was nothing for them in a united Ireland separate from Britain. 'The Islanders acted as loyalists simply as an assertion of their own cultural identity' (p. 178).

A crucial period has been given its most thorough examination to date by B. M. Walker, in his *Ulster Politics: The Formative Years, 1868–86* (1989). In some respects Walker may give comfort to traditional nationalists. He argues that the polarization of Ulster into Catholic-nationalist and Protestant-unionist blocs was not inevitable (pp. 46, 265). In particular, he shows that in the late 1870s and early 1880s, under the influence of agricultural depression, a powerful combination of Presbyterian and Catholic tenant-farmers, headed by the Liberal Party, grew up in opposition to their Church of Ireland landlords. It was not till the general election of 1886 that the cleavage was established which has marked the north of Ireland ever since. However, where Walker parts company from traditional nationalists is that he does not find it necessary to explain this transformation as the result of outside manipulation. Indigenous forces were amply sufficient to account for it. The extension of the franchise in 1884 greatly increased the proportion of Catholics in the electorate (pp. 42–3), and over much of Ulster they no longer needed a Presbyterian alliance in order to win seats. The home rule issue overtook the land question in importance, and many Protestants who had been prepared to co-operate with Catholics on agrarian issues found it impossible to do so when an autonomous Catholic-dominated Ireland was in prospect. Nationalists did attempt to gain Protestant support, but their chances of getting it were reduced by the prominence of Catholic clergy in their organization, and their readiness to support the Catholic line in education (p. 262). Behind all this lay deep-seated mutual suspicions between Protestant and Catholic, masked but not destroyed by the years of partial co-operation in the cause of land reform (pp. 26–31, 259–61).

The most original study of Ulster loyalist ideology is provided by David Miller's *Queen's Rebels* (1978). At one level Miller's findings, like Walker's, might seem to hold out some comfort to nationalists. He stresses that Ulster unionists, right up to the time of partition, described themselves as Irish (pp. 109–12). The two-nations theory as an explicit argument to counter home rule seems to have been introduced by British rather than Irish unionists (p. 112). However, that does not mean that Miller believes the unionists really to belong to the Irish nation. He finds, rather, that the unionists were not thinking in such terms. Nationalism is an ideology of the nineteenth century. Ulster Protestants, for reasons which Miller elaborates, missed out on this phase in the development of most European peoples. They continued to operate on a pre-nationalist ideology, which Miller describes as contractarian. According to the contract-arian view, subjects owe allegiance to a sovereign, on condition that he fulfils his duties to them, the most important of which is protection. Because Ulster Protestants operated according to this ideology, they cannot be described as a nation. But neither can they be accepted as part of the Irish nation. Ireland contains two groups—a nation, and a community. Miller's argument is well supported by quotations from Protestant spokesmen of many different periods. At the time it came out, it provided the most satisfying exposition of unionist ideology to have been published so far. Indeed it has been described by another distinguished student of Irish history, Charles Townshend, as having 'a good claim to be the most important single contribution to any understanding of the Ulster problem' (Townshend 1988, 12).

Miller's conclusions have aroused some controversy. A historian at the University of Ulster, James Loughlin, in his book *Gladstone, Home Rule and the Ulster Question 1882–93* (1986), argues that, at least during the first home rule crisis of 1886, Miller's theory does not fit the facts. Drawing on a sample of thirty speeches made by unionist spokesmen, he argues that in none of them did the speaker explicitly refer to the contractarian theory described by Miller, while only nine speakers even implied a contractual relationship (p. 157). He finds more noticeable in the speakers 'the high degree of ideological and emotional commitment to Britain and what they saw as British values and traditions' (p. 156). He concludes that Ulster Protestants were more similar to the inhabitants of Great Britain in their national identity than Miller had appreciated. Loughlin's conclusions, however, have in their turn been challenged by Alvin Jackson in his book (1989, 8–10) referred to earlier in this chapter. Jackson argues that Loughlin's sample of speeches was untypical, and, basing himself on a study of the whole period 1884–1911, concludes that unionists did possess a distinct Ulster identity, and that their identification with Britain was more qualified than Lough-lin alleges. In my view Miller and Jackson win this particular controversy.

However, though Miller, Loughlin, and Jackson may differ in how they conceptualize unionist ideology, they are in agreement on the seriousness with which that ideology was held. The idea that it was an artefact of British manipulation is one which none of them countenances. Indeed Loughlin's book is largely devoted to explaining how Gladstone could have so misread the situation as to imagine that the Ulster problem was less serious than it really was. The conclusions of Miller, Loughlin, and Jackson carry weight because they are the three historians who have looked most exhaustively at unionist attitudes in the union period.

There can then be no doubt where the balance has lain in recent historical study of Ulster. Back in the 1950s, on the meagre historical evidence then available, it had been possible for Gallagher and Barrington to reach opposite conclusions—one claiming that partition had been the result of British manipulation, and the other that it was the result of deep-seated divisions within Ireland itself. Without denying that the unionists received important support from Britain, the bulk of recent scholarship has put more stress on the internal strength of Ulster unionism.

The best introduction to the current state of historical scholarship in this area is a little book by a historian at University College Dublin, Michael Laffan, entitled *The Partition of Ireland, 1911–1925* (1983). Laffan points out the supremacist streak in unionist ideology, and the double standards employed by British politicians. He notes that the settlement reached in 1921 was only one of several possible, and was too favourable to the unionists for their own good (pp. 123–4). But that did not mean that the nationalist case was established.

Nationalists glossed over the distinctive culture and traditions shared by a million Ulster protestants. They attached to Britain all the responsibility for unionists' time-honoured preference for rule from London or Belfast over rule from Dublin, a preference which preceded Conservative and other British support, was always partly independent of it, and to an extent survived it. (p. 123.)

Dr Laffan's first chapter, in which he describes Irish society before partition, is entitled 'Two Irish Peoples'. 'Partition', he says, 'was a solution, one of several possible solutions, to a problem which went back centuries: the clash of interests between two "nations" and two religions in Ireland' (p. 1).

'REVISIONIST' HISTORIOGRAPHY: NATIONALIST ATTITUDES TO NORTHERN IRELAND

Recent historical scholarship is not confined to the union period. A number of scholars have turned their attention to the history of Ireland since 1920, a process which has been helped by the opening of archives, in both parts of Ireland and in Britain. One topic which has attracted considerable interest has been the policy and attitudes of southern politicians to the northern State.

So far, this interest has concentrated overwhelmingly on Éamon de Valera. Such an emphasis is not ideal, because for a rounded picture of southern policy it would be necessary to look at other statesmen besides him. But it is a good place to start, since de Valera towered over Irish politics for so many decades. He was president of the Republic from 1919 to 1922, a leading figure even while in opposition from 1922 to 1932, and then prime minister for twenty-three of the twenty-seven years 1932–59. During two intervals when he was out of power (1948–51, 1954–7) his ideas seemed to dominate the northern policies of the governments then in office. It was not until after his retirement that signs of new thinking began to appear under Lemass.

The modern study of de Valera began with the publication of the biography by Longford and O'Neill in 1970. The most comprehensive examination of his views on the north has been provided in John Bowman's magisterial work, *De Valera and the Ulster Question, 1917–1973* (1982). Bowman's work can be supplemented on particular issues by a number of recent books: the studies of de Valera by T. Ryle Dwyer (1980, 1982*a,b*) and by Lee and Ó Tuathaigh (1982), a volume of essays edited by O'Carroll and Murphy (1983), the examination of Anglo-Irish relations in the 1930s by Deirdre McMahon (1984), and others.

These works confirm that de Valera passionately believed in the tenets of traditional nationalism—that partition was wrong, and that it was the fault of Britain. What they do in addition is to explore more fully the ways in which he reconciled these beliefs with the evident support for partition among northern unionists.

De Valera, like other traditional nationalists, believed that the unionists were really Irish, and would come to recognize the fact if the British prop were withdrawn. To quote one statement out of many possible ones, in 1933 he told a correspondent of the *Christian Science Monitor* that, if British influence and British financial contributions were withdrawn, 'the force of common interest, the natural interdependence of the two parts of the country and the sentiment of nationality would work irresistibly for the restoration of the unity destroyed by British policy in 1920' (quoted in Bowman 1982, 115–16).

The weakness in de Valera's position has been explored by Lee and Ó Tuathaigh (1982). They quote other statements by de Valera to show that he disapproved of reunification by force because of the depth of bitterness which it would leave behind (pp. 114–15). But, in that case, why did he also say that the division in Ireland was due to British machinations?

De Valera's anticipation of generations of smouldering resentment seems exaggerated in the light of his analysis of the origins of the conflict. It is only if his analysis is wrong, and the conflict drew its inspiration from deep, instinctive, and indigenous racial and religious hatreds that de Valera's prophecy can carry conviction. If his analysis is right, his predictions are unconvincing. If his predictions are convincing, his analysis is suspect. (p. 120.)

However, the belief that the unionists were really Irish was not the only weapon in de Valera's armoury. He would not abandon his stand even if the unionists rejected unity, because in his view the territorial unity of Ireland took precedence over their wishes. De Valera was a believer in natural boundaries, in some cases at least. In 1939 he quoted with approval a speech of Mussolini's:

There is something about the boundaries that seem to be drawn by the hand of the Almighty which is very different from the boundaries that are drawn by ink upon a map:- Frontiers traced by inks on other inks can be modified. It is quite another thing when the frontiers were traced by Providence. (Quoted in Bowman 1982, 302.)

It followed from this that if unionists were not prepared to accept that Ireland was their country, then they should be induced to leave, and be replaced by Irishmen living in England. (This forgotten aspect of de Valera's policy was first recalled by T. Ryle Dwyer in his *Eamon de Valera* (1980, 112). For further examples see Dwyer 1982*b*, 197, 166, 169; Bowman 1982, 209, 260, 318–19.). The objection to this policy was that there was no evidence that the Irish in Britain wished to return to Ireland, any more than the Ulster unionists wished to go to Britain. Yet in the interests of carto-graphic symmetry de Valera was prepared to contemplate inducing both groups to go where they did not wish. He nowhere explained why territorial neatness was so much more important than the wishes of the people concerned.

One of the kinder verdicts on de Valera's northern policy is given by Bowman, but in a form which is likely to irritate traditional nationalists almost more than outright criticism. Bowman completes an exhaustive appraisal of de Valera's policy by concluding that it was more flexible and less doctrinaire than his reputation would have led one to expect. In reality, de Valera was 'predominantly pragmatic and occasionally heretical or revisionist' (p. 330). He was less extreme than some of his followers would have liked. For instance, in the 1930s he rejected all the more intransigent pro-posals—organizing Fianna Fáil in Northern Ireland, allowing northern representatives to sit in the Dáil, or bringing up partition in the League of Nations (pp. 133–6). However, because of his rhetoric he continued to be regarded as the exponent of anti-partitionist orthodoxy (pp. 330–1).

What about nationalists other than de Valera? As already explained, they have not yet been studied with nearly such thorough-ness. However, a start has been made by Clare O'Halloran in her book *Partition and the Limits of Irish Nationalism* (1987). O'Hal-loran deals in outline with the whole period from 1922 to the New Ireland Forum of 1984, but the great bulk of her book is concerned with the period 1922–37. For that period, she discusses not just the views of de Valera and Fianna Fáil, but at even greater length the attitudes of Cosgrave and the Cumann na nGaedheal/Fine Gael parties, as well as those of non-party writers.

O'Halloran's account shows that nationalists of all kinds were baffled by the same problems as taxed de Valera. None of them was prepared to abandon the central tenet of nationalism, that Ireland ought to be united. But none of them had any better idea than de Valera about how to reconcile this aim with the evident refusal of Ulster unionists to have anything to do with it. Some hoped for the economic development of the Irish Free State to such heights that the northerners would be glad to come in (O'Halloran 1987, 44, 159–63). Others comforted themselves by arguing that the border was so unnatural that unity was inevitable (pp. 158–9). Some argued that the unionists, despite their protestations, were really Irish and not British, and could be brought to accept their true nationality as they had done in the eighteenth century (pp. 36–41). A few even saw the study of Irish culture and the Irish language as a common interest which could act as a bridge to unity (pp. 170–5). But, on the whole, the attitude of southern nationalists to the north was irritation. It did not fit in with their ideology, and there was nothing they could do about it. This irritation could spill over to encompass northern nationalists. The most novel of O'Halloran's findings is that northern nationalists aroused almost as much hostility in the Irish Free State as did northern unionists (pp. 57–92, 131–56). As she puts it (p. 92), they were regarded with a 'mixture of resentment and guilt'.

Recent historical writing, then, has not been favourable to the traditional nationalist interpretation. Authors who have explored the nineteenth century have found that the roots of the unionist tradition are older and sturdier than nationalists were traditionally disposed to admit. Scholars who have investigated the nationalist attitude to Northern Ireland since partition have been struck by the internal inconsistencies of the position—insisting that Ireland was really one nation, yet unable to find any convincing way of reconciling that claim with the refusal of unionists to accept that they belonged to that nation. These findings are all the more significant because the majority of the authors who have developed them come from the nationalist tradition.

RECENT NATIONALIST WRITING

It would be wrong to assume that recent events and recent historiography have killed traditional nationalism. A trickle of publications continues to appear which show little change from the attitudes dominant among nationalists down to the 1950s. Three authors who believe that the British presence remains the core of the problem are Tom Collins in *The Centre Cannot Hold* (1983), Des Wilson in *An End to Silence* (1985), and Gerry Adams, President of Sinn Féin, in his two books *The Politics of Irish Freedom* (1987) and *A Pathway to Peace* (1988). It is fair to say that none of the three writers even claims to have written a work of deep research. They do not grapple with the evidence surveyed in preceding sections of this chapter. However, since this point of view retains popular support, comprehensiveness requires that an example of it be discussed. The author I have chosen is Gerry Adams, whose prominence as a politician makes him deserving of attention.

Adams is a wholehearted traditional nationalist. For him, the root of the problem is the British presence. He sustains this case in two ways: by appeal to principle, and by arguing from the practical ill effects of the British presence. The principled argument is that Ireland has a right to self-determination, and that the British presence prevents the Irish people from exercising that right (Adams 1988, 26). Unionists do not have the same right to self-determination: 'they are a national minority; a significant minority but a minority nevertheless. To bestow the power of veto over national independence and sovereignty on a national minority is in direct contravention of the principle of self-determination' (1988, 41). The practical argument is that the British presence has not brought peace to Ireland, has propped up sectarianism, has damaged the economies of both parts of the island, and has stunted the development of class politics (1986, 88–96). It enables Britain to maintain not just a colonial control over Northern Ireland, but a neo-colonial control over the Republic (1988, 32). Adams comes close to saying that all the evils in the island, north and south, stem from the British presence:

Partition and the British connection distorts our politics, sets restrictions on our economic growth, and dictates our social outlook and our cultural values.

   Partition divides our people not just in the six counties but between the six counties and the twenty-six counties.

   Partition saps our national morale and diverts our energies as a nation and as well as the 'carnival of reaction' which it established and maintains in the six counties, partition has a real and in-depth effect on the affairs of the rest of the island. (1988, 10.)

Adams admits that the unionists have material interests in maintaining the British link, and are not going to be persuaded to change their mind by argument (1988, 57). But he believes that once the British prop is removed they will face reality (1986, 89). They will then be able to 'embrace, enrich and enjoy a heritage which is in a very real sense theirs' (1986, 126).

   Both strands of Adams's case are open to question. The claim that the unionists are an Irish minority, without the right of self-determination, is to assume what needs to be proved. We have seen in Chapter 4 that northern Protestants are much more likely to describe themselves as 'British' or 'Ulster' than Irish. We have seen earlier in this chapter that nearly all historians who have looked at Ulster during the union period have been struck by the strength and durability of the distinct Protestant identity. We shall see in Chapter 8, where Marxist interpretations are discussed, that some Marxists see the Ulster Protestants as a distinct nation. There is a great weight of evidence here which needs to be faced by anyone with views like Adams's, but he does not even attempt it. His account of the growth of unionist feeling among nineteenth-century Protestants (1986, 115–17) is superficial. He attributes it to landlord manipulation, the machinations of the Presbyterian divine Henry Cooke, and the manœuvres of British Conservatives. These factors existed, but they are not the ones which historical research has uncovered as crucial. More important have been the real differences in religious values, national identity, and economic interest.

Adams's second line of argument, that the practical effects of the British connection have been disastrous, is also more contentious than he realizes. It can be conceded at once that partition has brought costs, particularly to the Catholic minority in the north, as we shall see in the next chapter. But to jump from this to saying that all the evils in Ireland, north and south, can be traced back to the British presence is to go beyond the evidence. It is to assume in the first place that partition was simply engineered by the British, and had no significant indigenous roots. It could be argued on the other side that the strength of Protestant feeling was such that an attempt to unify Ireland in defiance of it might have led to more violence, more misery, and more long-term problems for the island than its division between two States.

Furthermore, even supposing that partition is the product of British policy, the question still arises: were its effects so uniformly malign? The work of economic historians is more ambiguous on this point than Adams might expect. Mary Daly, in her *Social and Economic History of Ireland* (1981, 138) argues that the local consequences, except in Derry and to a lesser extent Newry, were probably slight. David Johnson, in his *Interwar Economy in Ireland* (1985, 7) has gone further and suggested that partition 'may well have benefited economically both parts of the island'—the rationale behind this conclusion being that the two parts of Ireland had divergent economic interests, and that partition enabled each to follow the policies which suited it best. Kennedy, Giblin, and McHugh, in their book *The Economic Development of Ireland in the Twentieth Century* (1988) do not include partition in their comprehensive set of explanations for the indifferent performance of the Irish economy. The claim that partition has stunted the development of class politics, too, seems an exaggeration. It has force in the north, where the salience of the national issue has inhibited all efforts to emphasize socio-economic questions. But, in the south, there are plenty of reasons besides partition to account for the weakness of left-wing forces. Michael Gallagher, for instance, in his study of the Irish Labour Party (1982, 8–23) offers a fifteen-page explanation for its weakness which does not mention partition. He points to the conservative, Catholic, rural, and individualistic nature of Irish political culture.

The most valuable parts of Adams's work are the autobiographical passages. He helps one to understand how a young man growing up in Catholic west Belfast could be attracted to republicanism. But he does not face the objections which anyone who does not already hold that doctrine might raise against it.

I can find only one recent work in the academic literature which can be placed even on the margin of the traditional nationalist school. Seán Cronin's *Irish Nationalism: A History of its Roots and Ideology* (1980) is based on a thesis submitted to the New School of Social Research in New York. The book contains a considerable amount of research, and some of the information it provides, particularly in the appendices, make it of permanent value even to those who find its argument unsatisfactory. In parts of the book the author appears to subscribe to the traditional nationalist line. He states that 'it is the fact of England's presence that leads to the violence' (p. 207), and adds that 'the ideology of Irish nationalism will continue to ripple the political waters until its conception of nationhood is achieved' (p. 236). But in other places he appears to distance himself from such views. In his introduction (p. 24) he cites approvingly Hans Morgenthau's claim that the nation-state has outlived its usefulness and is obsolete, which would seem to imply that the objective basis for the movement to obtain an all-Ireland nation-state is on the wane. Later (pp. 221–2) he notes that nationalist ideology is indeed on the wane in the Republic of Ireland. His chapter on 'Northern Ireland in the 1970s' contains some sharp criticisms of republican ideology, as well as that of other actors on the scene (pp. 206–11). All in all, readers may finish this book confused about where the author stands. Although he has sympathy for the traditional nationalist view that the British presence is at the core of the problem, it is not clear how wholeheartedly he subscribes to it.

Some might expect me to mention here another author well known for his writing on the Northern Ireland problem. Desmond Fennell is the author of four relevant books—*The State of the Nation* (1983), *Beyond Nationalism* (1985), *Nice People and Rednecks: Ireland in the 1980s* (1986), and *The Revision of Irish Nationalism* (1989). Some of Fennell's statements might lead one to classify him as a traditional nationalist. He has on occasion seen the British–Irish conflict as fundamental: 'the root of all the violence in the North is the fact that 600,000 Irish people (mostly Catholics, but including some Protestants) are forced to live under a constitution which denies their existence and foists Britishness upon them' (Fennell 1986, 42). He has written in harsh terms of British misrule in the north, and warmly of the republican rebellion against it (1983, 79, 96; 1986, 12, 42, 46–7, 96, 124–5, 140). On his own showing, he worked in the 1970s with Provisional Sinn Féin, and wrote for the republican organ *An Phoblacht* (1985, 157, 179). He has published an attack on revisionist history (1989, 62–70). At the same time, however, he rejects some traditionalist beliefs. He does not believe that the people of Ireland comprise one nation. In Ireland, 'there is one nation, the Irish nation, and part of another nation, namely, the British nation' (1986, 44). He sees the problem as one of 'devising a state in which both these communities can share' (1983, 117). He is critical of those nationalists who see the Ulster unionists as 'somehow, unknown to themselves, part of the Irish nation' (1986, 57). He writes favourably (1989, 10) of the report of the New Ireland Forum, which, as I shall argue in the next section, is more of a departure from traditional nationalism than a restatement of it. As he says himself, he is not easy to label. 'In the eyes of some people, I am anti-nationalist, and in the eyes of others, an extreme nationalist' (1986, 55). In his most recent book he states his position as being neither traditional nationalist nor anti-nationalist (1989, 11). We can accept that he is not a traditional nationalist as I have defined the term.

THE NEW IRELAND FORUM, 1983–1984

The most authoritative restatement of the nationalist ideal in recent times was presented by the New Ireland Forum of 1983–4. The forum comprised representatives of the four main constitutional nationalist parties in the island of Ireland: the Social Democratic and Labour Party (SDLP) from Northern Ireland, and Fianna Fáil, Fine Gael, and Labour from the Republic. It received written submissions from 317 individuals and groups and heard oral evidence from 31 of these (New Ireland Forum 1984a, para. 1.6). It also commissioned a number of research papers. Unlike some of the authors reviewed in the last section, it could not be accused of reaching conclusions without having done any research. Buttressed by government funding and a full-time staff, it was in a position to make a weightier contribution to the discussion on Northern Ireland than any previous body on the nationalist side since the All-Party Anti-partition Conference of the late 1940s. The question arises: how far did it stick to traditional nationalist doctrine, and how far did it strike out on a new line?

From the outset it was evident that the Forum was going to have difficulty in giving a clear answer to this question. In its opening session, on 30 May 1983 (New Ireland Forum 1983–4, no. 1), the four party leaders took sharply divergent lines. Three of them expressed views a considerable distance from the old nationalist claim that the problem was primarily the fault of the British. Dr Garret FitzGerald, the taoiseach and leader of Fine Gael, saw the heart of the issue as 'the existence in Northern Ireland of two senses of identity—the Irish/Irish sense of identity of the nationalist minority, and the British/Irish identity of the unionist majority' (p. 6). The leader of the Labour Party, Dick Spring, said that traditional nationalist as well as traditional unionist politics had failed (p. 19), and argued that society in the Republic, just as much as in Northern Ireland, would have to change if they were to be serious about their aspiration to unity. The leader of the SDLP, John Hume, saw the core of the problem as 'the belief by the Protestant tradition in this island that its ethos cannot survive in Irish political structures' (p. 23), and recognized that the Protestant tradition was not merely theological, but contained 'also and perhaps more importantly a strong expression of political allegiance to Britain which we cannot ignore and which we cannot wish away any more than unionists could wish away our deep commitment to Irish unity' (p. 23). He saw this as an intractable difficulty which the Forum must face.

A different view was expressed by Charles Haughey, leader of the Fianna Fáil party, then in opposition but still the largest single party in the Republic. He said it was 'the British military and political presence which distorts the situation in Northern Ireland and inhibits the normal process by which peace and stability emerge elsewhere' (New Ireland Forum 1983–4, no. 1, p. 8). Or again: 'The present situation in Northern Ireland is not primarily the fault of anyone living there. It is the cumulative effect of British policy in Ireland over many hundreds of years' (p. 8). And later: 'partition . . . was never legitimate from a democratic point of view and cannot be made so' (p. 10). He rejected the idea, which the other three leaders had implicitly or explicitly accepted, that developments in the Republic had anything seriously to do with the problem: 'We need apologise to nobody about the character or performance of our State, and we do not intend to do so. . . . If there are blemishes, they are small ones' (p. 10).

It is not surprising, in view of the divergent attitudes of the parties, that the final report of the Forum (New Ireland Forum 1984*a*) should contain a good deal of ambiguity. Traditional nationalists could feel they were vindicated by phrases such as those which referred to the 'arbitrary division of Ireland' (para. 2.2), or the failure of the British government in 1920 'to accept the democratically expressed wishes of the Irish people' (para. 3.3). The nationalist identity and ethos was defined as including a 'democratically founded wish to have that identity institutionalised in a sovereign Ireland united by consent' (para. 5.1.8), but the unionist identity was not defined as including a wish to have it institutionalized in the United Kingdom (para. 5.1.9). Above all, the party leaders agreed that 'the particular structure of political unity which the Forum would wish to see established is a unitary state' (para. 5.7). Newspaper reports at the time stated that this stipulation was insisted on by Mr Haughey, and that otherwise he would not have signed the report (e.g. John Cooney in the *Irish Times*, 3 May 1984).

Nevertheless, there are other passages in the report which suggest an openness to new interpretations. Though a unitary State was the preferred solution, the report explored two other options—a federal/confederal State (Chapter 7), and joint authority wielded over

Northern Ireland by both London and Dublin (Chapter 8). The signatories also declared that they remained 'open to discuss other views which may contribute to political development' (para. 5.10). The examination of joint authority—in which Fianna Fáil shared—is perhaps of special significance. It implied an acceptance that the total withdrawal of Great Britain might not be necessary for a solution of the Northern Ireland problem. Indeed much of the argument in Chapters 4 ('Assessment of the Present Problem') and 5 ('Framework for a New Ireland: Present Realities and Future Requirements'), seemed to be pointing in the direction of joint authority as a solution. The unionist as well as the nationalist identities were explored with some sympathy. It was recognized that the former included a sense of Britishness (para. 4.9.1). 'The Need for Accommodation of Both Identities in a New Approach' (para. 4.11) was accepted, and it was conceded that 'Irish nationalist attitudes have hitherto in their public expression tended to under-estimate the full dimension of the unionist identity and ethos' (para. 5.1.10). It was only in the later part of Chapter 5 that the argument slid into advocating a 'new and sovereign Ireland' (para. 5.2.3) as the desired solution. This did not follow from the preceding discussion, and can be attributed to the need to forge a compromise between Fianna Fáil and the other three parties.

Clare O'Halloran has argued, in her able book (1987) discussed earlier in this chapter, that the report of the New Ireland Forum is fundamentally a restatement of old nationalist attitudes. In view of the fudging on critical points which the divergence of opinion between the political leaders made necessary, the report can be interpreted in this way. But in my view, the innovations in its approach decisively outweigh the continuities with old-style nationalist views. Despite what Mr Haughey said in his opening statement, the report does not see the British presence as being at the heart of the Northern Ireland problem. The core is seen as lying in the clash of two identities. The contrast with Frank Gallagher (1957), who saw the unionist identity as a fabrication of the British, is fundamental. I would prefer to see the report of the New Ireland Forum as not lying within my definition of a traditional nationalist interpretation, but rather as belonging to the internal-conflict interpretation which I shall discuss in subsequent chapters. I shall give further consideration to it there.

A CONTINUING BRITISH RESPONSIBILITY

The traditional nationalist interpretation, in the form in which it was expressed by writers such as Gallagher or statesmen such as de Valera, is now rarely found in the literature on Northern Ireland. Scarcely anyone who has put himself/herself to the discipline of writing in a scholarly manner on the problem now stands over the one-nation theory. The majority of writers, even among those who would broadly be in the nationalist tradition, accept that the greatest obstacle to Irish unity lies within the Ulster Protestant community. However, it is important to stress the limits of what has been conceded. To accept the points made in the preceding pages does not mean accepting that the British have always been in the right. In particular:

Firstly, it does not mean saying that the 1920 settlement was just. Granted that there were two communities in Ireland, the Government of Ireland Act 1920 did not hold the balance fairly between them. As we shall see in the next chapter, it gave the unionists more territory than they were entitled to on a head-count, and failed to provide effective safeguards against the oppression of minorities.

Secondly, it does not mean denying that a historic responsibility rests on Britain for the deeper roots of the crisis. When every plea in mitigation has been made, the British record in Ireland has been a sorry one. Indeed it can be a source of pain to conscientious Englishmen. As Canon John Baker, then Sub-Dean of Westminster and subsequently Bishop of Salisbury, put it in a sermon at the time of the first hunger-strikes in 1980:

No British Government ought ever to forget that this perilous moment, like many before it, is the outworking of a history for which our country is primarily responsible. England seized Ireland for its own military benefit; it planted Protestant settlers there to make it strategically secure; it humiliated and penalised the native Irish and their Catholic religion; and then, when it could no longer hold on to the whole island, kept back part to be a home for the settlers' descendants, a non-viable solution from which Protestants have suffered as much as anyone. (Baker 1980.)

It does not follow that Bishop Baker had adopted the traditional nationalist view that the British presence was currently responsible for the divisions in Ireland. Indeed in a later paper (Baker 1982, 20) he wrote that the legacy bequeathed by England to Ireland 'bears the distinguishing mark of true evil, namely that there is no right answer to the problem it poses'. But in that paper again he expressed the guilt which an honourable Englishman can feel when confronting the Northern Ireland problem. (For another example of the anguish felt by an English person in coming to terms with the British record in Ireland, see Joan Tapsfield (1983).)

Finally, to reject the traditional nationalist interpretation does not mean exonerating recent British policy from blame for the current crisis. The Forum report contains a section highly critical of British policy (paras. 4.1–4.4), which it accuses of creating deadlock, reinforcing sectarian loyalties, giving insufficient recognition to the Irish identity of northern nationalists, and of following security policies which have made the situation worse. Nor are such criticisms confined to nationalist writers. Anthony Kenny, Master of Balliol College, Oxford, in his book *The Road to Hillsborough* (1986, 33), notes that security policy since the abandonment of internment in 1975 'increased rather than diminished Catholic alienation'. Dervla Murphy, an author strongly critical of the Provisional IRA, states in her travel book on Northern Ireland, *A Place Apart* (1978, 252–3), that 'in every Catholic area, urban or rural, grim stories are told to illustrate the corruption and savagery of the Brits'. Kevin Boyle and Tom Hadden, two academic lawyers whose book *Ireland: A Positive Proposal* (1985) I shall discuss later as an example of the internal-conflict interpretation, argue that British policies 'have contributed to a deepening sense of alienation among many Catholics both from Britain and from the majority community' (pp. 76–7). The particular shortcomings that they point to are (1) abuses in the security field, (2) the failure to secure an effective voice for Catholics in the government of Northern Ireland, and (3) the continuing difference in levels of unemployment and deprivation in the two communities.

British policy has been criticized with particular sharpness by Padraig O'Malley, in his brilliant book *The Uncivil Wars* (1983). Since I shall be citing this book in several contexts, I shall say a word about it here. O'Malley, a political scientist at the University of Massachusetts, carried out in the early 1980s an exhaustive series of interviews with the leaders of every grouping of importance to Northern Ireland—the leaders of British and of Republic of Ireland parties, as well as of the different parties and paramilitary groups in Northern Ireland. He then clinically examined the inconsistencies in each position. He was absolutely even-handed, and treated the

British no more severely than he did the other actors in the situation. When he put his finger on the weakness in the British position, then, his words should be taken seriously. He summed it up as follows: 'None of the parties to the conflict trusts Britain, and with good cause. Because she will not declare herself, no one knows where she stands' (p. 254). He called on Britain to spell out how she sees the long-term future of Ireland (pp. 255, 358).

O'Malley made an excellent point. Britain's long-term objective in Ireland is unclear. Furthermore, it has never been clear, from the time of partition onwards. The very measure which created partition, the Government of Ireland Act 1920, also contained provisions whereby the two parts of Ireland could eventually come together. The conditional nature of the British claim has been restated in several recent documents. The consultative paper on *The Future of Northern Ireland* (Northern Ireland Office 1972, para. 77), issued shortly after the imposition of direct rule, stated that 'no United Kingdom Government for many years has had any wish to impede the realisation of Irish unity, if it were to come about by genuine and freely given mutual agreement and on conditions acceptable to the distinctive communities'. The Sunningdale agreement of 1973, between the British and Irish governments, included a declaration by the British government that 'if, in the future, the majority of the people of Northern Ireland should indicate a wish to become part of a United Ireland, the British Government would support that wish' (quoted in Wallace 1982, 100–1). Finally, the Hillsborough agreement of 1985 reaffirmed that commitment:

The two Governments ... declare that, if in the future a majority of the people of Northern Ireland clearly wish for and formally consent to the establishment of a united Ireland, they will introduce and support in the respective Parliaments legislation to give effect to that wish. (Anglo-Irish Agreement 1985, Article 1.)

As Adrian Guelke has pointed out in his book *Northern Ireland: An International Perspective* (1988, 4, 197–8), this situation is anomalous by international norms. For a State to make its claim to a given area explicitly conditional on the consent of the people is unusual. Most States are defined in territorial terms.

The conditional nature of the British claim enables different people to draw different conclusions. On the one hand, unionists fear that it masks a covert desire to bring about Irish unity. As the deputy leader of the Democratic Unionist party, Peter Robinson, put it in a House of Commons debate on the Hillsborough accord, 'the agreement is intended to trundle Northern Ireland into an all-Ireland Republic' (quoted in Kenny 1986, 114). On the other hand Sinn Féin argued, in an exchange of documents with the SDLP, that the undertaking in the Hillsborough agreement was a smoke-screen, that Britain had strategic, economic, and political reasons for wishing to stay in Northern Ireland, and that she intended to do so (*Irish Times*, 7 September 1988). Thus different actors have been able to draw opposite conclusions from the same evidence. British policy has succeeded in maximizing distrust all round.

However, a judgement on British policy must include a recognition of its positive aspects. In the first place, there is British economic aid to Northern Ireland. By the mid-1980s, this was being calculated as amounting to around one-third of public expenditure in the region (Kennedy *et al.* 1988, 113; Wilson 1989, 85). True, there is some ground for disagreement about this figure: the Ulster-born economist Tom Wilson (1989, 85–6) suggests that on certain assumptions it might be significantly reduced. But even if a lower figure is accepted the degree of aid is still massive, and but for it everyone in Northern Ireland, Catholic as well as Protestant, would be much worse off. The other way in which the British presence may have helped is by reducing the risk of civil war. This claim rests on the assumption that if Britain were to withdraw, outright conflict would be the result. This assumption will be examined in Chapter 10. I shall just state here that in the opinion of the majority of authors who have examined the problem it is indeed likely that the British presence prevents the conflict from becoming worse. If so, then that is a plus which must be set against all the minuses outlined in preceding pages.

The weight of recent writing, then, does not sustain the traditional nationalist view that the current conflict is *primarily* between Britain and Ireland. To make the point clearer, a parallel might be drawn with the Israeli–Arab conflict. Israel receives massive aid from the United States, and American foreign policy is clearly tilted in favour of Israel. But that does not mean that the United States is the primary cause of the conflict. Indeed, it could be argued that a withdrawal of American interest in the area might strengthen the most intransigent elements in Israel and actually make the situation worse. For the same sorts of reasons, it is possible to combine a critical attitude towards British policy in Northern Ireland with a recognition that the root problem cannot be defined as the British presence. Indeed it is possible to argue that, with all its faults, the British presence prevents worse from happening in Northern Ireland.

7

The Traditional Unionist Interpretation

THE DEVELOPMENT OF THE TRADITIONAL UNIONIST INTERPRETATION

The traditional unionist interpretation can be summed up in two propositions: (1) there are two distinct peoples in Ireland, unionist and nationalist (or Protestant and Catholic); and (2) the core of the problem is the refusal of nationalists to recognize this fact, and to accord to unionists the same right of self-determination as they claim for themselves. Far from seeing Britain as the core of the problem, unionists tend to see the mainland British as unreliable allies who are too prone to give in to the nationalists.

The unionist view of Northern Ireland, like the nationalist, can be traced back to the earliest days of the region itself. One of the first, and still among the best, statements of the case can be found in Ronald McNeill's *Ulster's Stand for Union* (1922). Hugh Shearman wrote two books in the 1940s: *Not an Inch: A Study of Northern Ireland and Lord Craigavon* (1942), and *Anglo-Irish Relations* (1948). William A. Carson published a short book, scarcely more than a pamphlet, called *Ulster and the Irish Republic*, in 1957. The most comprehensive presentation of a pro-unionist point of view was published by a Dutch academic geographer, M. W. Heslinga, in his book *The Irish Border as a Cultural Divide* (1962). It is interesting that the fullest statement of the Ulster unionist case should come from a foreigner. Some might say that this illustrates the inarticulateness which unionists have always displayed, as compared with their nationalist counterparts. However that may be, it is probably true that Heslinga's work can be taken as the best counterpart to Frank Gallagher's *The Indivisible Island* (1957), which we discussed in the last chapter. Between them, the two books illustrate the nationalist/unionist argument as it stood before the troubles began.

Heslinga argues that, despite the political secession of the greater part of Ireland in 1921, the British Isles remain in many ways one unit (pp. 14–16, 81, 93–4). Basing his conclusions partly on his own observation, and partly on an exhaustive study of the secondary literature available at the time he wrote, he argues that, in so far as there are differences between various parts of the archipelago, they are between north and south rather than between west and east, and that the Republic is in temperament and culture closer to England than to Northern Ireland (pp. 96–7). Though he accepts that there are similarities between north and south in Ireland (p. 81), there are also many differences (pp. 68–75). The great difference between most of Ireland and the rest of the archipelago is religion (p. 204): it does indeed divide most of Ireland from Britain, but also south from north within Ireland. Heslinga sees Ulstermen as forming a separate nation (p. 62). While he does not feel obliged to stand over the details of the border (p. 49) he considers that it 'represents, however arbitrarily, an important spiritual divide' (p. 78). Heslinga does not come to any overt political conclusions, which he may have felt were inappropriate in what was in origin an academic thesis, but it is clear that in the argument between traditional nationalists and traditional unionists his sympathies are with the latter. To him, the partition of Ireland is the natural consequence of deep-seated differences, and he sees no merit in the claim that Ireland should be one State.

The traditional unionist view, like the traditional nationalist, was given plausibility by previous historical experience. It was the fact that Northern Ireland in its early decades appeared to be constantly under pressure from south of the border. The IRA campaign against the infant entity in 1921–2 was co-ordinated from across the border. The IRA campaign of 1956–62 was launched from across the border and largely confined to border areas. Twice—in 1938 and again in 1948—Dublin governments launched a propaganda campaign against partition. Ulster unionist views of the threat from the south have been perceptively analysed in Dennis Kennedy's book *The Widening Gulf: Northern Attitudes to the Independent Irish State 1919–49* (1988).

However, just as the traditional nationalist view has come under pressure in recent years, so has the traditional unionist. If it became harder for nationalists to see the core of the problem as British interference in Ireland, so it became harder for unionists to see the core of the problem as the southern Irish demand for an end to partition. It is the northern minority, not the southern regime or population, from which discontent has welled up in the past two decades. Indeed this has been recognized by more thoughtful unionists. The historian A. T. Q. Stewart, in his work *The Narrow*

Ground: Aspects of Ulster, 1609–1969 (1977) sees the problem as primarily internal, and as having been such from the start:

The planters were frontiersmen, and naturally displayed frontier attitudes where their lands bordered on those of the native septs. But even more important to them was the problem of the enemy in their midst. From the outset they faced the menace of a fifth column. This was, and still is, the very essence of what is called the Ulster problem. (p. 47.)

Or again:

Most people, if asked to define the chief symptoms of the Northern Ireland troubles, would say it is that the two communities cannot live together. The very essence of the Ulster question, however, is that they *do* live together, and have done for centuries. They share the same homeland and, like it or not, the two diametrically opposed political wills must coexist on the same narrow ground. (p. 180.)

However, the traditional unionist interpretation, to perhaps a greater degree than the traditional nationalist one, lives on. Explanations of this fact may vary. One prominent Official Unionist with whom I raised it replied that it was harder for a community under siege to reconsider its attitudes than one which was not under the same pressure. More critical observers might say that unionists have all along displayed greater rigidity and less imagination. Perhaps the most realistic explanation is that the case for uniting Ireland is still being put—even if not on the simplistic grounds of the past—and that unionists therefore still feel constrained to explain why they wish to remain separate from the Republic. But whatever the reasons, the fact seems clear enough. I shall mention just a few of the more articulate representations of the unionist point of view. Hugh Shearman has published two articles (1970, 1982) in *The Year Book of World Affairs*. The Revd Martin Smyth, Imperial Grand Master of the Orange Order, presented a paper to the Social Study Conference in 1974, which has since been published in the conference proceedings (Smyth 1975), and which represents a serious and temperate attempt by a northern Protestant to explain his position to a mainly southern audience. A group of northern lawyers and businessmen presented a paper entitled 'The Unionist Case' (McCartney *et al.* 1981) to members of the Irish government and opposition on 8 October 1981. I shall be using the seven-page photocopied Press hand-out, though the document was extensively reported in the papers of the following day. Two American academics, Galliher and DeGregory, interviewed a number of Protestant churchmen and politicians, and reported their findings in *Violence in Northern Ireland: Understanding Protestant Perspectives* (1985). Another publication worth noting is *Ulster: The Facts* (1982), by Ian Paisley, Peter Robinson, and John D. Taylor. Though this short book appeared over the names of three prominent unionist politicians, it was, I understand, largely written by two authors with academic qualifications. It cites scholarly literature, and can be considered the fullest recent attempt to give the unionist case a factual basis. From such sources as these we can build up a picture of the traditional unionist case as it is currently stated.

UNIONIST ARGUMENTS

The unionist literature explains the considerations which cause northern Protestants to favour maintaining themselves as a separate unit, distinct from the Republic. It stresses the very things that the traditional nationalist interpretation plays down—that there are unionist as distinct from British reasons for maintaining the border. These considerations can be grouped under three headings: religious, national, and economic. I shall discuss them in what seems to be their ascending order of importance.

The *economic* argument is, quite simply, that Northern Ireland is far better off as part of the United Kingdom than it would be as part of a united Ireland. The Republic of Ireland is portrayed as a weak economy, kept from collapse by high emigration, to join which 'would be to join economic hopelessness and a huge debt' (Paisley *et al.* 1982, 50–2). The south's decision to secede from the United Kingdom is criticized as entailing the loss of British social services and regional economic support (Shearman 1982, 183). However, it would be a mistake to put too much emphasis on the economic argument. Some authors do not mention it at all (McCartney *et al.* 1981). Others stress that it is only a subordinate part of the unionist case (Smyth 1975, 26; Galliher and DeGregory 1985, 54). Unionist literature makes it clear that the other two factors matter more.

The *national* argument asserts that unionists feel themselves to be of British nationality. Speaking of the unionist's ties with Britain, McCartney *et al.* (1981, 5) say: 'he is psychologically bound to her with bonds of blood, history and common adversity which cannot be bartered away in some logical package no matter how attractive that might seem'. Paisley, Robinson, and Taylor (1982, 52) say:

There is finally the fundamental nature of the Republic's secession from the United Kingdom and from the Commonwealth. To both, a large section of the community in Ulster has strong and positive loyalties. They do not wish to abandon their allegiance or change their nationality. Such a reluctance is not peculiar to Ulster. People feel that way about their country and its loyalties in most parts of the world.

A pamphlet from the moderate New Ulster Movement, *Two Irelands or One?* (1972a, 5) puts the same point:

To a large majority in Northern Ireland, British nationality seems as natural as the air they breathe. They travel on British passports, join the British armed forces or civil services, use the term 'our' when they are talking about things British. They erect memorials in their towns, schools and institutions to those who have died in the British forces during two world wars.

To the argument that unionists should accept the will of the Irish people as a whole, the reply is made that Ireland has never been united except under British rule, and that there is no reason why, when the southern Irish left the United Kingdom, the northern Irish had to follow them (Paisley *et al.* 1982, 39).

An aspect of the national argument which arouses particular heat among unionists is its rejection by the south in the 1937 Constitution. The claim in that Constitution that the whole of Ireland is the national territory is seen as giving legitimacy to the IRA's campaign of violence. 'The Northern Unionist objects not only to the fundamental nature of the claim to the territory of Northern Ireland, but to the pseudo-legality which it affords to the Provisional I.R.A.'s campaign of violence in the North' (McCartney *et al.* 1981, 2). 'The claim to sovereignty over Northern Ireland provided an ideological umbrella which gave shelter to several campaigns of terrorist outrages against the people of Northern Ireland, directed and organised from within the Republic' (Paisley *et al.* 1982, 41).

The argument on which most authors place greatest stress is the *religious* one. The objections have been partly to specific items of law which enshrine Catholic values, such as the prohibition of divorce, the difficulties in the way of obtaining contraceptives, Church control of education, and the existence of a literary censorship (McCartney *et al.* 1981, 5; Paisley *et al.* 1982, 50). But it does not follow that change in these areas would dissolve the difficulty. Unionist attitudes are based more on perceptions of an atmosphere than on particular grievances. Martin Smyth (1975, 30–1) complained of 'the system of authoritarian uniformity' which he detected in the south, and which spread into many activities which had nothing to do with religion. McCartney *et al.* (1981, 3) saw the Catholic Church in the Republic as being 'in such a position of entrenched power because of the control it exercises indirectly through the minds and attitudes of the faithful, as to be able to dictate policy to the State on matters which the Church considers essential to the maintenance of its position'. Galliher and DeGregory (1985, 71–9) found that many Protestant leaders were deeply suspicious of the power and intentions of the Catholic hierarchy.

A point made in almost all the unionist literature is that the Protestant population of the Republic has halved since independence. Some writers put this down to discrimination (Paisley *et al.* 1982, 50; Shearman 1970, 45), but even a relatively restrained writer concludes from it that 'the Republic is not a country in which the average Protestant thrives' (Smyth 1975, 29).

THE POSITION IN THE REPUBLIC

The unionist case derives from a particular view of the Republic. It therefore requires to be checked against research actually done on the Republic, of which there is by now a considerable volume. I shall consider it under the same three headings as the unionist arguments have been put—economic, national, and religious—but in reverse order. Since the religious area has been the most extensively discussed, I shall divide it into two sections: the position of the Protestant minority, and the position of the Catholic Church in the wider society.

Religion: The Position of the Protestant Minority

The position of the Protestant community in the Republic has, like other topics with a bearing on the Northern Ireland crisis, been extensively studied in recent years. At the time the troubles began, the most recent work was a pamphlet by Michael Viney, *The Five Per Cent* (1965), which is still of value. In more recent years it has been joined by a number of bigger works. The Revd Michael Hurley edited a volume on *Irish Anglicanism 1869–1969* (1970). Jack White published *Minority Report: The Anatomy of the Southern Irish Protestant* (1975). James McLoone edited the papers of the 1984 Social Study Conference on *Being Protestant in Ireland* (1985). The most substantial study is the Canadian sociologist Kurt Bowen's *Protestants in a Catholic State* (1983). Bowen actually confines himself to members of the Church of Ireland, but, since the Church of Ireland comprises roughly 80 per cent of all Protestants in the Republic (Bowen 1983, 3), his findings can be considered broadly applicable to the Protestant minority as a whole. An aspect of the Protestant situation has been explored in Donald Akenson's study of the Irish education system, *A Mirror to Kathleen's Face* (1975, 109–34).

There are, naturally, differences of interpretation between these books. The most favourable picture of the Protestant position is perhaps painted by Bowen (1983), who subtitles his work 'Ireland's Privileged Minority'. The least friendly is provided by Akenson, who argues that 'Protestants were tolerated and well treated as a religious minority but were penalized and ill-treated as a *cultural* minority' (p. 118). His reason for reaching this judgement is that he sees the policy of compulsory Irish in schools as being particularly damaging to the Protestant minority. This is perhaps to underestimate the degree to which it was unpopular among many Catholics as well — and also the extent to which some Protestants had participated in the language revival (McLoone 1985, 58–9). However, there is on the whole a greater degree of consensus among writers on the position of Protestants in the Republic than there is on many topics which I examine in this book.

The consensus in this literature is that southern Protestants are not a downtrodden group. The charge of discrimination against Protestants in the south, which northern unionists are prone to make, is not supported by these writers. White (1975, 169) and Bowen (1983, 96) treat it as a rare phenomenon, while Viney (1965, 10) denies its existence.

All authorities agree that Protestants are substantially over-represented in the upper reaches of the socio-economic scale (Viney 1965, 10; White 1975, 162–3; Bowen 1983, 84–92). It is true that the Protestant advantage is much less sharp than it was at the establishment of the State in 1922, but Bowen demonstrates that the change has occurred, not by squeezing Protestants out of commerce and the professions where they are relatively strong, but by building up a public sector in which Catholics dominate (p. 81).

The decline of Protestant numbers, on which unionist writers lay so much stress, has been examined by Bowen (1983, 20–47), by an American demographer, Robert E. Kennedy (1973, 110–38), and by an Irish demographer, Brendan Walsh (1970, 1975). In the early years after independence, a number of pressures combined to make the atmosphere uncongenial to many Protestants (Bowen 1983, 33–7), and their emigration rate was higher than that of Catholics (Bowen 1983, 29; Kennedy 1973, 113–16). But since 1946 the main reasons for the Protestant decline in numbers have been a high death-rate—the result of an unfavourable age structure—and a low birth-rate (Walsh 1970, 14, 18; 1975, 555). The Protestant emigration rate has actually been below the Catholic one—50 per cent lower in the intercensal period 1961–71 (Walsh 1975, 555). Shearman (1982, 183) has attempted to counter this point by stating that 'although aggregate Protestant emigration was lower than average, it was higher than average in the lower age groups'. But a glance at the census data shows that this was true only in the age groups 0–14, where the numbers involved were small in both communities, and where the higher Protestant proportion can perhaps be explained by the continuing tradition among some southern Protestants of sending their children to school in Northern Ireland or England. All in all, the evidence does not suggest that Protestants feel the country is one in which they are unable to thrive.

It would be a mistake, however, to go to the other extreme and argue that Protestants, as a religious minority, had nothing to complain of at all. There was one other demographic pressure on Protestants, besides the high death-rate and low birth-rate just mentioned—this was attrition through mixed marriages. All sources agree that this has caused a great deal of bitterness (Viney 1965, 23–9; White 1975, 129–34; Bowen 1983, 45–6, 168–9; McLoone 1985, 31; Galliher and DeGregory 1985, 72–3). White (1975, 129) explains the reasons:

There is no single cause that contributes so much to the embitterment of inter-faith relations as the rule of the Roman Catholic Church concerning mixed marriages. In any circle of Protestants, of any age-group, in any part of the country, this is the first reason that will be advanced to justify segregation in education and in social activities. Protestant parents do not want their children to mix with Catholics because they may marry Catholics; and if they marry Catholics, then the church will insist on an undertaking that the children of the marriage shall be brought up Catholics. ... As Protestants see it, their children are being placed in a situation of emotional blackmail, in which the price of love is the sacrifice of their own convictions.

In recent years the Catholic Church's regulations have softened, and in any case a higher proportion of Catholic spouses now appear ready to ignore their Church's requirements (Bowen 1983, 44–5). But these are recent developments, and it is uncertain how far they have gone. In the past, when a Protestant married a Catholic, he or she could usually be sure that the children would be brought up Catholics. This meant an unquantifiable but significant demographic loss to the Protestant community.

Religion: The Role of the Catholic Church in the Republic

The political role of the Catholic Church in the Republic has, like the position of the Protestant minority, been the subject of extensive recent research. In the late 1960s the only general surveys available were Paul Blanshard's polemical work *The Irish and Catholic Power* (1954), and a volume edited by Desmond Fennell, *The Changing Face of Catholic Ireland* (1968). These have now been joined by the present writer's *Church and State in Modern Ireland, 1923–79* (Whyte 1980), by Dermot Keogh's *The Vatican, the Bishops and Irish Politics, 1919–39* (1986) and, particularly for the period since about 1970, by John Cooney's *The Crozier and the Dáil: Church and State in Ireland 1922–1986* (1986). Father Liam Ryan contributed an important article on 'Church and Politics: The Last Twenty-Five Years' to *The Furrow* (1979). A philosopher's approach to the subject is provided by Desmond Clarke's *Church and State: Essays in Political Philosophy* (1985). A judicious survey by an academic lawyer has been offered by G. W. Hogan (1987). Papers have been published on the abortion and divorce referenda of 1983 and 1986 (Randall 1986; Girvin 1986a, 1987; O'Leary 1987; O'Leary and Hesketh 1988). Dermot Keogh and Seán Faughnan have published articles on the framing of the religious clauses in the Constitution of 1937 (Keogh 1987; Faughnan 1988). The wider position of the Catholic Church in Irish society has been examined by a sociologist, Tom Inglis, in *Moral Monopoly: The Catholic Church in Modern*

Irish Society (1987). As is only to be expected, a spectrum of opinion is displayed. Clarke (1985) and Inglis (1987) take the most critical view of the Church; my own book is among those taking a gentler one. However, there is sufficient common ground for these works to be considered together.

There is fair agreement that the influence of the Church has not been uniform throughout the history of the independent Irish State. My own view, as recorded in 1980, was that it had followed a trajectory, increasing during the early decades of independence, and declining from the 1950s (Whyte 1980, 372–4, 417). Inglis (1987) agrees that there has been some decline in recent years (pp. 77, 90–3, 213, 224–7). In the earlier period, the State enacted laws enshrining Catholic values on contraception, divorce, and censorship. On divorce, Keogh (1986, 128) has discovered from the archives that episcopal opposition went even further than appeared from the public record. Archbishop Byrne of Dublin informed the government in 1923 that 'the Church ... could not even sanction divorce for non-catholics for the reason that all persons who had been baptised are members of the Church and under its jurisdiction'. Successive governments paid homage to the pope, or proclaimed Ireland to be a 'Catholic nation' (Whyte 1980, 48, 158). The fundamental rights clauses of the 1937 Constitution were based on Catholic social teaching, and, while the final decisions about their phrasing were de Valera's, it is now known that they were framed only after extensive consultation with Catholic churchmen (Keogh 1987; Faughnan 1988). By 1949 one veteran Protestant nationalist, Thomas Johnson, could write to another, Ernest Blythe, saying that the revival of militant Catholicism gave credibility to the unionist fear that home rule would mean Rome rule—a fear that he would once have rejected (Bowman 1982, 276). Yet he was writing before the most celebrated exercise of episcopal power: the mother-and-child scheme crisis of 1951, when the government abandoned a health scheme, and the minister responsible for it resigned, after the hierarchy had condemned it as contrary to Catholic social teaching. (The account of this episode in Whyte 1980, 196–238, should be supplemented by the more recent research in McKee 1986, and Barrington 1987, 167–251.)

In the following years, however, a number of the measures which enshrined specifically Roman Catholic values were modified or repealed. The Censorship Board, once noted for its frequent banning of books which seemed incompatible with a conservative Catholic morality, was reformed by stages in 1956–7 and 1967 (Whyte 1980, 316, 344). The clause in the Constitution recognizing 'the special position of the Holy Catholic Apostolic and Roman Church as the guardian of the Faith professed by the great majority of the citizens' was repealed in 1972 (p. 389). The prohibition in an Act of 1935 on the sale or import of contraceptives was progressively watered down, by a court case in 1973 (p. 409), and then by Acts of Parliament in 1979 (p. 416) and in 1985 (Cooney 1986, 89). The mass media became far more ready to question Church influence, and developed as an alternative source of values (Inglis 1987, 90–3). The bishops themselves modified their position (Ryan 1979), and in an important statement issued in 1973 made clear that they did not insist that what was considered wrong by the Church need be prohibited by the State (Cooney 1986, 129–31).

In the 1980s, however, the pace of change faltered. Two referenda were held which had the effect of enshrining, or maintaining, traditional Catholic values in the Constitution. In the first of these (1983), the Constitution was amended so as to prohibit the enacting of any law permitting abortion. (Abortion was already illegal in Ireland.) In the second (1986), a proposal to introduce a limited form of divorce was rejected. Not everyone who discusses these episodes sees them in identical terms. Randall (1986, 84) goes further than some when she writes: 'the "liberal platform" has received a serious setback: some might indeed question whether it still exists in more than potential'. O'Leary and Hesketh (1988, 59) are more cautious than some when they speak of a situation 'in which liberal and traditional values exist side by side in a complex relationship'. But there is a consensus that the trend towards liberalization has at least been checked. 'Those who supported change were unrepresentative of a considerable section of Irish society' (Girvin 1987, 97). 'A majority of Southerners are quite happy with the status quo. Their desire to maintain the "Irish way of life" is simply a euphemism for a society and a State which happily embraces Catholic traditions and reflects Catholic moral values' (Hogan 1987, 94).

In both the abortion and divorce referenda, the Protestant Churches supported the 'liberal' side—that is, they opposed the entrenching of the ban on abortion in the Constitution, and they favoured the end of the constitutional ban on divorce. In both cases the Catholic hierarchy (while respecting the rights of those who conscientiously differed) supported the 'conservative' side. The fact that the side supported by the Catholic Church won the day suggests that, in the event of a conflict of values, the Catholic view will prevail. In neither case did the prospect that the outcome might affect northern Protestant attitudes to the Republic cut much ice with the electorate. Indeed the then taoiseach, Garrett FitzGerald, admitted that to make the repercussions on Northern Ireland an issue would have been 'counter-productive' (Hogan 1987, 96 n. 114).

Assessments have differed on the role of the Catholic Church in the Republic. On the one hand, Clarke (1987, 116–17) argues that to enshrine the values of a majority group in law is illegitimate, while Inglis (1987, 6) sees the Church as a 'compulsory and coercive organisation that, regardless of the intentions of individual members, has limited Irish discourse and practice'. The Catholic bishops, on the other hand, have defended the existing situation. In their submission to the New Ireland Forum (Irish Episcopal Conference 1984, 18–19) they argued that Catholic influence in a country like Ireland was natural:

Every legal system throughout the world bears the traces of majority opinion and of the public ethos and the majority consensus. This is true of Protestant countries as well as of Catholic countries. It is true of non-Christian countries as it is of Christian countries. A Catholic country or its government, where there is a very substantial Catholic ethos and consensus, should not feel it necessary to apologise that its legal system, constitutional or statutory, reflects Catholic values. . . . The rights of a minority are not more sacred than the rights of the majority.

To be fair, the bishops seem on reflection to have concluded that their statement was unnecessarily stark, because in a subsequent oral presentation to the Forum they put their position in more positive terms. Bishop Cahal Daly of Down and Connor began that presentation with a ringing defence of the rights of northern Protestants:

The Catholic Church in Ireland totally rejects the concept of a confessional state. We have not sought and we do not seek a Catholic State for a Catholic people. We believe that the alliance of Church and State is harmful for the Church and harmful for the State. . . . We are acutely conscious of the fears of the Northern Ireland Protestant community. . . . What we do here and now declare, and declare with emphasis, is that we would raise our voices to resist any constitutional proposals which might infringe or might imperil the civil and religious rights and liberties cherished by Northern Protestants. (New Ireland Forum 1983–4, no. 12, 2.)

However, as the session went on it became less certain how much the bishops had actually conceded. Bishop Daly qualified his statement by adding that 'we do feel bound to alert the consciences of Catholics to the moral and social evils which, as experience elsewhere shows, follow from certain kinds of legislative enactment' (p. 3). Members of the Forum then sought to elucidate what this might mean in a concrete case. Three different speakers—Séamus Mallon of the SDLP (pp. 11–12), Senator Mary Robinson of the Labour Party (p. 23), and Professor John Kelly of Fine Gael (pp. 38–46)—pressed the bishops to state how they would view divorce legislation in the context of a thirty-two-county Ireland. It is fair to say that none of them got a straight answer.

Opinions will differ on the merits of the criticisms made by writers such as Clarke and Inglis on the one hand, and the defence of the current situation made by the Irish hierarchy on the other. Personally I have sympathy with the bishops' view that a majority ethos is bound to mould the laws of any country. I shall just add that, from the point of view of northern Protestants looking south, the bishops' defence of the situation is perhaps less reassuring than Clarke's or Inglis's criticism of it. Such Protestants might agree with the bishops that it is natural that a majority ethos should prevail. But they might conclude that, in that case, they would prefer to remain in their own State with its Protestant majority than join a State which would have a Catholic majority.

Nationality

At the foundation of the State, most Protestants were unionists and found it difficult to identify with the new entity. All authorities agree that this has changed, and that most southern Protestants see themselves as unhyphenated Irish, without hankerings after the British connection (Akenson 1975, 148; White 1975, 4; Bowen 1983, 70–1, 198–200; McLoone 1985, 26, 63, 90). Indeed, Protestants have been found at all levels of the State up to the highest. An often-quoted example is that two of the six presidents of Ireland have been Protestants—Douglas Hyde (1938–45) and Erskine Childers (1973–4). All this might be cited as a reassurance to northern unionists that, if they were to accept a united Ireland, they would come to feel at home there.

On the other hand there is evidence that, notwithstanding the decades that have passed since independence, Protestants still do not see the State as theirs in quite the same way as Catholics. Protestants are still much under-represented in the public service. As White has noted (1975, 162): 'not many Protestants thought of making a career in the Irish civil service. No doubt some were deterred by the need to qualify in Irish; but this may have been less a real obstacle than a symbol of a service in which they expected, instinctively, to feel out of place.' A researcher who has worked for the Fair Employment Agency in Northern Ireland notes that 'if the North's fair employment legislation applied to the South, then the FEA could, on the statistical evidence, seek a major investigation of public sector employment' (Osborne 1983, 14). A sociologist, Hilary Tovey (1975), researching attitudinal differences between Protestant and Catholic schoolchildren in Cork, found that they did not relate to the concepts of Ireland and Irishness in the same way. While both groups had a positive attitude towards Ireland, this was matched with positive feelings towards England among Protestants, and negative feelings among Catholics. A national survey (Fogarty *et al.* 1984, 177) found that, while 68 per cent of Catholics questioned said they were 'very proud to be Irish', only 35 per cent of Protestants said so—though it must be admitted that Protestant numbers in the sample were small.

The New Ireland Forum, however, by its willingness to recognize the British identity of northern unionists has introduced a fresh note (New Ireland Forum 1984*a*, para. 4.9.1). It is possible that, if the discussion of Irish unity ever were on the cards, the reconciliation of national identities might now prove to be one of the less intractable problems.

Economics

The economic case for union between Northern Ireland and Britain has turned through 180 degrees in the course of the past century. At the time of the home rule controversies of 1886, 1893, and 1912–14, Ulster unionists saw themselves as a flourishing industrial community whose future lay, not in union with the backward agricultural south of Ireland, but in retaining the link with industrial Britain. In the words of an Ulster Unionist Council document before the First World War, unionist resistance to home rule was 'the revolt of a business and industrial community against the domination of men who have no aptitude for either' (quoted in MacLaughlin and

Agnew 1986, 253). Since then, however, the staple industries on which Ulster's prosperity grew—shipbuilding, linen, rope-making, engineering—have declined or disappeared altogether, and nothing adequate has been found to replace them. As was shown in Chapter 3, recent writers on the Northern Ireland economy paint a bleak picture. The case for union with Britain now is that Northern Ireland needs the support of a major economic power in order to stave off collapse.

The economic argument is probably stronger in its present form than its older one. It can be argued that, in the past, Ulster unionists exaggerated the danger from the possible economic policies of an all-Ireland government. Such a government would have depended heavily on Ulster for revenue, and that fact would have been a prudential check on its following policies which might damage Ulster's prosperity. But the present situation of Northern Ireland is so catastrophic that it is beyond the power of the Republic to give financial aid on the scale required—all the more so in view of the Republic's own economic difficulties. The point has been well illustrated from an unexpected source. The New Ireland Forum commissioned a study on the economic consequences of Irish unity, prepared by an economic consultancy firm, Davy Kelleher McCarthy Ltd. (New Ireland Forum 1984*b*). The study was deeply pessimistic about the effects of uniting Ireland in the absence of subvention from Britain or elsewhere. Its findings were summarized in a foreword by two distinguished economists, Norman Gibson and Dermot McAleese:

A total and precipitate absence of such transfers would in our view require what can only be described as catastrophic economic adjustments. The disappearance and non-replacement of the British subvention would result, as already indicated, in an immediate loss of income equivalent to about 8 per cent of the GDP of the combined economies. The net result could as a first round effect be a fall in disposable income of around IR£2,000 million. Losses on a similar large scale would be expected to persist for many years and unemployment would increase substantially in both economies. Any attempt to offset these effects through foreign borrowing would be doomed to failure. Further accretions of foreign debt to an already high stock of borrowing would exacerbate the problem of high taxation and would soon become unsustainable. In such circumstances, it is doubtful if foreigners would be prepared to lend even if the authorities were willing to borrow. (pp. 12–13.)

These conclusions applied whether the arrangements envisaged were unitary or federal. Only if Northern Ireland came under joint authority, which would entail a continuing British presence and British subvention, would the results be less drastic (p. 13). In short, the opinion of the consultants was that the reunification of Ireland was simply not practicable, unless a foreign subvention was obtained, at least for a time. (These conclusions, it is worth pointing out, are mirrored by those of another writer who personally favours a united Ireland: Rowthorn 1987, 131.)

Indeed, if unionists were to read more of the careful and unsentimental research being done on society in the Republic, largely by local scholars, they would find additional ammunition for their case. Some of this research shows the Republic to be, not just a relatively poor society, but also a relatively unequal one—as compared with the United Kingdom in general, and (where material is available) with Northern Ireland. Kennedy, Giblin, and McHugh, in their work *The Economic Development of Ireland in the Twentieth Century* (1988, 129) cite a number of studies which show that inequality of income is somewhat greater, and social mobility is less, than in the UK. Another study, of the two parts of Ireland as a whole, indicated that, while England and Wales had more mobility than either part of Ireland, Northern Ireland had more than the Republic (Miller 1986, 234). One southern scholar (McCashin 1982, 216) has identified education and housing as two areas in which State policy in effect reinforces inequality, by disproportionately aiding the middle classes. In neither of these sectors is State policy so regressive in Northern Ireland. Osborne and Cormack (1985, 338–40), comparing higher education north and south, note that there is a substantially higher proportion of students from working-class backgrounds in Northern Ireland than in the Republic. Brett (1986, 121) has shown that public housing is available to a much larger proportion of the population in the north than in the south—37 per cent as against 12 per cent in 1981.

In short, one might claim that the economic arguments for union with Britain, though they are the ones least stressed by unionists, are the ones which have most cogency. The religious and national objections could be reduced, by careful design of institutions. But the economic objections are beyond the capacity of the Republic of Ireland to meet unaided.

Appraisal

The case just deployed hardly accounts for the vehemence with which northern Protestants reject any kind of unity with the Republic. For that we have to go to some of the factors—particularly perhaps the psychological ones—explored in Part I of this book. None the less, the discussion shows that the Protestant case is not without foundation. Indeed, as we saw in Chapter 4, even some northern Catholics are doubtful about a united Ireland. After all, some of the arguments just deployed, particularly the economic ones, would be of concern to Catholics as well as Protestants. Some at least among southern nationalists have been prepared to admit that the kind of State that has been built up in the Republic is one which northerners could reasonably find unattractive. The Forum report acknowledged that the southern State had developed with 'insufficient concern for the interests of the people of Northern Ireland' (New Ireland Forum 1984*a*, para. 3.12), and that the south can be seen 'as being unduly influenced by the majority ethos on issues which Protestants consider to be a matter for private conscience' (para. 5.1.3). A future taoiseach, Garret FitzGerald, went further. In 1978 he declared that the Republic was 'so partitionist a state that northern Protestants would be bloody fools to join it'. (*Irish Times*, 13 February 1978.)

OBJECTIONS TO THE TRADITIONAL UNIONIST CASE

Nevertheless, there has been no stampede on the part of outside observers to accept the traditional unionist case. That case has a weakness of its own—quite different in nature from those of traditional nationalism—but sufficient to deprive it of general sympathy.

This weakness is the failure to take account of the division within Northern Ireland. Unionist spokesmen too often write as if the other community did not exist. The fault is worst in the older books. McNeill (1922) repeatedly spoke of 'Ulster' or 'Ulstermen' when he meant only unionist Ulster or unionist Ulstermen. Carson (1957, 55) spoke of 'Ulster's steady and oft signified determination to remain part of the United Kingdom', when many people in Ulster had no such determination. Since the troubles began it has been harder to ignore the existence of the nationalist minority, yet some unionists still come near to doing so. Paisley, Robinson, and Taylor (1982), for instance, play down the extent of division within Northern Ireland. They speak of a shared Ulster identity (pp. 47, 60), and claim that it is unrealistic to speak of 'two communities' in Ulster (pp. 35, 59). Elsewhere they speak of the desire of the 'overwhelming majority' to stay British (p. 39).

The objection to such statements is that they make the conflict incomprehensible. If the population of Northern Ireland is so overwhelmingly of the one way of thinking, then why should there be any problem? The truth is that that population is deeply divided. The big difference between the Republic and Northern Ireland is not that one is nationalist and the other unionist, but that one is homogeneous and the other mixed. In Northern Ireland there is a large and deeply disaffected minority, who have rights too. Any interpretation which ignores or plays down the existence of this minority is going to strike outsiders as unconvincing.

The nature of the division as it currently stands was explored in Part I of this book. However, it did not emerge without cause. A good deal of research has recently been done on the nature of the regime which the Unionist Party maintained in Northern Ireland between 1921 and 1972. This will be examined in the following pages.

THE DRAWING OF THE BOUNDARY

A clear example of unionist reluctance to deal fairly can be seen in the location of the boundary of Northern Ireland. Granted that there was a distinct community in the north-east of Ireland, and supposing that it had a right to self-determination, that right could not be used to justify the border where it now stands. For the border was so drawn as to corral within it not only almost all areas with unionist majorities, but also considerable areas with nationalist ones. If the county is taken as the unit, there were at the time of partition unionist majorities in only four of the six counties of Northern Ireland. If some smaller unit had been chosen, then parts of Tyrone and Fermanagh might have been reclaimed for unionism, but considerable parts of other counties would have been lost to nationalism.

The anomaly worried the British. With the opening of archives in the 1970s, the inside story became available of how the measure partitioning the country was framed (Mansergh 1974, 41–8; Lawlor 1983, 44–51; Fanning 1989). The British Cabinet saw the partition of Ireland as a temporary measure, and its original proposal was that Northern Ireland should consist of the nine counties of the historic province of Ulster, in which unionists had only a narrow majority, and which would make eventual unity all the more likely. This was rejected by the unionists, who felt that nine counties was more than they could safely control. Instead they demanded six, in which they felt more secure. Sinn Féin was boycotting the Westminster Parliament, and the unionists were the only bloc of Irish MPs of any size in the House. The Government felt that it could not be sure of the passage of its measure unless one at least of the Irish parties accepted it, and so it acquiesced in the unionist demand. But ministers felt uneasy. The assistant secretary to the Cabinet recorded in his diary a meeting of the British Cabinet in September 1921 to discuss the conduct of negotiations with Sinn Féin. There was general agreement that the boundary of Northern Ireland was the weakest part of their case (Jones 1971, 108–11). During the actual negotiations Lloyd George defended the six-county unit on the ground that it was only provisional, and that the number of nationalists contained in the new entity made it all the more provisional. As he said to Arthur Griffith, 'in order to persuade Ulster to come in there is an advantage in her having a Catholic population' (p. 131).

I have come across no comparable agonizing among unionists. Their only worry was how much territory they would be able to control. The idea that it might be unjust to ask for more territory than was actually unionist apparently never entered their heads. The fact might be used by their critics to argue that unionists sought, not equality, but supremacy.

THE RECORD OF THE UNIONIST STATE, 1921–1968

In this section I shall discuss the allegations of discrimination which were made against the unionist regime almost constantly, from its inception in 1921 until 1968, when under the combined pressure of the civil rights movement and the British government, it began to undertake reforms.

Even before the troubles began in 1968, there was a literature on this subject. Indeed it was almost the only area of Northern Ireland society and politics which had been at all extensively explored. On the nationalist side, the later chapters of Frank Gallagher's *The Indivisible Island* (1957) are devoted to the topic. The Campaign for Social Justice's pamphlet *The Plain Truth* (1964, 1969) produced an updating of some of Gallagher's statistics, and an expansion of some of his charges. On the other side, unionist writers such as Carson (1957) and Walmsley (1959) attempted a rebuttal of such points. When the troubles began in 1968, and an efflorescence of literature on Northern Ireland ensued, much of it dealt with the topic of discrimination, generally reaching conclusions damaging to the unionist regime. Perhaps the most telling was the report of an official commission appointed by the government of Northern Ireland to inquire into the origins of the disturbances (Cameron 1969). This commission, which consisted of a Northern Ireland Protestant, a Northern Ireland Catholic, and a Scottish judge as chairman, concluded that there was rising and well-founded resentment among Catholics at inequities in housing allocation, discrimination in local government employment, the gerrymandering of local government boundaries, and a partisan law-enforcement system (para. 229).

After that, for some years scholarly interest in the question died away. A sign of renewed interest, however, came with the publication in the *British Journal of Sociology* for 1981 of an article by a sociologist working in the United States, Christopher Hewitt, entitled 'Catholic Grievances, Catholic Nationalism and Violence in Northern Ireland during the Civil Rights Period: A Reconsideration', in which he argued that the extent of discrimination had been much exaggerated, and that 'the old system was not particularly inequitable' (p. 377). This produced an indignant rejoinder from another sociologist, Denis O'Hearn (1983), who argued that discrimination was 'systematic and pervasive' (p. 444). Further contributions followed from Hewitt (1983, 1985, 1987), and from O'Hearn (1985, 1987), with a commentary by Kovalcheck (1987). So far as it goes, I would consider the controversy inconclusive. O'Hearn damages some of Hewitt's arguments, but fails to dent others.

However, the participants on both sides have confined themselves unduly to quantitative material. They use statistical tests on, for instance, occupational or electoral data, to establish whether or not discrimination occurred. They make little use of the non-statistical material which has become available in recent years. With the opening of archives in the 1970s, a great volume of information on the inner workings of the unionist regime, at any rate during its first thirty years, became available, and historians have already done substantial research on it. The most important contributions are to be found in Bew, Gibbon, and Patterson's *The State in Northern Ireland, 1921–72* (1979), which draws on the new material for its earlier chapters; Patrick Buckland's massive study of the early years of the State, *The Factory of Grievances: Devolved Government in Northern Ireland 1921–39* (1979); Michael Farrell's detailed study of security policy, *Arming the Protestants: The Formation of the Ulster Special Constabulary and the Royal Ulster Constabulary 1920–27* (1983); and Brian Barton's study of the early career of a leading unionist politician, *Brookeborough: The Making of a Prime Minister* (1988). For the more recent period in which archive material is not yet available, memoir and other evidence has added to our knowledge. If this qualitative material is added to the quantitative data assembled by Hewitt and O'Hearn, some of the questions which they leave unresolved can be answered with more assurance.

For instance, the archives make clear that some of the imbalances developed in the early years of the state were systematic and deliberate. Discrimination was indeed rife against Catholics in the civil service (Bew *et al.* 1979, 77; Buckland 1979, 20–3). The B Specials were indeed a sectarian force, which a Westminster civil servant described in 1922 as 'purely partisan and insufficiently disciplined' (Farrell 1983, 153; cf. Bew *et al.* 1979, 49–50, 58–9). Local-government boundaries were indeed gerrymandered (Buckland 1979, 331–46). Barton (1988, 64) quotes the secretary of Tyrone Unionist Association as writing to his counterpart in Fermanagh in 1922 that he was 'gerrymandering at night'. True, some of the new evidence provides a more nuanced picture. Bew, Gibbon, and Patterson (1979, 76–93) detect a division in the Unionist Party between populists, who were shamelessly discriminatory, and anti-populists, who had more impartial standards—though the populists usually won. For a more recent period, an example can be taken from the memoir evidence. Patrick Shea was a Catholic civil servant who eventually reached the rank of permanent secretary. His autobiography, *Voices and the Sound of Drums* (1981) provides a fascinating picture of what life was like for a Catholic who tried to work within the system. The impression he leaves is that his civil-service superiors were always, and his political superiors were sometimes, fair; but that, when the latter chose to be unfair, there was nothing the civil servants could do for him. He was barred from promotion for many years by one particular minister, and it was only by securing transfer to another department with another minister that he eventually made further progress (pp. 177–84). While the fresh evidence may not uniformly sustain the bleak picture offered by O'Hearn, neither does it support the benign view offered by Hewitt.

Several surveys of the extent of discrimination now exist. The subject arouses strong emotions, and there is more disagreement on it than on many others. At one extreme can be found authors such as Rowthorn and Wayne (1988, 28–38), who depict it as pervasive. At the other extreme are authors such as Paisley, Robinson, and Taylor (1982, 63–8), who claim that nothing was wrong at all. There is, however, a bunching towards the centre among writers who have tried to assess the evidence on both sides. John Darby (1976, 77–8) concluded that 'some of the allegations of discrimination against the Unionist governments are not supported by evidence and that others have been exaggerated', but that none the less 'there is a consistent and irrefutable pattern of deliberate discrimination against Catholics'. Patrick Buckland, in his *History of Northern Ireland* (1981, 72), wrote:

The Unionist regime was neither as vindictive nor as oppressive as regimes elsewhere in the world with problems of compact or irredentist minorities. ... The fact remains that, owing to local conditions, the power of the government was used in the interests of Unionists and Protestants, with scant regard for the interests of the region as a whole or for the claims and susceptibilities of the substantial minority.

Birrell and Murie, in their book *Policy and Government in Northern Ireland* (1980) several times refer to the problem of discrimination, and, while they provide no quotable passage summing up their conclusions, leave the impression that they would come close to this view. I have myself published a paper entitled 'How much Discrimination Was There under the Unionist Regime, 1921–68?' (Whyte 1983b) in which I reach a similar conclusion.

The most recent contribution to the literature can be found in a book by a distinguished economist of Ulster Protestant background, Tom Wilson's *Ulster: Conflict and Consent* (1989). Wilson devotes four chapters (pp. 98–148) to discussing various areas of contention—industrial location, unemployment, housing, and education. He appears anxious to present pleas in mitigation where these are practicable, and consequently paints a picture rather more benevolent towards the unionist regime than that accepted by the authors just quoted. However, he does not claim that the regime was anywhere near blameless, and has harsh things to say about particular aspects of its policy—for instance, discrimination by local authorities (p. 117) and the siting of the New University of Ulster at Coleraine instead of in the much larger (but mainly Catholic) city of Derry (pp. 146–7).

In so far as there is a consensus in the literature, then, it is that the picture is not black, nor white, but grey. The verdict is quite sufficiently damaging to the unionist regime. I said in the last chapter that recent research on the union period, 1801–1921, has not been favourable to the traditional nationalist interpretation. It can equally be said that recent research on the post-1920 period has not been favourable to the traditional unionist interpretation.

There is one other twist to the argument that should be examined before we leave this topic. A fall-back position for unionists might be that, though discrimination happened, it was justified. Though this position has not, so far as I know, been taken in any publication, it has occasionally been taken in conversation or in oratory. Heslinga (1962, 65 n.) was told by unionists 'that there is no government in the world which does not discriminate, in one way or another, against a political grouping which reserves its loyalties for a foreign government'. Barritt and Carter (1962, 123) found that among the justifications offered for the gerrymandering of Derry city was that 'local government ought not to be in the hands of those who seek to engage in treason against Her Majesty'. Or, to take a more celebrated case, Sir Basil Brooke, future prime minister of Northern Ireland, in a speech in 1933 advocated discrimination on such grounds:

A great number of protestants . . . employed Roman catholics. He felt he could speak freely on this subject as he had not a Roman catholic about his own place. . . . He would point out that the Roman catholics were endeavouring to get in everywhere and were out with all their force and might to destroy the power and constitution of Ulster. There was a definite plot to overpower the vote of unionists in the North. He would appeal to loyalists therefore, wherever possible, to employ good protestant lads and lassies (cheers). (*Fermanagh Times*, 13 July 1933, quoted in Barton 1988, 78.)

Unionists, in short, might argue that if Catholics got less than equal treatment it was their own fault. If they had been prepared to recognize the State in the way that southern Protestants had been prepared to recognize the Irish Free State, then there would not have been the same need for unionists to be on their guard against Catholics.

There is something in this argument, but it begs the question of how best to treat a recalcitrant minority. Not every Catholic in Northern Ireland was disaffected. One of the most interesting findings from recent work in the archives is that a section of Catholics were prepared at the outset to collaborate with the new Northern Ireland State, but that instead of being encouraged they were rebuffed (Bew *et al.* 1979, 64–70; Buckland 1979, 20–3, 203–4; Farrell 1983, 106, 146–50, 179–81, 189–91). It would surely have been wise policy to encourage the growth of such collaborators, but the government, if anything, did the opposite. Even as late as 1959, a suggestion by a prominent unionist, Sir Clarence Graham, that the time might have come to recruit Catholics to the Unionist Party, provoked a rejection from the head of the Orange Order and a dismissal from the Prime Minister, Lord Brookeborough (Harbinson 1973, 43–4). By its actions the unionist regime had ensured that the nature of the problem would not be as it liked to make out. It liked to portray itself as a liberal democratic regime under threat from an unreasonable territorial claim. That was not the heart of the problem. The problem was one of the relationship between majority and minority within Northern Ireland.

A CONTINUING IRISH RESPONSIBILITY

The preceding pages show how seriously the traditional unionist argument has been damaged. It is not enough to show that unionists have reasonable objections to being united with the Republic, and to assume that that explains the crisis. The trouble is that a large minority within Northern Ireland has reasonable objections to the way in which it has been treated, and its grievances must also be addressed.

That does not mean that the Republic is exempt from all blame for the crisis. Just as one can reject the traditional nationalist interpretation and still argue that Britain has a share of the responsibility for the conflict, so one can reject the traditional unionist interpretation and still accept that the Republic has a share of the responsibility. That responsibility will be much less than Britain's, because Britain is the sovereign power with actual control over Northern Ireland. But none the less it exists, and some authors have been severe on the course followed by the Republic.

The strongest critics, naturally enough, are among the unionists. Paisley, Robinson, and Taylor (1982) depict the Republic as a place which gives a haven to terrorists (p. 43), and which has waged a 'long campaign of lies and smearing' against Northern Ireland (p. 48). Such claims need hardly be taken as a balanced assessment of the situation, particularly in view of the degree of security co-operation which now exists between the United Kingdom and the Republic.

There is, however, a more sophisticated criticism of the Republic, to be found more widely than among unionists. This is that the Republic retains a provocative claim to Northern Ireland despite the fact that its people are now ambivalent about pursuing that claim. The evidence for stating that the people are ambivalent comes from opinion polls, which have been analysed by a number of authors (Rose *et al.* 1978, 31–9; O'Brien 1980, 19–34; O'Malley 1983, 80–4; Cox 1985; Mair 1987, 89–92; Garvin 1988, 106–9). Their conclusions are substantially similar. All agree that, in principle, the ideal of reunification retains majority support in the Republic. But a much smaller proportion of the population is prepared to suffer any serious inconvenience to help that to happen. Three surveys, in 1978, 1980, and 1984, asked whether people would be prepared to pay more taxes in order to achieve unity: all three showed a majority against (Mair 1987, 91). Other surveys have shown that Northern Ireland comes low in the list when electors in the Republic are asked what they consider the most important political issues (O'Malley 1983, 84; Cox 1985, 35). Mair (1987, 105) sums up the attitude of voters in the Republic as follows: 'unity would be nice. But if it's going to cost money, or result in violence, or disrupt the moral and social equilibrium, then it's not worth it.'

Such attitudes are not surprising. There would be serious costs attached to unification in current circumstances. The economic burden has been examined earlier in this chapter. The political burden could be massive also, as resentful Protestants and radicalized Catholics joined a State which has adapted its administration and its party system to mesh comfortably with its political culture. As Tom Garvin has put it (1988, 109):

If such an offer [of a united Ireland] were to be seriously and publicly made by the British government ... it would have devastating, and possibly destabilising effects on the Republic. .... The structure of the Dublin state is predicated on the unspoken assumption of indefinite continuance of partition, as is its party system. Furthermore, the Republic has developed a corporate identity of its own that sudden reunification would threaten; an analogy would be requiring the United States to absorb Mexico.

Why, then, is the claim maintained? Conor Cruise O'Brien, in his book *Neighbours* (1980, 45), has suggested that to retain it has advantages from the point of view of politics *in the Republic*.

It gives equivocal voice to equivocal aspirations. It leaves Britain with the responsibility for Northern Ireland—indefinitely. It leaves the government of the Republic free to criticize Britain's discharge of those responsibilities—also indefinitely. This combination has a powerful, though unavowed, appeal to certain shrewd political minds.

That puts the point unkindly. A more realistic way of stating it might be that, even if a majority in the Republic no longer care strongly about the territorial claim, a substantial minority still do, and to abandon the claim would be to stir up trouble for any Dublin government. Others might feel that though the claim is in principle bargainable, it should not be abandoned without obtaining a much more substantial quid pro quo (joint authority, perhaps?) than any that has so far been offered. But, however convenient this stance may be within the Republic, it has negative consequences in Northern Ireland. It embitters the unionists, makes them more suspicious of any arrangement involving the Republic because the latter may use it as a stepping-stone towards unity, and thus delays a settlement. Padraig O'Malley (1983, 357) has gone so far as to suggest that there cannot be peace until the south confronts its own reality and steps away from the dream of unification.

However, that is far from saying that the Republic's attitude is the primary cause of the conflict. The point can be illustrated by returning to the Middle Eastern analogy which I used at the end of the last chapter. I argued there that it would be unreasonable for Palestinians to see the United States as the principal authors of their plight, however much the latter prop up the Israeli regime. Similarly, it would be unreasonable for Israelis to see the other Arab States as the principal authors of Palestinian hostility, no matter how much aid some of them may give to the Palestinians. Just as the conflict between Israelis and Palestinians is primarily just that, and cannot be explained as an artefact of some outside interference, so the conflict between the communities in Northern Ireland is just that, and cannot primarily be explained by the interference of either Britain or the Republic of Ireland.

A COMPARISON OF THE TRADITIONAL NATIONALIST AND TRADITIONAL UNIONIST INTERPRETATIONS

Unionists and nationalist ideologies, in their traditional forms, were irreconcilably opposed. Nationalists insisted that the State of Northern Ireland was illegitimate, and that the blame lay with Britain for dividing the Irish nation. Unionists retorted that they were a distinct people from the nationalists of the south, and that the blame for continued conflict lay with the nationalists for refusing to accept that fact. Yet we can now see that they shared a key assumption. To use the language popularized by the philosopher of science Thomas S. Kuhn, they were operating within the same paradigm.

Both believed that there was some natural unit of self-determination. Nationalists saw the island of Ireland as a geographical and historical entity, and the natural unit of self-government. Unionists saw themselves as a distinct community concentrated in one part of the island, with as much right to self-determination as the nationalists. The argument between them was about which was correct. The difficulty with the principle of self-determination is that there are no generally agreed criteria for applying it. Geographical, historical, and cultural factors can point in different directions, and when this happens there is no consensus on how to reconcile them. Ever since the principle came into vogue in the late nineteenth century, it has proved enormously difficult to apply in practice. Ireland is just one of dozens of cases round the world, from Belize to West New Guinea, where disputes have arisen over the appropriate unit of self-determination. United Nations declarations proclaiming the principle are no help, because they simultaneously proclaim the principle of territorial integrity (Bailey 1988, 54–6). Indeed the international trend in recent years has been towards accepting that the problem is intractable, and instead stressing protection for the rights of minorities in whatever political unit they find themselves (Capotorti 1979; Bailey 1988, 57–64).

What we can now see more clearly is that, in the Irish case too, appealing to the principle of self-determination is not by itself enough to solve the problem. In Northern Ireland, two communities are intermingled. On the one side, a Catholic or nationalist minority exists in the north-east of Ireland, with well-founded grievances about how they have been treated by the Protestant majority. On the other side, a Protestant or unionist community exists in the same area, with reasonable anxieties about how they might fare in an all-Ireland context. The task for statesmanship is to devise arrangements whereby the opposing sets of anxieties and grievances can both be assuaged. In doing this, the location of the boundary may be an instrument, because tensions may be exacerbated or ameliorated according to where the boundary is placed. But redrawing the boundary—either by putting it somewhere else in Ireland, or by placing it along the North Channel between Britain and Ireland—will not of itself resolve the problem. Wherever it is placed, there will still be two communities in the same region, harbouring contrasting hopes and fears.

The point can be illustrated by comparing the works of Frank Gallagher (1957) and of M. W. Heslinga (1962), which we have picked out as the best expositions of the traditional nationalist and traditional unionist views respectively. Both are concerned with lines on the map. Gallagher sees one overwhelmingly important division in the archipelago—between Ireland as a whole and Britain as a whole. Heslinga on the other hand sees the archipelago as criss-crossed by fault lines, as well as having a good deal of unity. In so far as one fault line is stronger than any other, he sees it as being the division between the Catholic part of Ireland and the rest of the archipelago, whether British or Irish. If one has to choose between the two, Heslinga's picture, because more complex, is nearer to the truth. But it has the crucial weakness that it does not take account of the intermingling of populations. Within the north-eastern part of the island of Ireland, there are two communities, not one, and, although one (the Protestant) is in a majority, the Catholic minority is substantial enough, and has grievances serious enough, to warrant special treatment. Any adequate theory of the Northern Ireland problem must go beyond looking at lines on maps, and examine the people who live in the area which the map lines circumscribe.

In Chapter 9, we shall start to look at theories which take account of this fact. But first we must look at the class-conflict theories put forward by some Marxists.

8

Marxist Interpretations

TRADITIONAL MARXISM

Marxist analysis of the Irish problem goes back to Marx and Engels themselves, whose writings on Ireland were numerous enough to have been collected in book form (Marx and Engels 1971). However, the first writer to apply Marx's ideas to Ireland systematically was James Connolly (1870–1916). Connolly's works were still influential in the 1960s, when the troubles in Northern Ireland broke out. They were kept in print long after the writings of contemporaries who at the time had had a wider influence, like Arthur Griffith or D. P. Moran. I shall use the edition which was most easily accessible in the 1960s—the three-volume collection edited by Desmond Ryan, which was first published in 1948–51 and was later reprinted. In particular I shall use the second volume, entitled *Socialism and Nationalism* (Ryan 1948).

Connolly, as befitted a follower of Karl Marx, saw the fundamental conflict in the developed world as being between employer and worker, and had as his overriding aim a workers' victory. There is disagreement among Connolly scholars about whether he maintained these views all his life, or whether—as is argued for instance by Morgan (1988)—he became in his last few years more nationalist than socialist. However, we need not go into this controversy. It is sufficient for our purposes that, at least for most of his career, Connolly was a wholehearted Marxist, and that a coherent set of propositions, compatible with Marxist theory, can be extracted from his work. They can be stated as follows.

1. In the Irish context, a struggle for a workers' victory also meant a struggle for national independence. The British Empire was 'the most aggressive type and resolute defender' of capitalism (Ryan 1948, 9), and socialism could not be built in Ireland without a total break from Britain.

2. It was hopeless to look, as some Belfast socialists did, for salvation from the British labour movement. The backgrounds of the British and Irish movements were 'so essentially different'

(p. 105). In Britain, 'the Labour party is a party which, in order to progress, must be continually breaking with and outraging institutions which the mental habits of its supporters had for centuries accustomed them to venerate' (p. 105), while in Ireland 'the working class are rebels in spirit and democratic in feeling' (p. 104).

3. True, the Protestant workers of the Belfast area seemed to wish to maintain British rule. This was a problem for Connolly, as he acknowledged:

According to all Socialist theories North-East Ulster, being the most developed industrially, ought to be the quarter in which class lines of cleavage, politically and industrially, should be the most pronounced and class rebellion the most common.

As a cold matter of fact, it is the happy hunting ground of the slave-driver and the home of the least rebellious slaves in the industrial world. (pp. 101–2.)

However, he had an explanation for that:

I have explained before how the perfectly devilish ingenuity of the master class had sought its ends in North-east Ulster. How the land were [*sic*] stolen from Catholics, given to Episcopalians, but planted by Presbyterians; how the latter were persecuted by the Government, but could not avoid the necessity of defending it against the Catholics, and how out of this complicated situation there inevitably grew up a feeling of common interests between the slaves and the slave-drivers. (p. 102.)

4. In Connolly's eyes the situation was so artificial that it could not last. Once home rule for all Ireland was achieved, 'the old relation of Protestant and Catholic begins to melt and dissolve' (p. 73), and Protestants would come to see their kinship with others. The interests of no economic class in Ireland, as a class, were bound up with the union. Even the landlords had made their peace with the farmers through the various land acts, and only the dying embers of religious bigotry buttressed unionism. The desire to make money would soon overcome the desire to waste time in rioting (p. 13).

5. There was just one circumstance in which Connolly's vision of the future harmony of the Irish working class would be destroyed. This was if Ireland were to be partitioned. Partition would be disastrous, because it would keep alive the national issue at the expense of class questions. 'All hopes of uniting the workers, irrespective of religion or old political battle cries would be shattered, and through North and South the issue of Home Rule will be still used to cover the iniquities of the capitalist and landlords class'

(p. 114). The result would be to strengthen the most conservative forces in both parts of Ireland, and, in one of Connolly's most quoted phrases, 'would mean a carnival of reaction both North and South' (p. 111).

Despite Connolly's warnings, partition was accomplished, and his successors in the Marxist tradition responded accordingly. For them it now became, not a potential evil to be fought against, but an existing evil to be undone (e.g. Jackson 1946). The only deviant voice on the left that I have noted, before the end of the 1960s, can be found in Strauss's history of Ireland from a Marxist point of view, *Irish Nationalism and British Democracy* (1951). Strauss suggested that northern Protestant workers' opposition to home rule could not solely be attributed to ruling-class manipulation (p. 234), and that unionist attitudes were nourished by 'solid interests' (p. 290). But these were only passing remarks in a book whose centre of interest did not lie in Ulster.

When the troubles began in 1968, Marxism was enjoying a revival in Western intellectual circles, and it is not surprising that a number of the early analyses were written from a more or less Marxist standpoint. Among works in this category can be included Bernadette Devlin's autobiography *The Price of my Soul* (1969), Owen Dudley Edwards's *The Sins of Our Fathers: Roots of Conflict in Northern Ireland* (1970), Liam de Paor's *Divided Ulster* (1970), The *Sunday Times* 'Insight' team's *Ulster* (1972), and Desmond Greaves's *The Irish Crisis* (1972). I shall not spend time discussing these works here, because more substantial Marxist works were soon to follow. I should like, however, to draw attention to a new turn to the argument provided by one of these works—Liam de Paor's *Divided Ulster*. De Paor's book was the first, so far as I am aware, to treat the Northern Ireland problem as a colonial one. As this analogy has since been frequently applied by left-wing and nationalist critics of the Northern Ireland State, it is worth taking a little space to discuss its validity.

THE COLONIAL ANALOGY

The treatment of Northern Ireland in particular, or of Ireland as a whole, as a colony had not always been part of the nationalist battery of arguments. At the time that most of Ireland was gaining its independence, nationalists were at pains to point out that Ireland was *not* a colony. As Griffith put it during the treaty negotiations of 1921, 'we do not feel ourselves to be a colony but a nation' (Jones 1971, 132). It was natural that he should wish to make the distinction, because at that period what happened to British colonies was that they evolved into self-governing dominions; Irish nationalists did not want that to be their terminus. But by 1970 the climate of opinion had changed. The British empire, like the French, Dutch, Spanish, and Belgian, had been largely decolonized, and this had been accepted as just, or at any rate as inevitable, by the populations of the metropolitan States. To label a situation 'colonial' was to imply two things: first, that it was illegitimate, and secondly, that it was unlikely to last.

The analogy is unquestionably valid in part. Settlers from Scotland and England did come over to Ulster in the seventeenth century, and settled there in much the same manner as their compatriots were settling in America. No one has thought to call the American settlements anything other than colonies. Some of the same individuals were involved in the Irish and the American schemes of colonization. The result, in Ireland at least, was to produce an enduring division of the population, as in other settler colonies such as South Africa and Algeria. The fact that Northern Ireland is legally not a colony, but part of the United Kingdom, does not destroy the analogy: Algeria was legally part of France, and Angola and Mozambique were legally part of Portugal, but that did not stop the French and Portuguese from eventually treating them as expendable, non-metropolitan parts of the State territory, and pulling out. Opinion polls show that much of mainland British opinion favours pulling out of Northern Ireland, which suggests that many Britons do not feel Northern Ireland to be really part of their country (Rose *et al.* 1978, 27–9; Jowell and Airey 1984, 33; Cox 1987, 348–51).

However, the colonial parallel has not been so convincing that it has generally been adopted by writers on the Northern Ireland problem. It is not easy to examine why, because those authors (the majority) who do not use it simply remain silent on the subject, and do not actually argue the case against employing it. Perhaps the alternative model that is in their minds could be described as the 'zone of ethnic conflict' model. The alternative way of looking at Northern Ireland is to see it as one of many areas in the world where two groups intermingle—in relative peace as in the South Tyrol or Malaysia, with greater bitterness as in the Lebanon, Sri Lanka, or the territories occupied by Israel. 'Ethnic conflict-zones' can often offer more intractable situations than colonies do. A colonial situation can be ended by the departure of the imperial power, but an ethnic conflict may remain as long as the two groups exist. Indeed, in many places the departure of the imperial power has been followed by a worsening of ethnic tensions (e.g. Nigeria, Sri Lanka, Cyprus, Lebanon). There does seem to be an implicit majority view in the literature that, while the 'colony' model illustrates some features of the Northern Ireland problem, the 'ethnic conflict-zone' model is more generally appropriate.

The colonial analogy is perhaps more apposite when applied to the whole of Ireland when under British rule before 1921. The majority of Irish people were indeed discontented with British government, and eventually, as has become the rule with colonies, threw off the metropolitan regime. The view of Ireland as a whole as a colony has been interestingly explored in such works as Michael Hechter's *Internal Colonialism* (1975), Ian Lustick's *State-Building Failure in British Ireland and French Algeria* (1985), and Raymond Crotty's *Ireland in Crisis: A Study in Capitalist Colonial Underdevelopment* (1986).

THE DEVELOPMENT OF TRADITIONAL MARXISM

As the troubles went on, the first wave of Marxist writings were superseded by two substantial works, which deserve fuller discussion. The first is Eamonn McCann's readable *War and an Irish Town* (1974, 1980—both editions have to be consulted because the second edition contains fresh material but unfortunately omits some of the most interesting bits of the first). McCann's book is based partly on the author's experience in his home town of Derry, but also includes much general information on the development of the Northern Ireland crisis. The second is Michael Farrell's *Northern Ireland: The Orange State* (1976, 1980), which contains extensive historical research, particularly into the Labour and nationalist oppositions, and which at the time it came out was the fullest history of Northern Ireland available.

These writers updated Connolly's interpretation to take account of the fifty-odd years which had passed since his execution. They argued that the 'carnival of reaction' which he prophesied had come to pass. Northern Ireland was governed by a capitalist class which kept the working class repressed and divided. Two main devices were employed by the capitalists to bring this about. The first was to beat the sectarian drum. Whenever Catholic and Protestant workers showed signs of uniting, employers riposted by stirring up Protestant fears of a Roman Catholic take-over. The second technique was differential discrimination. Though Protestant workers were exploited by their bosses, they were given a narrow but visible margin over their Catholic workmates. Anxiety to maintain this privileged position led them to ally with their bosses rather than with their fellow workers.

There can be no question but that both these techniques were employed. We have already examined the evidence for discrimination (above, Chapter 7), and although there is disagreement about its extent, there is widespread agreement that it was substantial. With regard to beating the Orange drum, this has been documented by writers who do not share the ideological assumptions of Farrell and McCann. Budge and O'Leary, in their history of Belfast politics (1973), provide examples of the exploitation of sectarian fears in the nineteenth and twentieth centuries (pp. 65, 76–94, 141–3). Harbinson (1973), in his history of the Ulster Unionist Party, sums up the Unionist technique for remaining in power as 'banging the big drum, waving the flag, and playing upon the emotions of the Protestant population' (p. 166).

However, to argue that the division of the working class can be wholly or mainly attributed to such devices is to make a large claim. It must be remembered just what is being asserted. For instance, Farrell (1976, 81), writing about the early days of Northern Ireland, states:

The Unionist leaders were not free agents: they had mobilised the Protestant masses to resist Home Rule and inclusion in the Free State, through the policy of discrimination and the ideology of Protestant supremacy. Now their followers were seeking their reward. If a lasting loyalty to the new state was to develop among the Protestant masses, they had to be given a privileged position within it.

This is to claim, not just that these devices strengthened the intensity of Protestant workers' feelings, but that they altered their direction. The implication is that the Protestant working class, if it had not been stirred up by 'the policy of discrimination and the ideology of Protestant supremacy', would have been instinctively Irish rather than British. That means brushing aside all the other reasons for Protestant attitudes—their religious fears, their feelings of identity with Britain, their belief that the prosperity of the industries in which so many of them worked depended on retaining the British link. It is also to ignore the whole thrust of recent historiography on Ulster under the union period, which we examined in Chapter 6. Indeed Farrell himself has subsequently modified his position. In his more recent work *Arming the Protestants* (1983) he notes that 'lower-class discontent with the Unionist leadership often expressed itself in a more extreme sectarianism than that of the pragmatic leaders' (p. vi). In other words he has conceded that, if the Protestant working-class broke loose from middle-class leadership, it might move, not towards anything like Irish nationalism, but in the opposite direction.

There is another weakness in this interpretation, at least in so far as it stresses the stimulation of sectarian fears as a technique for maintaining working-class Protestant loyalty. This is that those fears were not groundless. Nationalists did want an independent united Ireland, and in that Ireland the Catholic Church would be powerful. Our two authors cope with this problem in different ways. Farrell largely ignores it. He does not offer any discussion of the basis for Protestant fears, and the result is a serious weakness in his book.

McCann is more forthright. He accepts that Protestant workers in the north had ground for fearing the Irish nationalist movement as it developed (McCann 1974, 128, 143, 155, 177, 197). Indeed at times he seems to blame the Catholic Church as much as he does the unionist bourgeoisie for creating the conflict. However, he rescues the Connollyite one-nation perspective by arguing that, if only the republican left had been as hostile to the institutions of the south as it was to those of the north, northern workers would not then have seen the labour movement as alien, but would have appreciated that it had something for them as well—and on such a basis working-class unity could have been built. For instance:

It can seriously be doubted whether the Northern state could have survived the first two decades of its existence had not the 'Free State' become increasingly repellent to Protestants. The Unionist Party had to fight unceasingly and at times desperately to hold the support of the majority of

Protestants. That it succeeded was mainly due to the fact that the only alternative to the Union with Britain appeared to be sectarian Catholic rule from Dublin.
No one consistently canvassed a third alternative. No one was with equal vigour fighting sectarianism North and South, no one was actively supporting and attempting to politicize the economic militancy of Protestant trade unionists and, at the same time, seeking to destroy clerical conservatism in the South. (p. 202.)

This argument, however, could be criticized as containing a double dose of wishful thinking. It assumes that a serious anticlerical movement was possible in the Irish Free State, which in view of the dominant ethos in that country at that time seems unlikely. Secondly, it supposes that, if northern Protestant workers were to bolt from the control of their unionist bosses, they would bolt in a united-Ireland direction. This also seems unlikely. The record suggests that, when these workers did bolt, they were more likely to move towards a sectarianism more extreme than that of the unionist leadership. McCann, like Farrell, underestimates the tenacity and the autonomy of the Protestant workers' distinct identity.

As the troubles developed, it became increasingly difficult to ignore that identity. Traditional Marxism, like traditional nationalism, was being eroded, not just by the tides of historical scholarship, but also by the course of events. The theories which had comforted Marxists and nationalists—that Protestant workers did not really believe in unionist ideology, but had been bamboozled by the bosses (as Marxists would say) or by the British (as nationalists would put it)—became increasingly implausible in view of the fury shown by unionist workers at the civil rights movement and, later, the IRA campaign.

REVISIONIST MARXISM

For all these reasons, a strand of revisionist Marxism began to develop soon after the outbreak of the troubles. The pioneer in this development was a small grouping called the British and Irish Communist Organisation (BICO). In 1969 this body, then known as the Irish Communist Organisation, substantially accepted the traditional Marxist position. But then, in a series of pamphlets published between 1969 and 1972, it moved further and further away from this position until it adopted one almost diametrically opposed. (The evolution of BICO is outlined in two of its publications: *The Two Irish Nations* (1971*b*, 1–2), and *The Economics of Partition* (1972*b*, 71).)

BICO came to argue that differential economic development had produced two nations in Ireland: the Protestants of the north-east, and the Catholics of the rest of the island. In these circumstances, to claim that the Protestant or British bourgeoisies were dividing the working class was the reverse of the truth. It was the bourgeois Catholic nationalists of the south who played this role, by stirring up the Catholic minority in the north against acceptance of the State in which they lived, and thus preventing the development of working-class unity in Northern Ireland (BICO, *On the Democratic Validity of the Northern Ireland State* (1971*a*, 7)). BICO, and the authors associated with it, buttressed their case with a number of carefully researched historical pamphlets (BICO 1972*a*,*b*, 1973; *The Road to Partition* (1974); Carr 1974), showing that the separate identity of the northern Protestants had deep historic roots, and could not be explained away as the result of manipulation by a cunning bourgeoisie. These pamphlets, produced in photocopied form from an office in Belfast, are not well known outside Northern Ireland, but they have had an influence within it. They have been a more substantial contribution to the research literature than many of the professionally printed and expensively bound volumes which have come from academic presses elsewhere. An interesting characteristic of the BICO writers is that several of them come from Catholic and nationalist backgrounds.

BICO, perhaps, reacted too far. If Connollyite Marxism can be seen as a red variant of nationalism, then BICO's Marxism could be seen as a red variant of unionism, and shares unionism's defects. As we saw in the last chapter, the unionist case has failed to win general acceptance, not because its claim to a separate identity is denied, but because it takes insufficient account of the seamy side of the unionist regime. The same charge can be made against BICO. In some of its later publications, complaints against the Stormont regime were simply ignored (BICO 1975, 50). The civil rights movement of the late 1960s was dismissed as a republican tactic (BICO 1977, 52), and the loyalist strikers of 1974 were depicted as making a 'reasonable and moderate' demand (p. 75). If the unionist regime were really so pure as the BICO writers implied, it is hard to understand how it could have provoked so much bitterness.

Nevertheless, BICO seems to have raised sufficient doubts within the Marxist camp to trigger off a torrent of questioning about the traditional Marxist view. Since BICO started writing, a number of other revisionist analyses have appeared. I shall list them in roughly chronological order.

1. A Danish socialist, Anders Boserup (1972), accepted, like BICO, the reality of the unionists' separate identity. However, he saw the most important clash within Northern Ireland as being not between unionist and nationalist, but between moderate and extreme unionist. (At the time he was writing this clash was indeed more evident than it is today—the brands of unionism represented by Faulkner on the one hand, and Craig and Paisley on the other, were locked in combat, and it was not yet clear who would prevail.) He saw this conflict as based on the conflict between two different kinds of capital, one locally based and discriminatory, the other multinational and relatively enlightened. Moderate unionists such as Brian Faulkner articulated the interests of the latter. Boserup urged socialists to give them a tactical support.

2. Two writers in the French Marxist periodical *Les Temps Modernes*, Van der Straeten and Daufouy (1972), argued that Ireland was too small to be an independent economy, that the great mistake made by the Irish working class had been to separate itself from the English working class, and that its interests would be best served by a federal relationship with Britain. This was a rejection of one of Connolly's central contentions—that the circumstances of the British and Irish working classes were so different that the interests of the latter could be served only in an independent State.

3. Conor Cruise O'Brien is not a Marxist, but—at least in the early 1970s—he counted as a man of the left, and, since he made an important contribution to the controversy over Marxism, he can perhaps be included here. We have already seen in Chapter 6 that his book *States of Ireland* (1972) contained an important critique of traditional nationalism. The same book also contained a critique of Connolly's Marxism (pp. 89–99). O'Brien brings out Connolly's difficulty in dealing with the Protestant working class of north-east Ireland, who so stubbornly refused to behave in the way that Connolly said they ought. He shows that in his historical writings

Connolly coped with the problem by simply missing out nineteenth-century Belfast. O'Brien also points out how wrong Connolly's assumption of the weakness of working-class unionism has proved. On one occasion, Connolly told an Orangeman brandishing the Ulster Covenant of 1912 that 'your children will laugh at it'. But as O'Brien points out: 'the children have not laughed, nor are the grand-children laughing' (p. 97).

4. A Scottish nationalist who is also a Marxist, Tom Nairn, argued in an article originally published in 1975, and reprinted as Chapter 5 of his book *The Break-Up of Britain* (1977), that the United Kingdom was disintegrating anyway, that the Ulster Protestants, even if not a distinct nation in actuality, were so potentially, and that an independent Northern Ireland was the likeliest eventuality. His message to socialists was that they should accept that probability and work within it. It was not enough to say that Ulster Protestants had shown themselves to be hopelessly reactionary: to develop a nationalism was the only way they had of ceasing to be reactionary (Nairn 1977, 245).

5. A somewhat similar position was adopted by Belinda Probert in her work *Beyond Orange and Green* (1978). She accepted the reality of the distinct Protestant identity, and sought ways of developing class politics within that. Her message to her fellow socialists appeared to be that they should support the more class-conscious elements within the Protestant paramilitaries—by which she meant that section of the Ulster Defence Association which was pushing the idea of an independent Northern Ireland.

6. Bew, Gibbon, and Patterson in their book *The State in Northern Ireland, 1921–1972* (1979) offered an investigation of class relations within the Protestant community. Their book, as was shown in Chapter 6, contains much valuable historical research. It offers a thorough examination of divisions within both the Protestant bourgeoisie and the Protestant working class, showing that both were far from being homogeneous blocks. The theoretical chapters with which they open and close their book are more opaque, and it is not clear what positive message they wish to leave with their fellow socialists. It is clearer, however, what they do not wish to say. They do not approve of Connolly's interpretation, which they feel much underplays the objective basis of working-class unionism (pp. 4–10), and they disagree with current Marxist interpretations based on Connolly's belief that Ireland must be united

and Britain driven out. They consider that 'there is nothing inherently reactionary about the Protestant working class or, for that matter, a national frontier which puts Protestants in a numerical majority' (p. 221). Instead, they detect a secular labourist tradition in the Protestant working class which could in more propitious circumstances be fostered. However, republican efforts to undermine Northern Ireland make Protestants more reactionary than they need be. In these circumstances a British withdrawal would be followed by the establishment of another State, more reactionary than the one which exists at present (p. 221).

7. Two of the three authors of the book just noted have individually made important contributions to the history of Ulster during the union period (1901–1921). Peter Gibbon has published *The Origins of Ulster Unionism* (1975), a carefully researched study of nineteenth-century Ulster Protestants, which argues that Ulster unionism was not just 'a conspiracy of landed notables and industrialists to "dupe the people"' (p. 145), but had an objective social base, resting on an alliance of social groups whose origins preceded organized nationalism. Henry Patterson's *Class Conflict and Sectarianism: The Protestant Working Class and the Belfast Labour Movement 1868–1920* (1980) describes how labour politics developed, in Belfast as in other cities in the United Kingdom, in the late nineteenth century, and how labour leaders instinctively worked in a British context. This for them was the natural framework of reference—it was not something imposed by the manipulation of a crafty bourgeoisie. Patterson's picture of the Belfast working class has been confirmed and amplified by a massive Ph.D. thesis in the Queen's University of Belfast, shortly to be published in revised form—Austen Morgan's 'Politics, the Labour Movement and the Working Class in Belfast 1905–1923' (1978). It should give traditional Marxists food for thought that all the Marxist scholars who have looked seriously at the union period in recent years find themselves in the revisionist camp.

8. Meanwhile, at least one of the writers who started off as a traditional Marxist was showing an evolution in his thought. Liam de Paor's *Divided Ulster* (1970) was, at the time it came out, the best succinct statement of the traditional Marxist view. By the time a revised edition was published the following year, however, the author was showing signs of second thoughts. In the preface to that edition (de Paor 1971, p. xix), he stated that 'there *is* a unionist case',

a point which he had not conceded before. In a column called 'Roots', which he contributed to the *Irish Times* in the mid-1970s, he went further, conceding the reality of the separate Protestant identity. One of his most recent books is entitled *The Peoples of Ireland* (1986). The use of the plural indicates the rejection of the traditional Marxist (and traditional nationalist) view that there is only one people in Ireland.

The writers discussed in the eight preceding paragraphs can, with the addition of BICO and the subtraction of Conor Cruise O'Brien, who is not a Marxist, be grouped together as a 'revisionist Marxist' school. Like the traditional Marxists, they have their limitations. Though they unite in discounting the traditional view, there is no agreement among them on the alternative. Some (BICO, Bew, Gibbon, and Patterson) favour integration with Britain as the way forward. Others (Nairn, Probert, de Paor) prefer an independent Northern Ireland. The arguments used by some revisionists to a considerable degree cancel out those used by others, and indeed in their works they argue among themselves. (See, for instance, BICO's attack on Nairn in BICO, *Against Ulster Nationalism* (1977), or Bew, Gibbon, and Patterson's criticisms of BICO and Boserup (1979, 24, 132, 216).) However, the fact that such a school, inchoate though it is, has developed, shows how traditional Marxism has lost its cogency, even among many of those sympathetic in principle to the Marxist approach.

During the 1970s, then, the unity of the Marxist school of thought on Northern Ireland disappeared. The disarray can be illustrated by two anthologies which appeared at the beginning of the 1980s. The first consists of the papers from a seminar of Marxists interested in Ireland which had been held at the University of Warwick (Morgan and Purdie 1980). Of the ten contributions, four can be described as traditional and six as in varying degrees revisionist. The second comprises a special issue on Ireland of *Antipode* (1980), a periodical which subtitles itself 'a radical journal of geography'. Some of the articles in this issue are concerned with parts of Ireland other than Ulster, or concentrate on particular topics; but of those offering a general interpretation of Northern Ireland, I would classify three as traditional and three as revisionist.

DEVELOPMENTS IN THE 1980s

The development of a revisionist Marxist school has not prevented works with a traditional frame of reference from continuing to appear. Geoffrey Bell, a writer of Ulster Protestant background who has espoused views far removed from those general in his community, has published three books with a traditional Marxist framework. One analyses the tensions within the Ulster Protestant community (1976), a second examines the inconsistencies of British Labour policy towards Ireland (1982), and a third has argued the case for a British withdrawal from Northern Ireland (1984). The case for British withdrawal is also argued by most of the contributors to a work edited by Martin Collins, *Ireland after Britain* (1985). David Reed (1984) has claimed that British withdrawal would be beneficial for the left in Britain itself. Chris Bambery (1986) has written a brief general survey from a traditional Marxist point of view, and Ronnie Munck (1985) has written a longer one. It must be said about these books that they make little attempt to grapple with the objections raised by revisionist Marxists—not to speak of non-Marxists.

However, some of the recent works in this tradition are better than others, and I should like to pick out two for further consideration. The first is O'Dowd, Rolston, and Tomlinson's *Northern Ireland: Between Civil Rights and Civil War* (1980). I include this book among the traditional Marxist interpretations with some hesitation, because the authors do not explicitly state where they stand. In the introductory chapter O'Dowd notes the division of Marxists into two camps (p. 2), and goes on to state that the book's objective is 'to give concrete substance' to the argument between them (p. 3). The authors appear implicitly to support the traditional Marxist side of the argument, which is why I have included them in that camp. But they nowhere explicitly state which side of the case they favour. Nevertheless, whatever its theoretical limitations, the book is important for its empirical material. When it came out it was the first analysis of the development of Northern Ireland society under direct rule from Westminster. It showed that direct rule had made remarkably little difference to the structure of power in Northern Ireland, and that Catholics were still systematically the underdogs in almost every sphere. The kind of analysis in their book was unfamiliar at the time it came out, but has been largely vindicated by subsequent research into the economic gap between the communities (see above, Chapter 3). Thus their work is valuable even for those who reject their theoretical framework—or are puzzled to know what that framework is.

The second item that I should like to single out is John Martin's paper in *Capital and Class* (1982), entitled 'The Conflict in Northern Ireland: Marxist Interpretations'. This is perhaps the best review of the different Marxist schools to have been published. The author carefully and fair-mindedly weighs the merits of traditional and revisionist views. He notes the greatest weakness of the traditionalists—that they have underestimated the autonomy of the Protestant working class (p. 67)—but he finally comes down on the traditionalist side, because he sees what he considers an even greater weakness among the revisionists: namely, that they accept the progressive nature of the British State, thus ignoring its reactionary role in Northern Ireland (p. 69). This criticism, however, itself requires examination. First, it is not true that all revisionists accept that the British State has played a progressive role in Northern Ireland— perhaps only the BICO writers and, more uncertainly, Bew, Gibbon, and Patterson do so. Secondly, even if they did do so, it would not necessarily be without cause. Martin states: 'in Northern Ireland the state must reproduce sectarianism and sectarian division, if it were to do otherwise it would cease to be a capitalist state' (p. 69). But this implies that the sin of the State is to be capitalist rather than to be British. In that case would an Irish capitalist State do any better? It would face the same constraints as a British one, and have even fewer resources for surmounting them. Perhaps what matters, if one is arguing from Marxist assumptions, is that the State should be socialist, rather than what nationality it belongs to.

This brings us to a weakness of much traditional Marxist writing. It has never reconsidered what is the practicable unit of social transformation. Connolly argued that socialism could come in Ireland only if the country were independent of Britain, and he had reasons, plausible in his time, for believing so. Britain then was one of the great fountain-heads of capitalist power; London was the financial capital of the world. The benefits percolated right down to the working class, and the British labour movement was one of the most moderate in Europe. It was inconceivable that the revolution could begin there. But things are rather different in the 1990s. Britain has now dropped to sixth or seventh place among the world's economies. The British economy is penetrated by foreign multinationals to an extent which differs only in degree from that of Ireland, and the two islands, instead of being rivals, could to some extent be regarded as sharing a predicament. Moreover, Ireland by itself may be too small to sustain a revolution. Revolutionaries have the deepest suspicions of international capitalism, and they must fear that if, by some combination of circumstances, a revolutionary government were to come to power in Ireland, it would not be allowed to develop in peace, but would be destabilized just as Grenada or Nicaragua have been. The minimum viable unit of revolution is probably the archipelago as a whole, and even that may not be big enough. Yet some traditional Marxists continue to write as if the geographical relationships in the world have not changed since Connolly's time.

However, that is not surprising. One thing I have learnt from writing this book is that of all the groups writing on the Northern Ireland problem, traditional Marxists are by and large the most conservative.

While traditional Marxists have continued to publish, so have revisionists. I shall pick out two recent revisionist works for consideration. The first is Bew and Patterson's *The British State and the Ulster Crisis: From Wilson to Thatcher* (1985). This is in effect a sequel to *The State in Northern Ireland, 1921–72* (1979), discussed above, which these two authors wrote in conjunction with Peter Gibbon. They argue that the Northern Ireland State is not inherently reactionary—'the problem of the involvement of the British state in Northern Ireland lies not in its existence but in its specific forms' (p. 144). They deny that reform has been tried and has failed, but argue that it has not seriously been tried, and they suggest that a future left-wing British government could do much more (pp. 147–50). Their book can be read as a reply to O'Dowd, Rolston, and Tomlinson's (1980) implicit thesis that Northern Ireland is irreformable. As such it is not wholly convincing. One may wonder whether, if a succession of British administrations of varying hues have all made so little impression on the north's problems, this can entirely be due to mistakes made by particular administrators, or whether it does not imply some deeper structural factor at work. A better answer to O'Dowd, Rolston, and Tomlinson might be, not to deny that the situation in Northern Ireland is pretty well as bleak as they paint it, but to challenge them to present their alternative.

Another work which can be classified as revisionist-Marxist is *One Island, Two Nations? A Political Geographical Analysis of the National Conflict in Ireland* (1985), by a lecturer in geography at Maynooth, D. G. Pringle. This work answers the question in its title by stating emphatically that Ireland does contain two nations. The author offers two alternative ways of deciding what is a nation, which he describes as the checklist approach, and the self-definition approach (pp. 30–49). Whichever one uses, he concludes, the answer is the same. He offers a little comfort to nationalists and traditional Marxists by saying that the two nations crystallized only in the nineteenth century, and that the material conditions which led to their creation are now receding. To some extent he is banging at an open door: as was noted in Chapter 6, virtually no one who has put themselves to the discipline of researching on Northern Ireland still defends the one-nation theory. If a criticism can be made on his book—and indeed of the BICO defenders of the two-nation theory—it is that they put the case too much in economic terms. To stress economic divergence as the fundamental reason for the development of a different nationality in the north-east of the island from the rest of the country may be to place too little weight on cultural factors. If economics outweighed culture, one might have expected the Protestant farmers west of the Bann, whose material interests were much closer to those of their Catholic neighbours than they were to the workers and industrialists of the Belfast area, to have been drawn to nationalist Ireland, but in fact they were quite as staunch unionists as any other Protestants in Ulster. However, the book serves a purpose. Anyone who still believes in the one-nation hypothesis will find its arguments difficult to overturn.

AN APPRAISAL OF THE MARXIST CONTRIBUTION

Any fair-minded non-Marxist must agree that the study of Northern Ireland would be the poorer if no Marxist had written on it. Particularly in historiography, the Marxist contribution has been important. A large proportion, perhaps 50 per cent, of the best books on the history of Ulster have been written by Marxists of one school or another. The works by Farrell (1976, 1983) and McCann (1974, 1980), the books written jointly and severally by Bew, Gibbon, and Patterson, and some of the BICO publications, are

major contributions to the literature, which have provided illumina-
tion to Marxist and non-Marxist alike.

Some writers would criticize the Marxist approach for an excessive concentration on economic factors. Richard Rose's *Governing
without Consensus* (1971) can in its theoretical sections be taken as a
sustained attack on Marxist and other economic interpretations of
the Northern Ireland problem. Rose's key claim is that the conflict is
so intractable because it is *not* economic. Economic conflicts, about
the share-out of material benefits, are bargainable: conflicts about
religion and nationality are non-bargainable and therefore much
harder to resolve. It is Northern Ireland's misfortune that its
conflicts are about religion and nationality (Rose 1971, especially
300–1, 397–407). Ian Budge and Cornelius O'Leary, in their survey
of Belfast history (1973), discount the importance of economic
factors in causing the sectarian rioting which so often rocked that
city. They find it impossible to link the cycle of rioting with
economic factors, while almost every riot can be connected with
some political event. They prefer to stress non-economic factors,
and particularly the rise of the Orange Order, as causes of conflict
(pp. 91–5). Burton (1978, 156–62) analyses a number of Marxist
contributions, both traditional and revisionist, and accuses them all
of sacrificing 'the complexity of the problem . . . to maintain the
plausibility of a theoretical position' (p. 157).

The reaction against Marxism can be carried too far. To begin
with, not all non-Marxists would go as far as the writers cited in the
preceding paragraph in discounting the importance of economic
factors. Several have found a connection between economic factors
and political violence. Birrell, in a frequently quoted article on
'Relative Deprivation as a Factor in Conflict in Northern Ireland'
(1972) showed that rioting was more severe in those towns which
ranked highest on a number of indicators of deprivation. In Belfast,
the areas of greatest social need turned out, when plotted on maps
(Boal *et al.* 1974; Project Team 1977), to coincide roughly with the
areas of greatest disturbance. Few of the authors referred to in the
examination of the economic differential between Protestant and
Catholic contained in Chapter 3 of this book could be described as
Marxist, yet between them they demonstrate that a substantial gap
exists and that it is the source of much resentment.

Secondly, it would be unfair to depict all Marxists as being crude
economic determinists. They vary among themselves on how much

stress they put on economic factors. This division cuts across the division between traditional and revisionist. Among revisionists, Bew, Gibbon, and Patterson belong to the Althusserian school of Marxism, which stresses 'the relative autonomy of the superstructure'. They do not feel obliged to find an economic base for every political development, and indeed criticize some other Marxists for doing so (1979, 5–6, 132). Among traditional Marxists, O'Dowd, Rolston, and Tomlinson (1980) share with Bew, Gibbon, and Patterson a distrust of too simplistic class analysis. They reject the concept of sectarian superstructure resting on a class base: they prefer to see the two as inextricably intermingled. 'Class relations in NI were only experienced as *sectarian class* relations' (p. 25). Indeed since the early 1970s the distinction between at least the more sophisticated Marxists and other scholars has become increasingly blurred.

The most serious weakness of the Marxist approach is the inability of its practitioners to agree on their conclusions. As we have seen, Marxists can be grouped in two broad schools, each of which has further subdivisions. Among traditional Marxists, there are differences in the degree to which Protestants' fears of the Catholic Church are taken as genuine. Among revisionists the differences are much wider. There is no agreement among them on the nature of the British presence, or the best future for Northern Ireland. Indeed there was a serious case for eliminating this chapter, and distributing the authors whom I discuss in it among the other chapters, according to whether they come closest to the Britain-versus-Ireland, the south-versus-north, or the internal-conflict schools. I decided to keep them all together, because they share a common discourse, even if they do not reach common conclusions. They publish in Marxist periodicals, they read each other's works— and a few of them do not seem to read anybody else's. All the same, the fact that to dispense with a Marxist chapter was a serious possibility shows how incoherent the approach has become. This may be one reason why the Marxist approach does not enjoy more of a vogue. Like the traditional nationalist and traditional unionist approaches, it attracts the allegiance of only a minority of students of Northern Ireland.

9

The Internal-Conflict Interpretation

THE DEVELOPMENT OF THE INTERNAL-CONFLICT APPROACH

A political scientist at the London School of Economics, Brendan O'Leary, has pointed out in a stimulating article (1985) that a distinction can be made between endogenous and exogenous explanations of the Northern Ireland problem. The schools of thought covered in the three preceding chapters all offer exogenous explanations: the problem is the responsibility of the British, or the Irish, or the capitalists. We now come to a school of thought which stresses endogenous factors. This does not mean that the authors in this school dismiss the importance of outside forces: some lay considerable stress on the role of the British (and/or Irish) governments, and most recognize that one of the reasons for internal conflict is that the two communities in Northern Ireland relate differently to their neighbours, Britain and the Republic. But it does mean that they see the biggest source of the problem as lying within Northern Ireland itself.

This school of thought was surprisingly late in emerging. Until the 1960s all the literature that I know of on the Northern Ireland problem could be classified under one of the three preceding headings. The first book to be organized round the principle that the heart of the difficulty lay within Northern Ireland was Barritt and Carter's *The Northern Ireland Problem* (1962). This book, which has already been extensively cited in Part I of the present work, examined different areas of contention—social relations, education, discrimination, civil rights, and so on—drawing on information collected from both communities. Reread in the light of later events, it seems unduly complaisant towards the unionists, extenuating practices, such as the manipulation of electoral boundaries, which have long since been abandoned as untenable. The authors implicitly accepted this criticism when in the 1972 reissue of their book they added a preface and postscript which were distinctly more acerbic. This bias does not, however, destroy the pioneering quality of the book.

The approach which seemed so novel in 1962 was given a powerful fillip by the outbreak of the troubles in the late 1960s. The conflict so obviously was between two opposed communities with the British government trying more or less ineffectively to assuage it, that an internal-conflict approach became at once more plausible. Very soon, books and pamphlets were coming from the press based on this interpretation: the Northern Friends Peace Board's *Orange and Green* (1969), Max Hastings's *Ulster 1969* (1970), Martin Wallace's two books *Drums and Guns* (1970) and *Northern Ireland: 50 Years of Self-Government* (1971), Harold Jackson's pamphlet for the Minority Rights Group, *The Two Irelands* (1971), Harry Calvert's pamphlet for the United Nations Association, *The Northern Ireland Problem* (1972), and a whole range of pamphlets published in 1971–3 by the New Ulster Movement. Richard Rose's *Governing without Consensus* (1971), though planned before the troubles, adopted the same perspective and can be included here.

The internal-conflict interpretation was soon being put in an extreme form. The Cameron Commission (1969), appointed by the Northern Ireland government in March 1969 to investigate the causes and circumstances of the violence which had occurred since the preceding October, found in its conclusion (para. 229) seven general causes of the disorders. Six of these were Catholic grievances—about housing, discrimination, gerrymandering, the B Specials, the Special Powers Act, and the failure to get any redress of complaints—and one was Protestant fear of the threat posed by an increase in Catholic population and powers. There was no mention of any cause outside Northern Ireland.

The Cameron Report represents the high-water mark of the internal-conflict interpretation. It was the product of the special circumstances of 1968–9, when the civil rights movement, far from raising wider questions of national allegiance, was simply claiming British rights for British citizens. Events in 1969–72 brought the wider British and Irish contexts of the problem back into view—the deteriorating relationship between the Catholic community and the British Army; the rise of the Provisional IRA with its aim of reuniting Ireland; finally, the introduction of direct rule by Britain. But even after these events it was quite possible to insist that the core of the problem remained within Northern Ireland.

Certainly, many publications through the 1970s continued to do so. Conor Cruise O'Brien, in his *States of Ireland* (1972), provided an early example of the genre. Claire Palley, an academic lawyer then at the Queen's University of Belfast, provided a careful analysis of the situation in her paper *The Evolution, Disintegration and Possible Reconstruction of the Northern Ireland Constitution* (1972), in which she recognized important Irish and British–Irish dimensions to the problem, but put most stress on the interlocked communities within Northern Ireland. Morris Fraser, in his study *Children in Conflict* (1973), pioneered a psychological approach to the group antagonisms so obvious in Belfast. Richard Rose, in his second book on the region, *Northern Ireland: A Time of Choice* (1976) stressed the intractability of the internal conflict, and an inter-Church working party accepted it as central in their *Violence in Ireland: A Report to the Churches* (1976). John Darby, in his survey of the research to date, *Conflict in Northern Ireland* (1976), concluded an appraisal of interpretations of the problem as follows:

Whatever the values of the various theories about the conflict the one factor which emerges with greatest force is its Ulster character. Clearly it is also an Irish problem and a British problem, but its roots lie in the social, economic, cultural and geographical structure of Northern Ireland. Whatever political formulae are introduced to reduce its violent manifestations—whether a united Ireland, or union with Great Britain, or an independent Ulster—a peculiarly local conflict will still continue. (p. 196.)

The stream of works expounding an internal-conflict interpretation continued through the late 1970s and into the 1980s. A retired senior member of the Northern Ireland civil service, John Oliver, examined the possibilities for assuaging the community conflict in a pamphlet published by the London organization PEP (Political and Economic Planning), *Ulster Today and Tomorrow* (Oliver 1978*a*). Dervla Murphy, the well-known travel writer, explored the internal tensions of Northern Ireland in her book *A Place Apart* (1978). Aunger (1981) compared Northern Ireland with New Brunswick—a province whose divisions between French and English-speakers in many ways mirror the cleavages in Northern Ireland—and asked why New Brunswick was so much more peaceful. His answer lay in differences between the internal values and structures of the two areas. The Queen's University geographers Fred Boal and Neville Douglas, in their book of edited papers *Integration and Division: Geographical Perspectives on Northern Ireland* (1982) examined the nature of the community divide. The Jesuit periodical *Studies* devoted its Winter 1984 issue to a special number on 'Conflict and Reconciliation in Northern Ireland', in which the contributors, all of them Irish Jesuits, took as given the basically endogenous nature of the conflict. In 1985 two distinguished academic lawyers, Kevin Boyle and Tom Hadden, already well known for their researches on the Northern Ireland legal system, collaborated on a work entitled *Ireland: A Positive Proposal*, which was based on the assumption that Northern Ireland is 'a divided society in which two separate communities are locked in political conflict' (Boyle and Hadden 1985, 53). Their work gained weight from the fact that they had grown up in opposing traditions, Boyle coming from a Catholic background and Hadden from a Protestant one.

Most of the works which were examined in the review of interpretations of the community divide contained in Chapter 5 of this book can be seen as applying an internal-conflict approach. This would be true of Ken Heskin, *Northern Ireland: A Psychological Analysis* (1980), John Hickey, *Religion and the Northern Ireland Problem* (1984), Richard Jenkins, 'Northern Ireland: In What Sense "Religions" In Conflict?' (1985), Steve Bruce, *God Save Ulster!* (1986), and others. The only doubtful case is Michael MacDonald, *Children of Wrath* (1986). MacDonald takes a harsh view of British policy, which he sees as in practice maintaining the Protestant hegemony (p. 149). However, he criticizes British policy more for being ineffective and directionless than for being actively malign (pp. 31, 95, 151), and he accords the Protestants far more autonomy than does a traditional nationalist writer like Frank Gallagher or Gerry Adams. So on balance I include him in the internal-conflict school, though he is not far from the boundary between that and traditional nationalism.

A feature of the 1980s has been a growing number of reports and symposia from various bodies, official and unofficial, devoted to the Northern Ireland problem. The Royal Institute of International Affairs hosted a conference in 1981, attended by experts from England, the Republic, and Northern Ireland, whose proceedings were afterwards published as a book—*The Constitution of Northern Ireland: Problems and Prospects*, edited by David Watt (1981). In the same year two Irish groups dedicated to reconciliation, the Glencree and Corrymeela Communities, organized a conference in Belfast whose proceedings also appeared in book form: *Political*

Co-operation in Divided Societies: A Series of Papers Relevant to the Conflict in Northern Ireland, edited by Desmond Rea (1982). In 1982 the British government published a white paper, *Northern Ireland: A Framework for Devolution* (UK Government 1982), in which it put forward its proposals for the future of the region. The European Parliament commissioned a report on the situation in Northern Ireland, written by one of its Danish members (Haagerup 1984). The Official Unionist Party issued a discussion paper, *The Way Forward* (Ulster Unionist Party 1984). The constitutional nationalist parties, north and south, combined, as noted in Chapter 6, to issue the report of the New Ireland Forum (1984). A little later an unofficial but prestigious body, the British-Irish Association, commissioned an inquiry, chaired by Lord Kilbrandon and containing representatives of all the main political parties in Britain, as well as two members from Northern Ireland, to produce a United Kingdom response to the Forum report. Its findings were published later the same year (Kilbrandon 1984). The SDP/Liberal Alliance set up a commission to analyse the problems of Northern Ireland, whose well-researched report was issued the following year (Alliance 1985).

While all these documents concur in seeing important British and/ or Irish dimensions to the problem, they all give priority to the internal conflict. A series of quotations from these sources will illustrate the point:

Protestants insist on a settlement that gives them a dominant role in a British Northern Ireland, while Catholics will accept nothing less than a guaranteed share of power. . . . These are incompatible goals. (Watt 1981, 170.)

The conflict in Northern Ireland is one between different traditions, identities and allegiances. (Rea 1982, 1.)

This difference in identity and aspiration lies at the heart of the 'problem' of Northern Ireland; it cannot be ignored or wished away. (UK Government 1982, para. 17.)

A major cause [of the instability] is to be found in the conflict of identity of most members of the two communities and in the tradition of violence among extremists. (Haagerup 1984, 69.)

The basis of this conflict lies in the ultimate political aspirations of the two communities and in their sense of national and political identity and the allegiance that goes with it. (Ulster Unionist Party 1984, 2.)

The conflict of nationalist and unionist identities has been concentrated within the narrow ground of Northern Ireland. (New Ireland Forum 1984, para. 5.1.2.)

In Northern Ireland there is a manifest absence of that degree of political consensus which is essential if a society is to be at peace with itself. (Kilbrandon 1984, para. 3.4(*c*).)

The peculiar intractability of the Northern Ireland problem derives from its complex network of reinforcing allegiances, whereby national identity and religion, along with historical memories and socio-economic differences combine together to create powerful and antagonistic group loyalties. (Alliance 1985, para. 2.1.)

There are of course important differences of emphasis between the documents just cited. The Forum report is severe on the shortcomings of British policy:

The basic approach of British policy has created negative consequences. It has shown a disregard of the identity and ethos of nationalists. In effect, it has underwritten the supremacy in Northern Ireland of the unionist identity. Before there can be fundamental progress Britain must re-assess its position and responsibility. (New Ireland Forum 1984, para. 5.1.11.)

The Official Unionist document, for its part, shows suspicion of nationalist motives:

Constitutional nationalists appear to behave upon the basis that every form of pressure, short of direct force, is valid in order to obtain unionist consent [to Irish unity]. (Ulster Unionist Party 1984, 4.)

The other documents cited take up positions intermediate between these two.

Nevertheless, there are similarities between even the Forum and Official Unionist documents, let alone those in between. Both contrast with the traditional nationalist, or traditional unionist, views, whereby the basis of the problem would be removed if only Britain, or the Republic, gave up its claim to Northern Ireland. Both recognize that, even if the behaviour of the British (or Irish) governments had been different, there would still be a community problem within Northern Ireland—perhaps not of the same nature or intensity, but it would still be there. For that reason they have been classified here as adhering to the same broad interpretation, which I have labelled the internal-conflict approach.

THE BRITISH AND IRISH DIMENSIONS

To give primacy to the internal conflict does not mean ignoring the other conflicts that contribute to the Northern Ireland problem. The Cameron Report was exceptional in describing the conflict purely in internal terms. Subsequent writers have, as we have seen, generally recognized that British and/or Irish policies have contributed to the difficulties. Some writers, while on balance belonging to the internal-conflict school, put considerable stress on the external factors. I shall say a word about three of them. One is Padraig O'Malley, whose book *The Uncivil Wars* (1983) has already been referred to. The other two are political scientists at the Queen's University of Belfast, Adrian Guelke and Frank Wright.

O'Malley (1983) sees the conflict as one which at its most basic level pits one million Protestants against half a million Catholics (p. 10). In each of the interviews which form the core of his book, the discussion revolves round the nature of the conflict within Northern Ireland. At the same time he puts more stress than many authors on the wider context. He sees the problem as breaking down into three questions: 'first is the question of the external relations between Britain and Ireland; second, the question of the internal relations between Catholics and Protestants in Northern Ireland; and third, the question of the relations between the two parts of Ireland' (p. 4). The very fact that he interviews British and southern Irish politicians as well as representatives of the different viewpoints within Northern Ireland shows the importance he attaches to external influences. In his recommendations for progress (pp. 356–60) he sees things that both Protestants and Catholics within Northern Ireland should do—but he also has advice for the British and for the Republic.

Adrian Guelke, in his book *Northern Ireland: The International Perspective* (1988) explores 'the interconnection between Northern Ireland's sectarian divisions and the province's anomalous international status' (p. 195). Guelke is in no doubt about the reality of the community conflict in Northern Ireland: he does not consider that it can be explained as an artefact of either British imperialism or Irish irredentism. He notes that 'there is little basis in Loyalist Ideology or history for the supposition that Protestant resistance would dissolve if Britain withdrew its support for the Union' (p. 205), while on the other side he observes that in practice governments and public opinion in the Republic give low priority to unification (p. 108). However, he also considers that 'internationalisation has made the conflict more intractable' (p. 205). By internationalization he means most of all the influence of international opinion on the conflict (p. 2). He sees world opinion as considering the current status of Northern Ireland to be anomalous. British governments have specifically acknowledged Northern Ireland's right to secede from the United Kingdom. By international standards it is unusual for any State to grant a right of secession to part of its territory, and the fact that Britain has done so damages the legitimacy of British rule (p. 4). A number of consequences follow: the fears of Protestants are increased; the IRA is encouraged to continue its campaign; the government's response to that campaign is constrained; and even non-violent nationalists are encouraged to continue denying legitimacy to Northern Ireland (pp. 17–20). I doubt if all these consequences derive simply from the region's anomalous status: one might expect them largely to survive even if Britain were to declare Northern Ireland unconditionally part of the United Kingdom. None the less Guelke's analysis is important as showing how exogenous and endogenous factors can interact.

Frank Wright, in his difficult but profound book *Northern Ireland: A Comparative Analysis* (1987) is also interested in the interaction of internal and external factors. He treats Northern Ireland as one of a number of cases where an internal conflict is crucially shaped by the fact that it is a frontier region. The other cases cited are: Prussian Poland, Bohemia under Austrian rule, Algeria under French rule, and the American south. In all these instances he sees the same forces at work: a metropolitan power linked to an ethnic group in the area in question, which is being pulled by that ethnic group further than it wishes to go, but which cannot disown them altogether without giving up all control over the territory. Wright also compares Northern Ireland with two countries—Cyprus and Lebanon—where an internal conflict is exacerbated by the pull of rival outside powers. Of all these cases, the only one which has experienced anything like a benign outcome has been the American south, where no outside power has intervened to stir up the conflict. In all the others, the problem either festers (Lebanon), or has been 'solved' by mass flights of population (Prussian Poland, Bohemia, Algeria), or still festers despite mass expulsions (Cyprus). Wright's purpose is to show how Britain and Ireland, as the external forces involved in Northern Ireland, can avoid producing the same malign consequences as external actors elsewhere. He has drawn out his conclusions more clearly, though necessarily more briefly, in a subsequent article (Wright 1989).

CONCLUSION

The popularity of the internal-conflict approach has been quite recent. Before the troubles began, the bulk of the (admittedly very much more meagre) literature then available in Northern Ireland could be classified as traditional nationalist or traditional unionist. In the early part of the troubles, Marxist interpretations enjoyed a vogue. But the dominance of the internal-conflict approach was assured by the early 1970s, and has continued unabated since.

I can offer a couple of statistical exercises in support of this conclusion. First, I have made an analysis of those books which I have read on Northern Ireland that contain, implicitly or explicitly, an interpretation of the problem. The handful published before 1968 can all, except for Barritt and Carter (1962), be classified as traditional nationalist, traditional unionist, or Marxist. But the ones published since the troubles began present a different pattern. There are 155 such titles. I classify them as follows:

Traditional nationalist	11%
Traditional unionist	9%
Marxist	17%
Internal-conflict	63%

As a check on these figures, I offer an analysis derived from another source. The *Social Science Bibliography of Northern Ireland, 1945–1983* (Rolston *et al.* 1983) contains a section headed 'General Political Analysis', which lists 842 books, articles, and other items. If I exclude items which I do not know, or which in my opinion were wrongly included under this heading, this leaves 725 titles, 669 of them published in or after 1968. I classify these 669 titles as follows:

Traditional nationalist	8%
Traditional unionist	8%
Marxist	26%
Internal-conflict	57%

In both lists, Marxist items divide about two-to-one between traditional and revisionist Marxism.

There are some divergences between the two tables. Rolston *et al.* have discovered a higher proportion of Marxist items than I have. However, the agreements are more striking than the differences. In particular, we agree that the internal-conflict approach is by far the most popular.

Nor is the popularity of the internal-conflict approach confined to writers. It has spread to the politicians. Evidence of this can be found in an M.Sc. thesis in psychology completed by Anthony Gallagher (1982) at the Queen's University of Belfast. Early in 1982 Gallagher interviewed spokesmen for six major groups in Northern Ireland—the five main political parties (the Official Unionists, Democratic Unionists, Alliance Party, Social Democratic and Labour Party, and Sinn Féin), and the Ulster Defence Association. Among the questions he asked them was 'what would your party describe as being the Northern Ireland problem?' (p. 109). Two of the six respondents gave replies which diverged from those offered by the rest. The Sinn Féin spokesman gave a traditional nationalist or traditional Marxist answer: 'we see the problem as a colonial problem' (p. 111). The DUP spokesman saw the problem as primarily caused by the IRA:

A violent minority ... refuse to accept that the constitutional destiny of Northern Ireland has been settled ... democratically by the people of Northern Ireland and that violent minority have taken it upon themselves to, by bombs and bullets, seek to obtain what they cannot obtain by the ballot.

But the other four—OUP, SDLP, Alliance, and UDA—were close together in their analysis. All saw the core of the problem as a clash between two groups within Northern Ireland. I shall quote just two of them: 'there is a conflict between two different national identities and national aspirations' (OUP: p. 110); 'we see the problem as being ... a problem of identity, and ... of conflict of identity' (SDLP: p. 110); Although these statements come from political opponents, they are virtually interchangeable. Thus there is a wide measure of agreement among four out of six strands of political opinion in Northern Ireland about the nature of the problem. This may not get us very far—they are still far apart on the nature of the solution. But it is further evidence of the widespread acceptance of the internal-conflict approach.

To sum up: it seems clear that the internal-conflict approach is by far the most popular; that is is at least twice as popular as any other approach; and that it is more popular than all the others combined. It is not far from being a dominant paradigm.

Indeed the primacy of the internal-conflict interpretation is so marked that some readers may feel that I am hammering at the obvious. It is difficult for younger people to realize how strange such an interpretation would have seemed thirty years ago. As one of my younger colleagues, who has read this book in draft, said to me: '*of course* most unionists and most nationalists will recognise that the conflict is primarily internal'. If they do, however, this is quite a recent phenomenon. It would not have been so widely recognized before the troubles.

I can offer some examples of this fact, drawn from both sides of the fence. Seán Cronin, in his book *Irish Nationalism: A History of its Roots and Ideology* (1980), quotes a memoir by an IRA prisoner in Belfast prison from 1954 to 1962, Seán O'Hegarty. Speaking of republican ideology at that date, O'Hegarty writes: 'little if any emphasis was placed on the fact that the majority of the population wished to remain under the Crown. The fact that this sentiment might be transformed into formidable armed opposition against a united Ireland, or that it could provide the single most significant stumbling block to national unity, was completely overlooked' (p. 337). I can remember seeing in a St Patrick's Day parade in Dublin, sometime in the 1950s, an anti-partition float on which six small papier-mâché figures, representing the six counties of Northern Ireland, cowered under the lash of a brutal-looking model of John Bull. The fact that the majority of the population in four of those six counties wanted to be under John Bull's rule counted for nothing with the designers of the float. They evidently believed in some Platonic-form Antrim, Down, Londonderry, and Armagh, which remained part of the Irish nation even if the majority of the people living there had no wish to do so.

On the unionist side of the fence, there was until well into the 1960s a sign outside Great Victoria Street railway station in Belfast, which confronted passengers coming out of the train from Dublin. It said in capital letters ULSTER IS BRITISH. On looking back, this sign seems doubly misconceived. First, by implying that 'Ulster' had a uniform will, it did not state the truth. A more accurate formula would have been 'Northern Ireland is a mixture of British and Irish'. Secondly, the sign was in the wrong place. It was put where it would be the first thing that visitors from Dublin would see—as if people from the south were the problem. If the regime wished to convert people by propaganda, its slogans would more appropriately have been placed where the Catholic minority would see them. The latter was the group which, as events were to show before the 1960s were out, posed the real threat to unionist hegemony.

The internal-conflict interpretation, though it has become by far the most popular, suffers, like the other interpretations, from difficulties. The drawback of the traditional nationalist school is that it took insufficient account of the separate identity of northern Protestants. The drawback of the traditional unionist school is that it took insufficient account of the community divide within Northern Ireland. The limitation of the Marxist approach is that its practitioners have been unable to agree among themselves on what conclusions to draw from their method. A limitation of the internal-conflict school is that, though there is agreement in broad terms on the nature of the problem, there is no agreement on the nature of the solution. The various possible solutions, and the objections to each of them, will be examined in the next chapter.

III
Conclusions

10
Solutions?

INTRODUCTION

My purpose in this chapter is to survey possible solutions to the Northern Ireland problem, and to assess their merits. Such an exercise is not new. It has been done many times in the literature— for instance, by Palley (1972), Rose (1976), Oliver (1978a), Palley again in Watt (1981), Barritt (1982), Rea (1982), Boyle and Hadden (1985), and the SDL/Liberal Alliance commission on Northern Ireland (Alliance 1985). It has been done with particular comprehensiveness by Padraig O'Malley, who, in his book *The Uncivil Wars* (1983), interviewed representatives of every strand of opinion, and then clinically dissected the weaknesses in their arguments. However, there is a case for repeating the exercise. As time moves on, so new ideas may emerge or the balance of forces may shift, and an analysis written at the end of the 1980s may not reach quite the same conclusions as one written a few years earlier.

I shall examine ten different proposals or approaches which I have found in the literature. First, I shall discuss a proposal outside the constitutional sphere—the development of integrated education— which has been put forward by a number of observers. I shall then go on to discuss four possible constitutional frameworks: a united Ireland by consent; integration with Great Britain; an independent Northern Ireland; and power-sharing plus an Irish dimension. All of these options presuppose that some kind of compromise is possible. But what if it is not? The worst scenarios also need investigating. I shall then go on to three options which assume that compromise cannot be achieved: repartition; a united Ireland by coercion; and throwing up one's hands and saying that no solution is possible. I shall conclude by considering two approaches which have come into prominence in recent years. The first is to argue that, even if an overall settlement is not possible, small steps forward can be made. The second is to advocate some form of joint authority.

In this chapter I shall take as given the conclusion reached in Part II—that there is widespread consensus on the heart of the problem being an internal conflict between two communities within Northern Ireland. I shall therefore draw mainly on authors who accept that perspective. I shall, however, note points made by authors who adopt some other perspective, where these are pertinent.

1. INTEGRATED EDUCATION

As was shown in Chapter 2, there is an almost total division in Northern Ireland schooling, with Protestant children being educated in one set of schools, and Catholic children in another. As was also shown, there is a body of research evidence which suggests that this division exacerbates the community conflict. It is not surprising, then, that some writers should have advocated, as a way of ameliorating the conflict, the integration of the two school systems.

So far as I know, the topic was first broached by the then prime minister of Northern Ireland, Terence O'Neill, speaking at Corrymeela in 1966:

A major cause of division arises, some would say, from the *de facto* segregation of education along religious lines. This is a most delicate matter, and one must respect the firm convictions from which it springs. Many people have questioned, however, whether the maintenance of two distinct educational systems side by side is not wasteful of human and financial resources, and a major barrier to the promotion of communal understanding. (Quoted in O'Neill 1969, 113.)

As the troubles developed, so the case for integrated education came to be put more frequently. (A helpful survey of the main statements, for and against, can be found in Gallagher and Worrall, *Christians in Ulster* (1982, 153–72).) The fullest exposition of the case for integration was provided by the Belfast child psychiatrist Morris Fraser, in his book *Children in Conflict* (1973). Fraser argued that the vicious circle of prejudice and stereotyping was maintained by both school and home, and the advantage of integrated education is that it would allow the circle to be broken (p. 135). In integrated schools, children would meet members of the other group. Stereotypes would be challenged, and hostility reduced. Fraser supported this claim by evidence from other countries, and by his experience of special schools for the handicapped in Belfast, which are among the few schools where Catholic and Protestant mix (pp. 136–7). He stressed, however, that these beneficial effects were likely to apply only to younger children: by the time they reached 13 or so, stereotypes would have become too strong to be discarded (pp. 137–8).

The psychologist Ken Heskin (1980, 150) suggested further beneficial effects from integration. First, it would retard the process of ethnic discrimination—that is, the learning of cues by which one group gets to recognize the other. Secondly, it would reinforce in their values the majority of the population—who according to opinion polls favour integrated education—and would force those who favour keeping the communities apart into re-examining their attitudes.

Other researchers, however—as we saw in Chapter 2—have been more sceptical about the benefits of integrated education. As was shown there, the scholar who has done most to document the divisive effects of segregated education has been Dominic Murray in his book *Worlds Apart* (1985). Yet, precisely because of the depth of division which his study revealed, Murray is not an advocate of integration (p. 106). He feels that in Northern Ireland religion is too deeply enmeshed with political and cultural differences for integration to be practicable. To illustrate the point, he appends a list of questions which would have to be answered if one were even considering integration as a possibility:

Does it mean, for example, that integrated schools would prohibit any overt signs of religious or cultural aspirations? Which (if any) identity would be fostered? Would all clergy be deprived access? Which flags should be flown? Which prayers said? Which games played? Which songs sung? (pp. 134–5.)

Indeed forcible integration could well lead to the importation into the classroom of the wider community conflict.

Experiments in the educational field are possible. The small existing network of integrated schools could be expanded, so that those parents who desire such schooling for their children would find it easier to obtain. Murray suggests (1985, 129) that more could be done to improve contact between schools of different traditions. This had already been recommended by an inter-Church working party comprising both Protestants and Catholics (*Violence in Ireland*, 1976, 86–7). But to assume that changes in the education system could transform community relations in Northern Ireland is optimistic.

2. A UNITED IRELAND BY CONSENT

Most of those who seek a united Ireland do so from traditional nationalist or traditional Marxist premisses. However, it is possible to accept that the problem in Northern Ireland is primarily internal and still argue that the best solution would be in an all-Ireland framework. The report of the New Ireland Forum takes this line (para. 5.5). It argues that both traditions in Northern Ireland could benefit from the change. For nationalists, this is obvious; but even unionists, it is argued, would make gains. It would give them 'the opportunity to share in the leadership and to shape the future of a new Ireland'. It would provide economies of scale, and a framework in which the interests of both parts of Ireland, which are in many ways similar, could best be advanced in a European and international framework.

The problem with proposing unity by agreement as an aim lies, not in its theoretical desirability, but in the fact that agreement manifestly does not exist. As we have seen in previous chapters, the unionist community in Northern Ireland, for various reasons, some bad, some good, is passionately opposed to unification with the Republic. Its opposition has if anything grown in intensity over the last twenty years, and does not seem likely to lessen for many years to come.

In that case, two alternatives exist. One is to try to persuade the unionists to change their minds. The other is to seek to coerce them. These are best treated as distinct options, and I shall return to a united Ireland by coercion later in this chapter. For the moment I shall deal with a united Ireland by persuasion.

The persuasion, if it is to be effective, will have to come from Britain. Irish nationalists have been unable in a hundred years to find any arguments to convince unionists that their interests would be better served in a united Ireland. If a strong voice from Britain, however, united itself with theirs, then the situation might be different. The British Labour Party has since 1981 been committed to securing a united Ireland by consent, and in a recent policy document (Labour Party 1988) it has set out how it proposes to secure the agreement of unionists to a united Ireland. It proposes that, if a Labour government is in power, the following changes will be put through:

1. Highest priority will be given to measures providing for equality of opportunity in employment and an end to discrimination. Goals and timetables will be laid down (paras. 25–7).

2. Integrated education will be encouraged, and the funding of Catholic schools improved (paras. 29–30).

3. Job creation will be given the highest priority with the focus on areas of greatest unemployment [which in practice are Catholic] (para. 34).

4. Cross-border economic ties will be strengthened, and Labour will seek to agree with the Republic on joint approaches to the European Community (paras. 35, 58).

5. An extensive programme of legal reforms, as promised in a previous statement (Labour Party 1987) will be implemented (para. 37). The Prevention of Terrorism Act 1984, and eventually the Emergency Provisions Act 1978, will be repealed. Supergrass trials will be ended. Three-judge courts will replace the existing single-judge courts, and the party will work for the restoration of jury trials. Strip-searching will be ended. Measures will be taken to increase confidence in the RUC and to reduce the imbalance in recruitment. The independence of the complaints procedure will be enhanced. The RUC code of conduct will be published. An effective scheme of compensation for injury will be introduced. The use of plastic bullets will be ended. The rules with regard to the use of lethal force will be reviewed, as will delays in the holding of inquests.

6. Sexual and religious imbalances in the Northern Ireland civil service will be remedied, and special units set up to implement the change (paras. 44–5).

7. As appointments to public boards come up for renewal, appointments will be made to increase minority representation (para. 46).

8. The framework of the Anglo-Irish Agreement will be used to harmonize policy with the Republic, and the joint secretariat will be expanded (para. 51).

9. Moves will be made towards a common currency for the two parts of Ireland (para. 61).

10. Efforts will be made to create an all-Ireland industrial development authority, replacing the Industrial Development Agency in the Republic and the Industrial Development Board in Northern Ireland (para. 62).

11. Agricultural policy, north and south, will be harmonized (para. 63).

12. An all-Ireland energy authority will be pressed for (para. 64).

13. The railway system will be unified, a common road system planned, and a Belfast–Dublin air service introduced (para. 65).

14. The social security systems will be harmonized. A Labour government would continue to help finance the system after unification (para. 66).

15. Efforts will be made to harmonize curriculum development in schools, to improve co-operation in third-level education, and to unify student recruitment (para. 68).

16. Steps will be taken towards harmonizing company law and criminal law.

17. A Bill of Rights and/or an all-Ireland equivalent of the Standing Advisory Commission on Human Rights will be promoted (para. 70).

18. An all-Ireland structure for the RUC and the Garda will be considered (para. 71).

19. A Labour government will promise continuing financial support until the benefits of unification have been realized (para. 75).

It is promised that this programme will proceed 'even in the face of sustained opposition from some section of the community' (para. 17).

This is a more detailed programme for the reunification of Ireland than has come from any quarter previously. The weakness is that the Labour document nowhere explains why it is thought that such measures will secure unionist consent. They can be put through against unionist opposition, just as the Hillsborough agreement has been maintained against unionist opposition, but that is not the same as securing unionist acquiescence. None of the items in the Labour Party's list begins to address unionist objections on grounds of religion and nationality to joining a united Ireland. Indeed the reforms, if carried through, might do more to reconcile Catholics to living in the United Kingdom. To be fair, the document lays down two other objectives besides unification by consent. These are the reform of the institutions of Northern Ireland, and the harmonization of policies with the Republic. These will undoubtedly be advanced by the proposals listed above, and perhaps that is all that the drafters of the document realistically hope to achieve.

In discussing a united Ireland as a solution, I have not gone into details about what a united Ireland might look like. There are basically two options: a unitary State or a federal/confederal State. A federal or confederal State, as we saw from the survey data in Chapter 4, would be rather less unpalatable to northern Protestants and would therefore have somewhat more chance of being implemented. On the other hand, in such a system Protestants would still be free to run Northern Ireland largely as they liked, and there would be a danger that the abuses of the old Stormont system would be revived. For that reason northern Catholics would be more likely to prefer a unitary State. But under a unitary State it would be difficult to protect northern Protestants from being coerced into accepting Catholic-inspired legislation on any matter where Catholic and Protestant values diverged. Thus if by some miracle a united Ireland were to reach the stage of negotiation, the actual design of institutions would raise further difficulties. For anyone who wants to explore these variations further, useful discussions are available in Palley (1972, 462–74), Boyle and Hadden (1985, 28–30), and the report of the New Ireland Forum (especially Chapters 6 and 7). However, since a united Ireland by consent seems unlikely to occur, there is no need to spend further time on these issues.

3. INTEGRATION WITH GREAT BRITAIN

A quite different proposal for Northern Ireland is that for total integration with Great Britain. At present, Northern Ireland is governed by direct rule from Westminster. This is *de facto* integration, but it differs from *de jure* integration in being temporary. The intention of the British government, as enshrined in the Northern Ireland Constitution Act 1973, is that Northern Ireland should have its own executive and legislature, with powers devolved from Westminster. The argument of the integrationists is that the current temporary arrangements should become permanent, and that Northern Ireland should be governed like any other part of the United Kingdom.

Integrationists are to be found on both right and left. A current of opinion in the Conservative Party supports their case (e.g. Biggs-Davison 1982). There has been a similar current in the British Labour Party, as is disgustedly documented by Geoffrey Bell—a strong opponent of such views—in his book *Troublesome Business: The Labour Party and the Irish Question* (1982, 125–6, 141–4). Support for the demand in the academic literature is rather thin, but a couple of book-length examples can be found. One is Peter Brooke's work on *Ulster Presbyterianism* (1987). Another is Graham Walker's life of the Northern Ireland labour leader Harry Midgley, *The Politics of Frustration* (1985). Since Brooke's work treats mainly of the seventeenth and eighteenth century, with its integrationist conclusions reserved for the final chapter, while Walker's book covers much more recent times, I shall take Walker as my example of the integrationist case.

Walker is interested in Midgley as a case-study in the difficulties of building up a cross-community labour movement in a divided society like Northern Ireland. Midgley spent many years trying to build up the Northern Ireland Labour Party, but eventually gave up the struggle, joined the Unionist Party, and ended as a cabinet minister under Lord Brookeborough. Walker argues that his career would have been less frustrated if Northern Ireland had been part of the United Kingdom like Glasgow or Liverpool:

This is not to suggest that the task [of diminishing the force of sectarian appeals] would not have been much harder, or to gloss over the fact that sectarian tensions in Northern Ireland, unlike Glasgow and Liverpool, existed in the context of a conflict over national identity. It is simply to stress that provincial politics in Northern Ireland proved to be demonstrably unamenable to anything but sectarian considerations. Devolved government meant that most issues with a bearing on class interest were settled at Westminster; at Stormont there was no escaping the overriding importance of the national question. Had Northern Ireland been integrated with the rest of the UK this issue would probably not have been surrounded with such uncertainty, and, consequently, the respective fears and mutually exclusive aspirations of both communities would not have assumed such potent political force. (p. 217.)

Walker's analysis has a good deal in common with nationalist criticisms of the Northern Ireland State. Like nationalists, he sees the structure of that State as aggravating the sectarianism of society. Both he and they see the answer as merging Northern Ireland in some larger unit. But where they see the larger unit as the island of Ireland, he sees it as the United Kingdom.

The advantages of integration have been listed by another academic writer, Professor Paul Wilkinson (1986, 183). He notes four:

- It gives an unambiguous reassurance to Ulster's Protestant majority that their political status is not going to be sacrificed or bargained away. This will enhance public co-operation and support for Government Security Forces.
- It sends a clear message to the IRA and INLA murderers that they have *lost* the long-term political battle and this will serve to demoralize them. . . .
- It ensures that the rights of *both communities* in Northern Ireland are properly protected under Westminster and Whitehall, in a manifestly *non-sectarian* system of administration.
- It does not preclude attempts to resuscitate and develop proper institutions of local government in the Province.

Biggs-Davison (1982) adds a further point. He quotes survey evidence to show that integration would be acceptable, not just to nearly all Protestants but also to many Catholics.

Yet despite all these arguments, integration has never been adopted as policy by any British government. James Prior, Conservative Secretary of State for Northern Ireland from 1981 to 1984, states in his memoirs (1986, 192) that he ruled it out at a very early stage. He gives the following reasons for his decision:

I rejected integration because it would have made a bad situation worse. It offered as a permanent solution an approach favoured by only a minority of the Unionists—one section of the Official Unionists. It would have made the position of moderate, democratic Nationalists impossible, and played into the hands of the terrorists. It would have scuppered any hope of co-operation with Dublin. And it assumed that institutional change could have a much greater impact on attitudes and behaviour than Tories have traditionally believed. (p. 194.)

Another argument against integration was put in the white paper issued in the early stages of Prior's period in Northern Ireland: 'Northern Ireland's divided community, its geography and the history of its politics all make it impracticable to treat the Province as though it were in all respects identical to the rest of the United Kingdom' (UK Government 1982, para. 6).

Prior, like Wilkinson and Biggs-Davison, argues on the basis of the likely consequences within Northern Ireland. There is a further set of considerations to be taken into account: the effect of integration in Great Britain. Prior does not mention these, but many in all parties in Britain would see them as mainly negative. Richard

Rose (1976, 155) has listed some of the considerations which would weigh with the mainland British:

The bloody Troubles since 1969 have only emphasized the alienness of Ulster to Englishmen. . . . British politicians have no wish to end the institutional anomalies and uncertainties arising from direct rule by integrating what is now often regarded as an alien part of the United Kingdom. . . . Increased Westminster responsibilities in Ulster are formally opposed on the grounds that the problems there are atypical and unsuitable for Westminster's governance.

Rose added a further consideration which matters less at the beginning of the 1990s than it did in the mid-1970s, but which could come to matter again: that the trend elsewhere in the United Kingdom was not towards integration but towards devolution.

In recent years, the argument for integration has been given a new twist. Rather than insisting on institutional integration, its advocates have come to stress the importance of British parties organizing in Northern Ireland. The main pressure group making the new demand has been the Campaign for Equal Citizenship, founded in March 1986 (Roberts 1987, 315 n). The fullest academic statements of the case can be found in the publications of two political scientists—Hugh Roberts's article 'Sound Stupidity: The British Party System and the Northern Ireland Question' (1987), and Arthur Aughey's book *Under Siege: Ulster Unionism and the Anglo-Irish Agreement* (1989).

A starting-point for both authors is a rejection of the principle that Northern Ireland is fundamentally different from the rest of the United Kingdom. Roberts denounces the idea that 'Northern Ireland is a place apart for which anomalous arrangements must be made' (p. 327). Aughey criticizes the notion that 'the specific style of Ulster politics requires an unusual form of government' (p. 34). For both authors, the main thing that makes Northern Ireland different is the refusal of the major British parties to organize there. This leaves the region in the grip of introverted sectarian-based local parties. Roberts goes so far as to say that the party boycott is 'the fundamental reason for the continuing conflict in the province' (p. 335).

Both authors foresee great benefits if the main British parties were to organize in Northern Ireland. Aughey says that 'participation in national party politics would release the compressed energies of those confined to the "political prison" of provinciality' (p. 156).

Roberts argues that if the mainland parties were to extend to Northern Ireland, the result on both sides could be an uncoupling of policy preferences from sectarian bases. For instance, Catholic parties in Northern Ireland have failed to secure Protestant consent to unification. The British Labour Party seeks unity by consent, but has the advantage of being devoid of particular religious associations. The only hope of securing unity by consent is if the Labour Party 'undertakes to canvass a non-sectarian case for Irish unification amongst the Protestant population' (p. 332). Equally, Catholics can be won for the union only if the Conservative Party organizes in the region. As Aughey puts it, Catholics cannot be expected to associate with either the Official Unionist Party or the Democratic Unionist Party—the one linked to the Orange Order, and the other to Paisley's Free Presbyterian Church (p. 157). Yet opinion polls show that many Catholics favour the maintenance of the union: the arrival of the Conservatives in Northern Ireland would enable them to become unionists in their own way (p. 158).

The argument that the main difference between Northern Ireland and the rest of the United Kingdom lies in their party systems is not convincing. Nowhere else in the United Kingdom are communal tensions remotely so severe as they are in Northern Ireland. Nowhere else does one find the lethal mixture of a large minority with a well-founded and deeply felt sense of grievance, and a narrow majority with justifiable anxieties about what the future may hold. There are nationalists in Scotland and Wales, but they do not display the bitter sense of injustice felt by nationalists in Northern Ireland and, apart from a tiny fringe, they do not resort to violence. There are racial tensions in some English cities, but these do not call into question the nature of the State. The truth is that Northern Ireland *is* different, and the notion that special institutions are required to meet the contending needs and aspirations of its two communities is reasonable.

Experience in other divided societies does not suggest that mere changes in the party system can transform the situation. Institutional changes, to give a sense of equality to the contending cultures, have repeatedly been found necessary. Aughey claims that in other European countries regional differences in political culture are not held to require special institutions (p. 34)—but he is unwise enough to have chosen among his examples Corsica and the South Tyrol, both of which were given special institutions following a period of ethnic conflict. In the South Tyrol these amount to institutionalized power-sharing between the German and Italian communities—just the kind of arrangement which Aughey denounces for Northern Ireland. Italian parties organized in the South Tyrol, and French parties organized in Corsica, ever since the restoration of democracy after the Second World War, but that did not prevent ethnic conflict from spreading. Spanish parties organize in the Basque country without preventing ethnic conflict there: the Spanish government is seeking to restore peace by developing special institutions. Swiss parties organized in the Bernese Jura without preventing conflict: the special interests of the French Catholic minority have been safeguarded by carving out a new canton. In Belgium the three main parties organized across the linguistic divide, but that did not stop tension between Fleming and Walloon from rising in the 1960s. If the tension has been largely defused, it is because special institutions to safeguard each identity have been developed. The three traditional parties have each split into two on linguistic lines, so that improved relations have been accompanied by less electoral integration, not more.

Even if the main British parties did organize in Northern Ireland, one wonders how much difference it would make to patterns of electoral support. No one can know for certain in advance of the experiment being tried; but some indication may be found in opinion polls. A survey published in the *Belfast Telegraph* of 5 October 1988 asked respondents if they agreed with the idea that the main British political parties should put forward candidates for election in Northern Ireland. Sixty-five per cent of Protestants, and 45 per cent of Catholics, said that they did. But the survey then asked: 'if the main British parties did put forward candidates for election along with the traditional parties in Northern Ireland, which party would be most likely to attract your support?' In reply to this question, only 33 per cent of Protestants and 30 per cent of Catholics said that they would vote for any of the British parties, while 57 per cent of Protestants and 56 per cent of Catholics said they would continue to vote for one of the traditional Northern Ireland parties. In any case the Labour Party is unlikely to organize in Northern Ireland. The Conservative Party decided, at its annual conference in October 1989, in principle to do so, but it will be handicapped among Protestant voters because it is committed to the Anglo-Irish Agreement, and among Catholics by its opposition to a united Ireland, so its appeal may be limited. However, this is a subsidiary objection to the electoral-integration thesis. Even if the British parties swept the board in Northern Ireland, that would not alter the situation so long as the electors, in making their choice of party, were preoccupied by the same anxieties as possess them now. Those anxieties, as was demonstrated in Part I of this book, are manifold and deep-seated. It would need more than a mere change of party choice to root them out.

The works by Roberts and Aughey contain information which will make them valuable even to those who most disagree with their conclusions. Roberts provides an account of the actual practice of British parties towards Northern Ireland; Aughey offers the fullest survey so far published of recent unionist politics. But these virtues cannot disguise the threadbare nature of their case. Electoral integration is a dead end, and the attempt to explore it only postpones the search for a settlement.

4. AN INDEPENDENT NORTHERN IRELAND

If the polar opposites of integration into the rest of Ireland, and integration into the rest of the United Kingdom, are both impracticable, then perhaps some intermediate settlement might be more acceptable. One such settlement might be the establishment of Northern Ireland as an independent State. It could be seen as intermediate because it has something for both communities. It gratifies nationalists by getting rid of the British link, while it gratifies unionists by securing their independence from Dublin.

The idea has in fact received support from both sides of the community divide. To my knowledge its first appearance during the present troubles came in a pamphlet by Fergus McAteer, son of the veteran Derry nationalist Eddie McAteer, in a pamphlet entitled *Won't You Please Sit Down?* (1972). The best recent statement of the case comes from a southern Irishwoman of Catholic background, Dervla Murphy, in her pamphlet *Changing the Problem: Post-Forum Reflections* (1984). On the other side of the divide it has been advocated by a group linked to the Ulster Defence Association, the New Ulster Political Research Group (NUPRG), who put the case for it in a pamphlet, *Beyond the Religious Divide* (1979). In England, the proposal has been advocated by the former Labour Prime

Minister, James Callaghan, in the House of Commons on 2 July 1981 (Callaghan 1987, 500).

The case for independence is best put in the words of its advocates. The New Ulster Political Research Group (1979, 3) state that they were led to it because any proposal which involved London would be rejected by the minority and any proposal which involved Dublin would be rejected by the majority:

We believe there is one proposal which does offer peace, stability and reconciliation. It is the only proposal which does not have a victor and a loser. It will encourage the development of a common identity between the two communities, regardless of religion. It offers first class Ulster-citizenship to all of our people, because, like it or not, the Protestant of Northern Ireland is looked upon as a second class British citizen in Britain and the Roman Catholic of Northern Ireland as a second class Irish citizen in Southern Ireland.

Dervla Murphy (1984) offers additional arguments:

By successfully establishing an Independent NI, the British and Irish governments could release the Northern Irish into a wholly new world where the instinct of self-preservation would compel them to abandon the cultivation of sectarian division and concentrate instead on fostering that unity without which their new State would fall apart. Freed of the destructive pulls of the London and Dublin magnets, the two communities would soon find their interests naturally converging. (p. 17.)

However, there are risks attached to the setting up of an independent State. It would be frail economically. The NUPRG attached to their pamphlet (1979, 41–8) two papers by distinguished authorities, John Simpson and T. K. Whitaker, which argued that an independent Northern Ireland could be viable economically; but this was only on certain assumptions which some might feel to be too favourable, and anyway the situation of the region has deteriorated since then. Even if the economy as a whole survived, the economic gap between Protestant and Catholic, examined in Chapter 3, would not be diminished, and would lead to the same disagreements as it does at present over how far rectifying action should be taken by the government. A further danger is that the IRA would not accept the settlement, but would continue its campaign— which would lead to the same problems as at present, with Protestants complaining of inadequate security, and Catholics of unnecessary harassment. Both the NUPRG and Dervla Murphy take it for granted that the new governmental structures will ensure that one community does not dominate the other. But this does not mean that they will be free from tension. Like the power-sharing executive of 1974, they might be faced with fundamental differences between the two communities in perceptions of where injustice lay, and might find it impossible to reach an acceptable compromise. Independence does not automatically bring responsibility. In Sri Lanka the Tamils and Sinhalese have had forty years to resolve their differences and have not been able to do so.

The dilemma can be put in epigrammatic form. If there were enough trust between the communities in Northern Ireland, independence would probably be viable—but then it would probably not be necessary.

5. POWER-SHARING WITH AN IRISH DIMENSION

If an independent Northern Ireland seems impracticable, is some other compromise settlement possible? British governments appear to think so, because ever since 1972 they have been trying, with varying degrees of energy, to achieve one.

The fundamental British analysis of the situation was laid down in the green paper (so called despite the fact that its cover was white) published in October 1972, *The Future of Northern Ireland: A Paper for Discussion* (Northern Ireland Office 1972). This paper contained two important innovations. First, it insisted that any new institutions 'must seek a much wider consensus than has hitherto existed', and it added that there were strong arguments for saying that this would best be achieved by giving minority interests a share in the exercise of executive power' (para. 79). The second was that the paragraphs discussing relations with the Irish Republic were headed 'The Irish Dimension' (para. 76). This phrase has been used so often since that it has become a cliché. But clichés become such because they put a point well, and in 1972 the phrase 'Irish dimension' was a brilliant innovation. Up till then, most discourse about Northern Ireland had assumed that only two statuses were possible: that it should be part of the United Kingdom wholly independent of the Republic, or that it should be part of a united Ireland wholly independent of the United Kingdom. The new phrase signalled that the maintenance of Northern Ireland within the United Kingdom could accommodate a range of special relationships with the Republic.

The rationale for these innovations was not specifically spelt out in the green paper, but one can deduce that the intention was to give each community what it was perceived as most wanting. On the one hand Protestants were perceived as wanting above all the maintenance of the union with Britain, so that desire was not challenged—indeed the green paper repeated the assurance that Northern Ireland would remain part of the United Kingdom for as long as the majority wished (para. 39). On the other hand Catholics were perceived as wanting above all equal treatment within Northern Ireland. The commitment to a share in executive power and a recognition of the Irish dimension were intended to provide this.

If such considerations indeed lay behind the green paper, then the survey evidence which we examined in Chapter 4 lends them support. Indeed the white paper's compromise seems better attuned to what the two communities want than does the independent-Northern Ireland compromise. The survey data showed that the latter had little support in either community. On the other hand, power-sharing-plus-an-Irish-dimension offers both communities what the data suggest they most want. The surveys show that the overwhelming majority of Protestants wish to maintain the union, and under the green-paper philosophy they are guaranteed that. They also show that substantial numbers of Catholics would settle for an arrangement short of a united Ireland, provided they could be sure of a square deal within Northern Ireland; and a share in executive power plus an Irish dimension would help to ensure equality for them in Northern Ireland.

Despite its theoretical attractiveness, however, the solution of power-sharing-plus-an-Irish-dimension has not so far been successful. I shall not attempt to trace all the twists and turns of British policy since 1972, but I shall examine the two most determined attempts to put this philosophy into force. The first was the formation of the power-sharing executive in January 1974. An executive was formed comprising representatives of moderate Unionists under Brian Faulkner, of the SDLP, and of the Alliance Party. At Sunningdale in December 1973 its members had agreed, together with the British and Irish Governments, to set up a Council of Ireland, in which the governments and parliaments of the two parts of Ireland could deal with matters of common interest, on a basis of unanimity. It was shown at the Westminster general election of February 1974, however, that these arrangements did not have the support of most of the Protestant community. In May 1974, the power-sharing executive was brought down by a loyalist general strike.

The lesson to be drawn from these events was that any settlement must be proof against boycott by one or other of the northern communities. The lesson was applied in a later attempt to put into operation the philosophy of the 1972 discussion paper. This was the Anglo-Irish Agreement signed by the prime ministers of Ireland and the United Kingdom, Dr FitzGerald and Mrs Thatcher, at Hillsborough in November 1985. In this agreement the emphasis was put on the Irish dimension. An Intergovernmental Conference was set up, 'concerned with Northern Ireland and with relations between the two parts of the island of Ireland' (Article 2*a*). The two Governments promised to make 'determined efforts' to resolve any differences (Article 2*b*). In effect the British Government was conceding to the Irish Government a special role in Northern Ireland: something less strong than joint authority, but stronger than a mere right to consultation. If unionists did not like it, they could reduce the scope of the Intergovernmental Conference by agreeing to a measure of devolution (Article 2*b*), but it was made clear (Article 3) that any devolved institutions must be acceptable to the minority as well as the majority in Northern Ireland. Thus the unionists were given a choice: if they wanted to diminish the Irish dimension, they could do so by in effect agreeing to power-sharing.

The Anglo-Irish Agreement, unlike the power-sharing executive, has at least endured. As a method of reconciling communities, however, it has had less success. On the one hand Catholics complain that it has made little practical difference to the way they are treated. On the other hand unionists remain bitterly resentful that the agreement even exists. For at least two years they did their best to bring it down. Though there has more recently been a softening of attitudes among some unionists, it has not at the time of writing proceeded far enough to produce any results.

It remains an open question whether the British government's preferred method of advance—power-sharing plus an Irish dimension—can be made to work. Even if the constitutional parties in Northern Ireland were to agree, the problem of paramilitary violence would continue.

6. REPARTITION

One feature of the four constitutional arrangements which we have so far examined is that they assume that compromise is possible. The first two—a united Ireland and integration with Britain—are based on the assumption that one side or the other in Northern Ireland is not too serious about its national aspirations and can be induced to abandon them. The next two—an independent Northern Ireland or power-sharing-plus-an-Irish-dimension—are based on the assumption that both sides in Northern Ireland can be induced to settle for less than their maximum demands. This may well be true of substantial segments of both communities. But as long as important fractions of both remain intransigent, it is possible for the conflict to continue indefinitely. The experience of the troubles to date suggests that these determined minorities exist in Northern Ireland, and are not shrinking.

In that case, what alternative exists? One possibility would be repartition. If Catholics and Protestants cannot live together in Northern Ireland, then let them live separately, and let each community have control in the area where it is a majority. This solution has several times been proposed. The earliest instance that I know of is to be found in a pamphlet by a Conservative MP, Julian Critchley (1972). The Queen's University demographer Paul Compton suggested it tentatively in the volume of essays on the Northern Ireland problem edited by D. C. Watt (1981, 80-4). One of the world's leading authorities on the politics of divided societies concluded that, if power-sharing cannot be made to work in Northern Ireland, repartition may be inevitable (Lijphart 1977, 141). The fullest exposition of the case has been published by an economic historian at Queen's University, Liam Kennedy, in his booklet *Two Ulsters: A Case for Repartition* (1986).

Repartition has been successfully applied in other parts of the world. When a portion of the French-speaking minority in the Swiss canton of Berne proved dissatisfied with Bernese rule, a new canton of Jura was carved out for them by a succession of plebiscites in 1974-5. Belgium was divided into Dutch- and French-language regions in 1962 (though even there, the status of Brussels continues to give trouble). After the First World War several international boundaries (German–Danish, German–Polish, Austrian–Yugoslav) were determined by plebiscite.

However, these were all areas where the level of conflict was far below that attained in Northern Ireland. Other historical precedents exist which are much less reassuring. In India in 1947, Palestine in 1948, and Cyprus in 1974, partition was imposed, but only at the cost of great violence and massive displacement of population. The economic and psychological costs were devastating. The bitterness lasts till the present day.

There are great practical difficulties in applying repartition to Northern Ireland. Catholic and Protestant do not live neatly in different parts of the region. While it is true that Catholics are relatively more numerous in the south and west, there are innumerable exceptions. For instance, 100,000 Catholics live in west Belfast, far from any other majority-Catholic area. On the other hand, there are Protestant-majority pockets even in parts of Fermanagh and Tyrone. To draw a new boundary which takes account of this distribution would result in a long and straggling border, with tongues of Catholic territory extending into Protestant areas and vice versa, and probably with detached enclaves as well. The maps in Liam Kennedy's book (1986, 58–9), which I reproduce here with his kind permission, illustrate this well. He offers four alternative options. In three of them Catholic west Belfast survives as a detached enclave of Irish Ulster. In one of them, Protestant parts of Fermanagh survive as a detached enclave, and in two a long tongue of Protestant territory extends down from the eastern part of Derry city through west Tyrone. Such borders would be a nightmare to defend, and would also cause complications for the provision of public services. Many country areas would be cut off from the towns on which they currently depend for, among other things, hospitals and second-level schools. Yet to provide a straighter border would mean leaving large numbers of people stranded on what was for them the wrong side.

It is not surprising, then, that repartition has remained very much a minority proposal. True, if compromise finally proves impossible, things could reach the point in Northern Ireland where the only alternatives left are repartition and civil war. In that case repartition, as the lesser evil, would deserve to be taken seriously. Kennedy's statement of the case for it reads cogently, and he suggests various ways in which the risks could be reduced. However, in the view of most commentators, we have not yet reached the point where all hope of compromise must be abandoned. For the present,

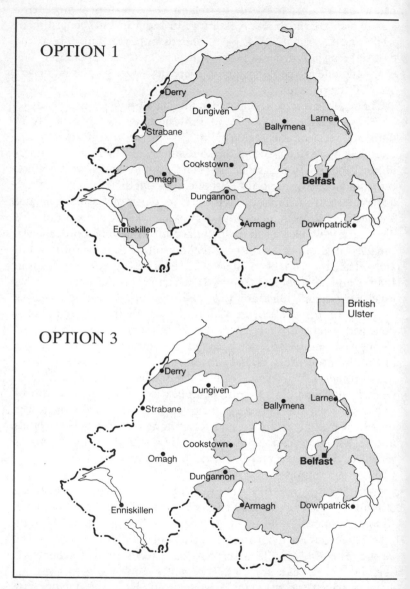

Map 10.1 Four repartition options

Source: Kennedy (1986, 59). Reprinted by permission.

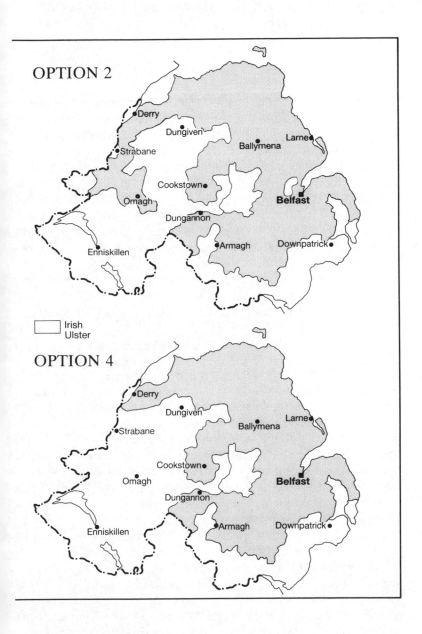

repartition has less support in the literature than any of the ten options discussed in this chapter.

7. A UNITED IRELAND BY COERCION

Another possible solution would be simply to coerce the unionists into joining a united Ireland. This strategy has been pursued by the IRA for nearly two decades. It is not absurd. Irish history shows that force has worked before. The Northern Ireland imbroglio is a drain on British lives, finance, and international prestige. Opinion polls have consistently shown that a majority of the British public are prepared to disengage (e.g. Rose *et al.* 1978, 27–9; Jowell and Airey 1984, 33; Alliance 1985, 118; Cox 1987, 348–51). It is not inconceivable that, if the pressure is kept up, some future British government would assess the national interest differently, and withdraw.

The big question is what would happen next. Traditional nationalists and traditional Marxists argue that, deprived of British support, Protestants would negotiate. For instance, Michael Farrell (1980, 333–4) has written:

At the moment Britain supplies two thirds of the full-time forces in the North and arms and pays for the rest as well as providing massive subsidies to run the area. With this backing it is easy to be intransigent. Deprived of these forces and subsidies and faced with the choice of accepting a united Ireland or fighting to establish a permanently beleaguered Protestant state few Protestants are likely to choose the latter.

This however, may be to underestimate the intensity of Protestant feelings. As was argued in Chapter 5, they seem to go beyond what is warranted by the real differences in interest involved, and to have deep psychological roots. In such circumstances, people may show more intransigence than could be justified on a rational calculus of profit and loss. Most observers believe that that is what is likely to happen. I shall take just a few examples from the many that might be cited. The Quaker author Denis Barritt (1982, 128) sees a British withdrawal as unlikely to bring peace. The distinguished anthropologist Leo Kuper, in his book *Genocide* (1981), considers that the presence of the British Army is one of the factors restraining genocide in Northern Ireland (p. 204), and that 'the removal of the British presence and the withdrawal of the British Army before a political solution is achieved would seem to be an invitation to bloodshed' (p. 206). The Alliance Commission on Northern Ireland (1985, 64–5) sees the likeliest result as being an independent Northern Ireland, civil war, and a new border. Boyle and Hadden (1985, 38) consider 'the more likely result would be the establishment of a provisional Protestant Government in Belfast and an untidy and bloody redrawing of the boundary between areas of Protestant and Catholic domination' and they note that 'no British or Irish government has accepted the case for unilateral withdrawal'. Frank Wright, in his *Northern Ireland: A Comparative Analysis* (1987) discusses chilling examples of similar situations elsewhere in the world which have degenerated into violence despite the wishes of many, perhaps most, of the people involved. Padraig O'Malley (1983, 248–51) offers an analysis of what might happen in the event of such a withdrawal: he argues that such a situation would strengthen the paramilitaries on both sides, and 'the stage would be set for an apocalyptic pogrom' (p. 250). Elsewhere (p. 95) he notes that Jack Lynch, when taoiseach, specifically disclaimed any desire for Britain to state a date for withdrawal because, as Lynch put it, 'there would be a possible build-up of preparedness by militants for that date'. A similar sentiment was expressed much more recently by the Irish Minister for Foreign Affairs, Brian Lenihan. He is reported as saying that 'the presence of British troops is an essential aspect of security in Northern Ireland at present' (*Irish Times*, 18 March 1989).

One of the fullest discussions of the possible consequences of British withdrawal has been provided by the SDLP, in an exchange of documents with Sinn Féin. The SDLP, after showing that the IRA campaign has hit hardest the nationalist people, and after pointing out that the campaign is unlikely to shift the present British Government, goes on to state:

Even if, of course, the stated objectives of the IRA were to be achieved in the manner which they have set out, we in the SDLP would argue that that would not bring peace to Ireland but would lead to much greater chaos and to permanent division and conflict among our people. . . .

In such a vacuum [i.e. of pending British withdrawal] the likelihood is that the British Army would become inactive. In the knowledge that their Government has decided to withdraw all responsibility does anyone think that soldiers would be prepared to risk their lives? Each section of the community would seize its own territory and we would have a Cyprus/

Lebanon style formula for permanent division and bloodshed. What would the 12,000 armed members of the RUC do? What would the 8,000 armed members of the UDR do? Is it not likely and natural in the emotionally charged atmosphere that would obtain, and in the absence of any acknowledged authority, that they would simply identify with the community from which most of them come and become its military defenders? And what would happen to the Catholic community in such circumstances, particularly in those areas where they are most vulnerable? (*Irish Times*, 12 September 1988.)

To this argument Sinn Féin did not even attempt an answer.

It is true that, in advance of trying the experiment of British withdrawal, no one can know for certain how it will turn out. However, one can assess probabilities, based on (1) the previous record of the group concerned, and (2) the evidence of comparable events elsewhere. As far as (1) is concerned, the previous record of the unionist community does not show evidence of flexibility. It has tended to be particularly intransigent, as Peter Gibbon pointed out in an article in the *Socialist Register* (1977, 87), when British support was uncertain, as in 1886, 1912, and 1921. He could have added 1974, and, if he were writing the article now, 1985.

As far as (2) is concerned, it is not easy to think of reassuring parallels in other parts of the world. One of the few that comes to mind is the end of independent Rhodesia, which occurred when South Africa told Ian Smith that it would no longer support him, and insisted that he make the best terms he could. On the other hand, it is possible to think of disturbing parallels—the bloodstained withdrawals of Britain from India in 1947, Palestine in 1948, and Aden in 1967, and of Portugal from Angola in 1975. It must be remembered that, for civil war to break out, it is not necessary for a majority of inhabitants to desire it. Quite small numbers of extremists on each side can force a situation where, by reprisal and counter-reprisal, the peacefully inclined majority are obliged to seek protection from, and then give support to, the paramilitaries of their own community. This is how civil war began in the Lebanon in 1975 (Gilmour 1983, 119).

To conclude, there is substantial consensus in the literature—greater than on many topics examined in this book—that a British withdrawal is more likely to bring greater bloodshed than a peaceful settlement. It is significant that no Irish government has ever asked for a simple British withdrawal.

So far, however, we have been discussing a scenario in which Britain simply withdraws. Supposing Britain not merely withdraws but, before withdrawing, actively coerces the unionists into a united Ireland? This scenario has been explored by Bob Rowthorn and Naomi Wayne in their book *Northern Ireland: The Political Economy of Conflict* (1988). They argue that Britain can offer both a stick and a carrot. The stick would be economic sanctions. 'Britain acting alone has the power to wreck the economy of such a new north-eastern state, and could do so at no cost to itself—simply by cutting off financial aid and imposing a trade boycott of the area' (p. 151). The carrot would be a continuing British financial subsidy, provided the unionists accepted Irish unity (p. 157).

This is a more realistic scenario for achieving a united Ireland than any so far put forward. Britain has resources which the IRA does not, and could apply a degree of pressure on the Protestants which would be irresistible. There would, however, be great difficulties in implementing such a plan. To do them justice, Rowthorn and Wayne recognize this, and devote a section of their book (pp. 140–65) to pointing out how the dangers could be met. They concede that the likely first result of such a policy would be a spate of attacks by unionists on Catholics, in the hope of forcing Britain to stay (p. 141). But they believe that, if Britain stands firm, emphasizes the economic advantages of acquiescence, and takes measures to minimize the attacks on Catholics, the policy can succeed. Among the measures they propose is that the Irish Army be invited in, and that the UDR and if necessary the RUC be disarmed. Their proposals, however, entail even greater risks than they realize. They overestimate the strength of the Irish Army. They ignore the difficulty which the British Army might have in disarming the UDR and RUC—forces in comradeship with whom it has served against the IRA. Most of all, they neglect to enquire whether the Catholics of Northern Ireland, who they admit would be in danger, are prepared to accept the risks which they so blithely propose on their behalf.

There are also ethical and legal difficulties for a British government seeking to coerce unionists into a State to which they do not wish to belong. The British Labour Party wishes to achieve a united Ireland, but its policy document shows that it believes it would be wrong in principle to secure that unity by coercion. 'Any democratic government should accept that where a change in sovereignty was in prospect which would affect directly the interests and citizenship of a part of its population, those thus affected should have a determining say in the question' (Labour Party 1988, para. 16). The document also points out that to abandon the requirement of consent would be to 'ignore the problems an Irish government would have in implementing unification in the absence of consent' (para. 17). Finally, a legal point is worth mentioning. It is that the majority in Northern Ireland could have a case against the government(s) of Great Britain and/or Ireland before the European Court of Justice. Boyle and Hadden (1985, 39) note that the transfer of territory from one State to another against the wishes of the majority of its inhabitants cannot be justified in contemporary international law.

8. NO-HOPE ANALYSES

We have looked at seven possible ways forward in Northern Ireland, and have found powerful objections to all of them. Perhaps the only realistic conclusion is that the Northern Ireland problem is hopeless? There is a tradition in the academic literature which reaches that conclusion. As early as 1971 Richard Rose, in his *Governing without Consensus*, concluded: 'in the foreseeable future, no solution is immediately practicable' (p. 21). Five years later, in his second book on the region, *Northern Ireland: A Time of Choice* (1976), he declared: 'Many talk about a solution to Ulster's political problem but few are prepared to say what the problem is. The reason is simple. *The problem is that there is no solution*' (Rose 1976, 139). He then proceeded to an extended survey of the possible options, showing the obstacles to each.

Other observers have been almost equally pessimistic. Frank Wright (1981), in a brilliant article, examined two competing claims—that British withdrawal is essential because otherwise the two sides will never have the incentive to work out a compromise; and that British withdrawal would be disastrous because it would lead to civil war. He suggested that the peculiar malignancy of the Northern Ireland situation is that the two claims are true at the same time (p. 200). Donald Watt, editing the collected papers of a conference at the Royal Institute of International Affairs in London, noted that 'the book re-emphasizes the enormous complexity of the problem and the unlikelihood that any quick solution is available at all' (Watt 1981, 3). Moxon-Browne (1983, 178) made a point which seems obvious when stated, but which I do not remember having seen previously. This is that the Northern Ireland problem is not one, but a cluster of problems, and 'that a remedy addressed to one of them may exacerbate at least one of the others'. I myself have published a paper (Whyte 1981*b*) in which I argued that all parties to the conflict—unionists, nationalists, and British—were pursuing policies which made the conflict worse, but that political and psychological pressures made it impossible for them to do anything else. I am delighted to say that I think I have been proved wrong, at least so far as the London and Dublin governments are concerned, because the Hillsborough agreement of 1985 showed on their part a willingness to take risks which my analysis had shown they were locked into avoiding. But the particular risks which they took have not so far produced a settlement.

However, to say that there is no solution is the most pessimistic of all conclusions, not to be adopted till every other way forward has been conclusively blocked off. The authorities just cited nearly all come from a particular period, 1976–83, after the power-sharing executive had failed, and before Anglo-Irish negotiations had yet delivered anything. A somewhat more constructive note can be detected in the most recent literature. In the remainder of this chapter I shall consider avenues of advance which have received more attention in recent years.

9. THE PURSUIT OF INTERMEDIATE OBJECTIVES

As mentioned in Chapter 9, a crop of documents appeared in the mid-1980s, analysing, and prescribing for, the Northern Ireland problem. In chronological order they were:

1. The British white paper, *Northern Ireland: A Framework for Devolution* (UK Government 1982).
2. The Haagerup Report, presented to the European Parliament (1984).
3. The Official Unionist Party document *The Way Forward* (1984).
4. The report of the New Ireland Forum (1984).
5. The report of the Kilbrandon Committee, set up by the British-Irish Association (1984). This was in effect two reports,

because although the members of the Committee could agree on many points, they could not agree on all. On some crucial issues they divided into a majority of eight members and a minority of four. The minority were more sympathetic to the unionist case than were the majority.

6. The report of the SDP/Liberal Alliance Commission on Northern Ireland (Alliance 1985).

Some of these documents favoured courses which we have already examined. The Forum report recommended a united Ireland. The Alliance document favoured another attempt at power-sharing with an Irish dimension. The Kilbrandon minority favoured a modest form of power-sharing with a limited Irish dimension. However, others explored two ways forward which had not figured prominently in the literature before.

The first of these was that, rather than attempting to reach a final settlement now, the parties should concentrate on smaller but achievable goals. This was the philosophy behind the British white paper of 1982, with its proposal for rolling devolution. As the paper put it:

The object of the Government's proposals is to point to a way whereby, in spite of their acknowledged and continuing differences, the two sides of the community may achieve sufficient mutual respect, and make sufficient mutual accommodations, to participate more creatively in the public life of the Province. (para. 18.)

A similar philosophy can be found in the Official Unionist document *The Way Forward* (1984). The paper starts from the assumption that the aspirations of the two communities are irreconcilable, and that a full solution is therefore at present unattainable. It argues, however, that that is not a reason for doing nothing:

The Ulster Unionist Party, in putting forward this document for discussion, is proposing a policy whereby reconciliation and participation of all sections of the community can be attempted from the bottom up and not imposed from the top down. The object is for all representatives to participate in government in those areas which affect citizens' daily lives and concerning which the resolution of conflict may be more feasible than on those involving the future of Northern Ireland.

The document went on to suggest a Bill of Rights, and various administrative changes which it believed could be put through with cross-community support. While insisting that any changes should be within the context of Northern Ireland, it added: 'it is the responsibility of the majority to persuade the minority that the Province is also theirs'.

A similar approach was taken by Nils Haagerup (1984) in his report to the European Parliament. He concluded that 'there is no definite solution to the problems of Northern Ireland which could expect to satisfy everybody in Northern Ireland or the large majority of the two communities' (p. 69). However, he argued that this was no reason for doing nothing, and that 'alienation could partly be overcome if measures were agreed by the British authorities in Northern Ireland in co-operation with locally elected representatives without raising the constitutional question' (pp. 72–3).

Similar strategies are proposed in some of the academic literature. Padraig O'Malley (1983, 356) suggested that there should not be a search for a solution as such, 'but rather for a framework that will accommodate a range of alternative settlements'. James O'Connell (1988, 190) has argued that 'there is need not for solutions but for process'. Moxon-Browne (1983, 178), immediately after he made the point, quoted in the last section, that the Northern Ireland problem is not one but a cluster of problems, went on to suggest:

There is a strong case for trying to create an atmosphere where the problems themselves either change, or become redefined. . . . To seek *a* solution to *the* Northern Ireland problem is to pursue a mirage in the desert: a better ploy would be to irrigate the desert until the landscape looks more inviting.

The philosophy of proceeding by small steps was put into action by the Anglo-Irish Agreement of 1985. Neither party to the agreement claimed that it was a final settlement. Each recognized that further evolution was inevitable. They disagreed as to what that evolution might be. The Secretary of State for Northern Ireland, Tom King, caused dismay in Dublin by saying that it would ensure the maintenance of the union 'unto perpetuity' (*Irish Times*, 4 December 1985), and the Irish Government made clear that that was not its view. But it was certainly not a document which left things as they were. The fury with which it was greeted in the unionist community showed that it was perceived as tipping the balance of power within Northern Ireland.

The limitation to the strategy of progress by small stages was demonstrated by the same agreement. The trouble with this strategy is that it does not make clear what long-term settlement is anticipated. Yet a government's choice of intermediate stages is presumably influenced by its vision of the long-term future of Northern Ireland. If this is not articulated, then people's suspicions are aroused, and they will draw the most hostile conclusions from its actions. This was illustrated by the aftermath of the Hillsborough agreement. The suspicions felt on both sides towards Britain, to which we have already adverted in Chapter 6, were raised even beyond their habitual levels. Unionists opposed the agreement because it would lead to a united Ireland; Fianna Fáil and the Republicans because it would not.

The policy of advancing by intermediate stages is not a policy on its own. It is bound to be shaped by the policy-makers' view of where they would like to be heading. If they do not have any such view, then they will find that, by the particular choice of intermediate steps that they have made, they have constrained their options for the future.

10. JOINT AUTHORITY

Joint authority is the second proposal to have received increased attention in the last few years. It is not an entirely new concept. Desmond Fennell suggested in a newspaper article in 1971 that Northern Ireland become a condominium of Britain and Ireland (Fennell 1985, 156). The SDLP made the same proposal in 1972 (McAllister 1977, 56), but soon dropped it in view of its acceptance of the Sunningdale scenario, of a power-sharing executive plus an Irish dimension. A pamphlet by T. J. Pickvance (1975) advocated what was in effect joint authority, in the form of an autonomous Northern Ireland under the tutelage of both Britain and the Republic. His solution was commended by the Queen's University geographers, F. W. Boal and J. N. H. Douglas (1982, 355–6). But before 1984 interest in the idea was only spasmodic.

Interest in joint authority was encouraged by the discussion of the concept in the report of the New Ireland Forum (1984, 37–8). Joint authority was not the preferred option of the Forum, but the latter did see some advantages in the arrangement—in particular that it would accord 'equal validity to the two traditions in Northern Ireland and would reflect the current reality that the people of the North are divided in their allegiances' (para. 8.1). A sub-committee of the Forum examined the concept in more detail and, while its report was not officially released, it was leaked to the press, and has been published as an appendix to the Kilbrandon report (1984, 61–70). The subcommittee's report shows that joint authority would be compatible with the existence of a local assembly and executive. It also points out an additional advantage from the Republic's point of view over an independent united Ireland, whether federal or unitary—namely, that Northern Ireland would continue to have a claim on British financial support (p. 68).

The Forum report assumed (para. 8.10) that under joint authority the London and Dublin governments would have equal responsibility. In doing this, it was following international precedent. In nearly all the twentieth-century examples of joint authority, there have been two sovereign powers wielding, legally at least, equal power. Andorra is jointly subject to the President of France and the Bishop of Urgel in Spain. The New Hebrides were jointly subject to Britain and France. The Anglo-Egyptian Sudan was jointly subject to Britain and Egypt. The difficulty with this situation is that it provides no mechanism for the resolution of deadlock. It has worked in these cases, either because one of the co-domini is in practice dominant (Sudan), or because the territory concerned is so small and remote that neither power need make a great issue about disagreements (New Hebrides, Andorra). Neither of these comforting circumstances would exist in the case of Northern Ireland. The territory is relatively large and important, and, although Britain is undoubtedly more powerful than Ireland, the latter has enough independence to ensure that its government would not be content to play puppet to London. One could forecast, then, that if Northern Ireland were to become subject to joint authority on a fifty-fifty basis, there would be endless disputes and deadlocks between the sovereign powers.

However, joint authority does not necessarily have to be on a fifty-fifty basis. Here the Kilbrandon majority made a breakthrough in the modern discussion of the Northern Ireland problem. While they rejected joint authority as proposed by the Forum (pp. 29–31), they offered as an alternative what they described as 'co-operative devolution' (pp. 46–53). Under this scheme, Northern Ireland would be governed by a five-man executive, consisting of one representative each of the United Kingdom and Irish governments, and three representatives from Northern Ireland itself (who would presumably break down in the proportion of two unionists to one nationalist). This would import more flexibility than an equal sharing of power by two co-domini. As the Kilbrandon majority point out (pp. 48–9), there would be no automatic majorities on such an authority. While on some issues the line-up would no doubt be British plus unionists against northern and southern nationalists, on others the British might vote with the nationalists, and there could even be cases where the three local representatives would unite against the representatives of Britain and the Republic. The arrangement would also be proof against boycotting (p. 49). If the representatives of one community in Northern Ireland boycotted the meetings, that would simply enhance the weight of the other community.

The proposals of the Kilbrandon majority have been criticized by the Alliance Commission on Northern Ireland (1985, 66–7). The Commission argues that the Kilbrandon scheme would deprive the people of Northern Ireland of effective responsibility for their own affairs, that it would still be a form of direct rule, and that Britain would still be blamed for the problems of Northern Ireland. It also sees constitutional difficulties in Britain and the Republic.

However, these are objections to the specific form of joint authority advocated by the Kilbrandon majority. They would not necessarily apply to all forms of joint authority. The concept has been explored further in a paper by a political scientist at Keele University, Martin Dent (1988). Dent points out that the joint authority need not necessarily administer the region directly: it could delegate authority to an administrator, who would best be an outsider. If it was relieved of day-to-day management, it could be enlarged in size, and could include representatives of the people of Northern Ireland. Dent also suggests dividing power between the governing authority and a locally elected assembly, a proposal which would partly meet one Alliance objection to the Kilbrandon Report—that the people of Northern Ireland would not be responsible for their own affairs.

Finally, a couple of relevant points are made by an inter-Church working party on human rights in the United Kingdom and Ireland (Bailey 1988). Its report points out (p. 63) that there is one recent precedent for joint authority being shared between more than two partners. The Moroccan city of Tangier was under international control between 1923 and 1956. Its legislative assembly contained representatives of the local people and of no fewer than eight foreign powers. The report also notes (pp. 62–3) that there are a number of instances where an outside power has been given a say, falling short of joint sovereignty but going beyond a mere right of consultation, in the territory of another power. After the First World War, Germany and Poland signed a treaty providing safeguards for their respective minorities in Upper Silesia. Finland negotiated an agreement with Sweden regarding the status of the Åland Islands, which were under Finnish sovereignty but had a Swedish population. The United Nations has recognized the legitimate concern of Austria in the treatment by Italy of the German-speaking population in the South Tyrol. So joint authority does not have to be shared between two partners on a fifty-fifty basis. There are examples both of its being exercised by more than two parties, and of a balance of power which is somewhere in between fifty-fifty and one-hundred-to-zero.

Several points can be made in favour of joint authority. It responds to the analysis of the Northern Ireland problem as one of a clash of identities—an analysis which, as we saw in Part I, has attracted a substantial measure of acceptance. It is the logical goal towards which the Anglo-Irish Agreement of 1985 seems to be pointing, whether or not its signatories intended that fact. There is some ground for arguing that it is the point towards which various forces in the conflict appear to be converging—unionists' adamant refusal to be ruled by Dublin; nationalists' insistence on symbolic as well as practical equality in Northern Ireland; the declining interest of opinion in the south in outright unification; and possibly a British readiness for detachment from the problem without taking the risk of abandoning all say in how it should be handled.

On the other hand, there are enormous difficulties in the way of joint authority. In its commonest form of two sovereigns having equal powers, it is too rigid to work. In the innovative form pioneered by the Kilbrandon majority and developed by Martin Dent, where there may be more than two partners, and where power need not be divided equally between them, it is a relatively untried device, and much trial and error may be necessary before a proper balance between the parts is found. There would be difficulties in reconciling it with the much-repeated pledge by British governments that Northern Ireland may remain part of the United Kingdom so long as the majority of its people wish. True, it has never been precisely defined what membership of the United Kingdom means, and a formula might be found whereby joint authority was reconciled with such membership—but it would require prodigies of draughtsmanship.

A joint-authority framework would come under immense pressure from both sides. On the one hand, Protestants would look on it as a staging-post on the way to a united Ireland—the Official Unionists and the Democratic Unionists have already condemned joint authority on that ground (Kenny 1986, 58). If most Protestants have opposed the compromise of power-sharing-with-an-Irish-dimension, how much more likely are they to reject the compromise of joint authority, which is weighted more heavily against them. The only way it could be made relatively attractive would be if it were presented as a final goal and not a half-way house. The Kilbrandon majority in commending the arrangement recognized this need, and stated that 'co-operative devolution can only be made acceptable if it is clearly accepted as a durable solution, and not as a method of coercing unionists into a united Ireland' (1984, 51). That would entail the repeal of Articles 2 and 3 of the Republic's Constitution, and declarations from all parties in the Republic that they did not even seek a united Ireland unless it was with the freely given consent of a majority in Northern Ireland. Unless such an undertaking were forthcoming, joint authority is a non-starter. Even if it were forthcoming, the problem of IRA violence, and how best to meet it, would remain, and could be expected to heighten tensions between the communities in Northern Ireland.

It has been worth devoting some space to joint authority because, at least in the innovative forms proposed by the Kilbrandon majority and Martin Dent, it is the most original idea to have been thrown up in the last few years. It has been favoured by at least two other recent academic writers: Brendan O'Leary (1985, 40) and Frank Wright (1987, p. xiv; 1989). However, it remains very much a minority recommendation.

CONCLUSION

We have examined ten possible approaches to the Northern Ireland problem. All face serious difficulties. None has anywhere near approaching majority support in the literature. Just where consensus is most desirable it breaks down most completely.

One clue to the reason for this may be found in an idea which recurred in Part I of this book. This is that, small though Northern Ireland is, it contains a great variety of situations within it. There are places like south Armagh, which are defiantly nationalist. There are places like north Down, which are happily unionist. There are places like Buckley's Upper Tullagh, where unionist and nationalist intermingle, but without the bitterness that is to be found in some other areas. If any one of these types of place existed on its own, there would be no problem. If the whole region had been like south Armagh, Northern Ireland would never have been set up as a separate entity. If it had all been like north Down, the IRA would have found no chink from which to operate, constitutional nationalists would long since have despaired of ever converting such people, and Northern Ireland would probably have been integrated with the rest of the United Kingdom. If it had all been like Upper Tullagh, some compromise could long since have been worked out. But Northern Ireland contains south Armaghs and north Downs and Upper Tullaghs, and every conceivable variety of situation in between. Perhaps it is unrealistic to look for a single solution covering the region as a whole. Perhaps the search for a solution in future should envisage the possibility that different arrangements will be required in different areas.

11

Implications

In the final chapter of this book I wish to offer some reflections on the preceding material. I shall discuss in turn: (1) how far has common ground been established among researchers into the problem?; (2) why has research on the problem not been more effective in helping towards a solution of the problem?; (3) how far, notwithstanding the limited effectiveness of research to date, has research into the Northern Ireland problem been worth while?; and (4) is there any way in which future research can be made more fruitful?

HOW MUCH COMMON GROUND?

Researchers appear to have reached *unanimity* only on the barest matters of fact. Everyone accepts that Northern Ireland was established as a separate unit in 1921; that its government and Parliament were suspended in 1972; that the Anglo-Irish Agreement was signed at Hillsborough in 1985; and so on. But the moment we go on to examine the significance of those events, disagreement breaks in.

However, this does not mean that disagreement is total. There appears to be *substantial* agreement among researchers on a number of issues. By 'substantial' I mean that one interpretation emerges as a clear favourite, being supported by more writers than all the alternatives put together. Among such areas of substantial agreement are the following:

1. The conflict is to be seen primarily as one between the communities in Northern Ireland. This does not mean that the British or the Irish governments are exempt from responsibility, or that there is no class conflict: but it does mean that in the view of the majority of commentators, these are not the most important factors in the situation.
2. The two communities are deeply but not totally divided. Though the factors dividing them are more important than the factors uniting them, the latter do exist.

3. Catholics are at a substantial disadvantage, economically and socially, as compared with Protestants.
4. The division between the communities comprises a mixture of religious, economic, political, and psychological elements.
5. Protestants on average are more concerned to maintain the border than Catholics are to do away with it; although a substantial number of Catholics feel as strongly opposed to the border as most Protestants feel in favour of it.
6. In contrast Protestants are more uncertain about their national identity than are Catholics. Most Catholics describe themselves as 'Irish', while Protestants have been more inclined to tack between the labels 'British', 'Ulster', and even 'Irish'.

However, those are generalizations. The moment we attempt to bring more precision into the conclusions, we find a more *limited* amount of agreement:

1. While the majority of authors agree that the primary conflict is between two communities in Northern Ireland, even those who agree on this point vary among themselves about how much subsidiary responsibility should be attributed to British and/or Irish policy.
2. While most authors agree that the division between the communities is substantial but not total, they disagree among themselves on where to put the emphasis as between factors making for division and factors making for integration.
3. There is no consensus on the most appropriate labels to use for the two communities. 'Protestant' and 'Catholic' is one possible pair; 'unionist' and 'nationalist', or even 'Ulster British' and 'Ulster Irish' are other possibles. The religious labels are the most commonly used, but they are not universal.
4. While there is agreement that Catholics are at a disadvantage as compared with Protestants, there is less agreement on how extensive that disadvantage is, or the reasons for it. In particular, there is substantial disagreement on how far the disadvantage is due to discrimination.
5. While there is agreement that the conflict results from a mixture of religious, economic, political, and psychological factors, there is no agreement on their relative importance. In particular, there is a divergence of view on how much stress to put on religion.

There is widespread *disagreement* on some issues. The most important of these is the most practical—namely, what should be done? Even those who substantially agree in their diagnosis of the problem reach no consensus on how to resolve it.

Thus, after twenty years of study by hundreds of researchers, there is still only partial agreement on the nature of the problem, and none at all on the nature of the solution.

WHY HAS RESEARCH ON THE NORTHERN IRELAND PROBLEM NOT BEEN MORE EFFECTIVE?

If research could solve a problem, the Northern Ireland conflict should by now have been settled several times over. As was mentioned in the Preface, the amount done has been prodigious, and Northern Ireland is possibly the most heavily researched area in the world. Yet despite all this hard work, the problem endures. Why is this?

I shall suggest five reasons. The first is that people simply do not read research. This certainly seems to be true if one compares the distribution of opinion among researchers with the distribution of opinion in the wider public. Previous chapters have shown that, as far as researchers are concerned, traditional nationalists and traditional unionists are now very much in the minority. They are not so much of a minority in the wider public. One has only to read the letters to the editor in the newspapers of Dublin and Belfast to see that a considerable number of people still hold traditional views, and appear to be unaware of the research findings which have led more scholarly nationalists and unionists to modify their positions. The ignorance can go to the highest political levels. Gerry Adams in his two books (1986 and 1988) purveys a case hardly different from that of Frank Gallagher (1957) and ignores the evidence which has caused many scholars brought up in the nationalist tradition to query its assumptions. The Official Unionist Party, in its document *The Way Forward* (1984) denies that 'there is any foundation in reality for any feeling of minority discrimination or disadvantage', despite the massive evidence surveyed in a preceding chapter which shows that there is substantial foundation for such feelings. The best research in the world can be of no effect if those with power to influence the course of events show no interest in its findings.

A second reason why research may be ineffective lies in the bias of the recipients. Some people find it too painful to accept research which runs counter to their psychological needs. Jonathon Moore (1988) has described the fury with which some of the Irish in Britain have received revisionist historiography. Subjected to abuse and ridicule in their everyday lives, they 'have often found solace in reminding themselves of their victimised past'. Revisionist history threatens to deprive them of the heroes they need. Eamonn McCann (1974, 119) has found a similar reaction in the Catholic ghettos of Northern Ireland. 'Some people need myths, need them to glorify their history in order to push away the grim reality of the way they have to live now.' Nor is this reaction confined to the nationalist Irish. The difficulty which many unionists have in accepting that they ran an unjust regime, or that many British have in accepting that their Army sometimes misbehaves, may be examples of the same need to maintain a positive image of one's own group.

However, not everyone is prejudiced beyond reach of argument. Whatever about readers, certainly some researchers have been prepared to modify their views in the light of fresh evidence. I have come across a number of examples while preparing this book. Michael Farrell's second book, *Arming the Protestants* (1983) shows more understanding of the problems facing the new regime in Northern Ireland than his first book, *Northern Ireland: The Orange State* (1976). Patrick Buckland's earlier volumes, *Irish Unionism, i, The Anglo-Irish and the New Ireland 1885–1922* (1972), and *Irish Unionism, ii, Ulster Unionism and the Origins of Northern Ireland 1886–1922* (1973) showed a sympathy with unionism which was dented by his discoveries in the archives when he went on to examine the regime set up by the unionists in his book *The Factory of Grievances* (1979). The antagonists in the *British Journal of Sociology* debate on the degree of discrimination in Northern Ireland— Hewitt (1981, 1983, 1985, 1987) and O'Hearn (1983, 1985, 1987)— moved perceptibly closer to each other's positions, despite their combative tone. The most striking example of an ability to change one's mind is shown by the rise of the revisionist Marxists. Most of the members of this school began, to my personal knowledge, as traditional Marxists. But the weight of evidence persuaded them that the assumptions with which they started out could not be sustained. However, it must also be pointed out that the majority of Marxists remain in the traditional camp.

There is a third reason why researchers may not have been able to reach a greater measure of agreement on the nature of the Northern Ireland problem. This is that the evidence is not sufficient to sustain conclusions that are beyond question. Northern Ireland may be one of the most heavily researched areas in the world, but the research done there still falls far short of a comprehensive knowledge of the situation. Dozens of attitude surveys have been conducted, but the questions asked have been a small minority of the questions worth raising. Two dozen participant-observation studies have been carried out, but that leaves hundreds of locations which have not been investigated. And even if an attitude survey or a participant-observation study was exhaustive at the time it was carried out, the course of events would before long render it out of date. The complexity of human society is such that it could not be fully captured, even by a programme of research far more extensive than that carried out in Northern Ireland.

A fourth reason why agreement is difficult lies in the particular circumstances of Northern Ireland. Research is undoubtedly more difficult there than in more peaceful areas of the world. We have already come across examples. In Chapter 1 it was noted that attitude surveys seem to exaggerate moderate opinion and underestimate extreme views, and so must be treated with reserve. It was also noted that participant-observers have an understandable preference for peaceful areas of the region, with the result that strife-torn areas are somewhat underrepresented in the literature. A sociologist who has worked in Northern Ireland, Rupert Taylor, has collected a number of examples of how research can be hampered. Government may be reluctant to release sensitive data (Taylor 1988*a*, 129), and there are instances of it suppressing or delaying the publication of research (p. 130). In hard-line areas researchers may be an object of suspicion, and there have been cases of researchers being driven out or even shot (pp. 136–9). True, the difficulties can be exaggerated. Richard Jenkins, the anthropologist who studied Ballyhightown, has described the obstacles which he faced (Jenkins 1984). The suspicion shown to him by paramilitaries was one of them, but he puts more stress on the problems of a male in researching the female half of a community, and on the general problems of participant-observation research anywhere. I felt myself that Taylor's article, by concentrating on those research projects which have run into trouble and devoting little space to the considerable number which have not, made the situation seem somewhat bleaker than it really is. None the less, it is clear that special problems attach to research in Northern Ireland. Since Taylor published his article, there has been a further illustration of it. Robert Miller (1988), a sociologist who had done work for the Fair Employment Agency on the Northern Ireland civil service, has published an article showing the difficulties in which a researcher can innocently involve himself if he attempts to publish findings which are unpalatable to powerful institutions.

A fifth reason why there is no total agreement on the nature of the Northern Ireland problem lies in the limitations of the human mind itself. Even if everyone read all the research; even if everyone was completely unbiased in studying it; even if the amount of research done was far more extensive than it has been; there would still be the problem of comprehending it. The human mind is unable to grasp the full complexity of a social situation. We need an organizing principle, some thread to guide us through the intricacies. Publishers insist on this from their authors. University teachers insist on it from their graduate students. If the organizing principle is not there, the book or thesis becomes just a jumble of facts, which no reader will accept. However, an organizing principle entails emphasizing some theme which the author thinks important so as to clarify reality. That brings with it the inevitable corollary—that other factors, really present, will be de-emphasized so as not to obscure the dominating theme. To organize is to simplify. To simplify is to distort. Writers who simplify reality in order to clarify it are by that very action making sure that the picture they put across is incomplete.

An analogy might be drawn with that of a cartographer, trying to put on a plane surface a representation of the global surface of the earth. It cannot be done with accuracy. Whichever projection the cartographer uses will create a distortion. Mercator's projection will ensure that the cardinal points are always in the correct relative positions, but only at the cost of grotesque distortions in the relative size of land masses. An equal-area projection will ensure that the land masses have their correct relative size, but only at the cost of distorting their shapes. Projections have been devised which keep both size and shapes of land masses approximately accurate, but only at the cost of disrupting the representation of the much larger water surfaces of the globe.

Yet cartographers are less badly off than social scientists. Cartographers at least know the approximate real shape of the globe which they are mapping. They can calculate the degree and nature of distortion which their choice of projection will produce. Social scientists do not know the 'real' shape of the phenomenon they are studying. It is as if they are mapping, not a globe, but some planet of highly irregular shape whose true contours are not even known. To make the analogy more precise, we may also posit that the shape of the planet is constantly changing, but in an unknown manner. Researchers know, as they plot segments of this planet on two-dimensional maps, that they are certainly distorting the reality of a three-dimensional surface—but they do not know by how much or in what ways. Perhaps the only way forward is for different cartographers, working on different assumptions about the real shape of their planet, to go ahead with their mapping, and see which set of maps proves in the long run to be the most useful.

In a sense that is what has been done by the researchers whose work has been studied in preceding chapters. They can be seen as four different teams—the traditional nationalists, the traditional unionists, the Marxists, and the internal-conflict theorists. Each has in effect taken a different projection. The preceding discussion has shown that the internal-conflict theorists' projection is the one that has been accepted as the most widely satisfactory. But it is still only a projection—an attempt to put on a two-dimensional surface a three-dimensional reality. Other projections may depict parts of that reality more accurately—hence their continuing popularity with some researchers.

The critique just suggested applies, of course, to this book. I too have had to find a guiding thread. By adopting my fourfold classification of researchers, divided according to the conflict which they most stress, I too have emphasized one aspect of reality and therefore downplayed others. My simplification brings together in the same category authors who in their own view might have important differences. I put traditional and revisionist Marxists together. I included among internal-conflict theorists authorities who differ sharply among themselves on the weight to be put on different factors in the conflict. Any kind of classification is bound to create incongruities like these.

It would be worth completing this section by discussing other simplifications—other projections—which have been used. The first classification of interpretations of the Northern Ireland problem that I know of was made in a review article by the distinguished

Dutch political scientist Arend Lijphart (1975*b*). Lijphart, surveying six recent books on Northern Ireland, detected ten different models of the situation employed by the authors:

1. A binational or multinational State
2. A religiously divided society
3. A plural society. (The term 'plural society' had been used previously by M. G. Smith (1969) to describe a society which is deeply divided into subgroups, in which the subgroups do not have equal rights, and in which there is a lack of any basic consensus in society.)
4. A biracial society
5. A colony
6. A fragment society. (The term 'fragment society' had been used by Louis Hartz (1964) to describe settler societies outside Europe which had tended to become frozen in their values at the time of settlement.)
7. An arena of guerrilla warfare
8. An arena of class struggle
9. A pseudo-democracy
10. A besieged democracy

Lijphart concluded (p. 96) that 'Northern Ireland can be understood best as a plural society, our understanding being complemented by images of the country as a colony, a fragment society and a majority dictatorship.' There were limitations to taking Lijphart's list as the framework for this book. Some of his models shade into each other, and his list would need to be supplemented by models—such as Harold Jackson's (1971) 'double minority'—to be found in other works besides the ones which he reviewed. However, his article offers an alternative principle on which to classify interpretations.

The year after Lijphart published his article, John Darby of the New University of Ulster at Coleraine, in his book *Conflict in Northern Ireland: The Development of a Polarised Community* (1976), included a chapter (pp. 162–97) on 'Theories about the Conflict'. He classified them as follows:

1. Universal aspects
   (a) economic theories
   (b) racial/ethnic theories
   (c) caste theories

    (d) psychiatric theories
    (e) comparative studies
2. Irish aspects
    (a) the nationalist view
    (b) the unionist view
    (c) the two-nations theory

This is a more complicated organization than the one I have adopted, and some of the sub-categories are quite small: to take the extreme case, the heading 'caste theories' covers a single unpublished paper by Patrick McNabb (1971). However, it does enable Darby to bring out things which my classification obscured. In particular, his broad first classification into 'universal aspects' and 'Irish aspects' leads him to bring out a contrast in merit between the two. He notes:

Comparative studies and general theories of conflict are useful for providing insights. But it is noticeable that those researchers who approached the Northern problem from the basis of a more general theoretical background and who also took the trouble to examine the background to the problem in detail invariably were forced to make major readjustments to their original premises. Northern Ireland is at least as remarkable for its peculiarities as for its general characteristics. (p. 197.)

This squares with my own experience. I have read very widely in the general literature on conflict, hoping to pick up ideas which would help me to understand the Northern Ireland problem more clearly. It has been largely a waste of time. I have found it more profitable to read accounts of specific conflicts in particular places abroad, which have sometimes given me useful insights.

More recently, John Hunter contributed 'An Analysis of the Conflict in Northern Ireland' to the volume edited by Desmond Rea, *Political Co-operation in Divided Societies: A Series of Papers Relevant to the Conflict in Northern Ireland* (1982, 9–59). In this well-researched paper he classified theories of the conflict under four headings:

1. political theories
2. religious theories
3. economic theories
4. psychological theories

Hunter drew the conclusion that, while all these theories help to explain the conflict, some are more important than others, and he singled out the political ones (p. 53).

Hunter's four categories are identical with four that I have used myself—but in Part I of this book, where I was discussing the nature of the community divide, not in Part II, where I was discussing interpretations of the Northern Ireland problem. I consider that the classification which I use in Part II has some advantages. It brings out the contrasts between different authors' views of who the principal antagonists are. But Hunter's has advantages too. It enables him to concentrate more than I have done on the controversy about the relative importance of the religious and the political. Whichever classification we adopt there are, inevitably, gains and losses.

A more recent classification has been offered by Brendan O'Leary in his article 'Explaining Northern Ireland: A Brief Study Guide' (1985). He categorizes the explanations as follows:

1. Exogenous
   (a) nationalist
   (b) nationalist Marxist
   (c) unionist
   (d) unionist Marxist
2. Endogenous
   (a) atavistic
   (b) psychological
   (c) The 'no-nation' theory. (This is a reference to David Miller's theory (1978), according to which unionists are not a separate nation, but operate according to a pre-national, contractarian theory.)
   (d) an arena of relative deprivation
   (e) a plural society

O'Leary's schema is more successful in covering the exogenous than the endogenous theories. Among the latter there are a number which he does not examine. However, it has its strengths. In effect O'Leary groups together my first three categories—traditional nationalist, traditional unionist, and Marxist—into one super-category, the exogenous. This has the advantage of bringing out that endogenous theories—the equivalent of my internal-conflict approach—are comparable in importance to all the exogenous theories put together.

One might ask—why not combine the various classifications and so gain the advantages of all of them? The answer is that this would produce a schema so impossibly complicated that it could not be expected to hold the reader's attention. We are like cartographers choosing between different projections. If we use one, we cannot simultaneously use the others. We are, once again, up against the limitations of the human mind. It does not have the span to grasp simultaneously all the complexities of a social situation. We have to simplify. To simplify is to distort. That is why no social-science theory can ever be fully satisfactory.

HAS RESEARCH ON THE NORTHERN IRELAND PROBLEM BEEN WORTH WHILE?

If it is impossible to achieve fully satisfactory results, the question then arises—has research on the Northern Ireland problem been worth while? There is a case for saying that it has not. Despite the enormous amount of research done on the region over the last twenty years, its problems are as intractable as ever. One could draw a contrast with the last round of troubles in Ireland, in 1916–23. Then, there were no attitude surveyors, no participant-observers at work in the country. Yet the people muddled through to some kind of settlement. From Irish experience one might deduce that research actually does harm: that the more work is done on a problem, the longer it takes to solve it. I do not put that forward altogether seriously—there were other reasons besides a mere absence of academics why the last round of troubles proved easier to bring to an end. But it could be argued from Irish experience that research does not seem to do much good. Indeed in a previous publication, entitled *Is Research on the Northern Ireland Problem Worth While?* (Whyte 1983a), I did raise the question whether it had any value.

However, though I still feel oppressed by the disparity between the effort put into research and the results achieved, I feel that I may have been unduly pessimistic on that occasion. In the first place, one can point to cases where research has had a practical effect. The Belfast Areas of Need programme of the late 1970s developed from research undertaken in the Geography Department of Queen's University for the Community Relations Commission (Boal *et al.* 1974). Work done by all three of Northern Ireland's third-level institutions in the late 1970s provided ammunition for the early stages of the Fair Employment Agency's work. If I had to single out one item for its impact on policy it would be Edmund Aunger's article in the *Economic and Social Review* for October 1975 on 'Religion and Occupational Class in Northern Ireland'. By demonstrating the extent of the economic gap between Protestant and Catholic, this article opened up an area which could not easily be ignored by policy-makers. That does not mean that Aunger opened up this field single-handed. There were several other factors at work. The Van Straubenzee Report (1973) had already recommended setting up a Fair Employment Agency. Such an Agency was set up in 1976, thus providing an institution whose job it was to look at inequality of opportunity between the communities. The Fair Employment Agency might never have developed the clout which it actually did by the mid-1980s had it not been for the campaign in the United States to discourage American firms from investing in Northern Ireland except in circumstances where discrimination was outlawed. But it was Aunger's article which first provided a factual underpinning to complaints of economic inequality.

There are not many areas where the impact of research on policy is as clear as in Aunger's case. This does not mean that most research is without effect, however. Studies have been done in both Britain and the United States (well summarized in Martin Bulmer's book *Social Science and Social Policy*, 1986) on the impact of research on policy, and the conclusion appears to be that the effects are indirect and hard to observe. The most usual influence is according to what is called the 'enlightenment model', whereby researchers influence the climate of opinion in which policy is carried out. Nor does an increased volume of research necessarily make things clearer. As an American scholar, Carol Weiss (cited in Bulmer 1986, 39) has put it:

As more studies are done, they often elaborate rather than simplify. They generate complex, varied and even contradictory views of the social phenomena under study, rather than cumulating into sharper and more coherent explanation. The effect may be to widen and enrich our understanding of the multiple facets of reality, but the implications for policy are *less* simple and clear cut.

So, if researchers in Northern Ireland sometimes find that their results are confused or contradictory, they need not lose heart: their experience matches that of researchers in other parts of the world. Indeed the degree of consensus reached among researchers in Northern Ireland is, in comparison with cases one can think of elsewhere, quite gratifying. There are other areas of social research (for instance, on the reasons for Britain's economic decline and the remedies that should be applied) which generate sharper disagreement.

One way of judging whether the research done on Northern Ireland has been worth while is by asking ourselves what difference it would have made if the volume of research available in 1988 had been available when the troubles broke out in 1968. It might have meant that demands and expectations on all sides would have been more realistic. The civil rights movement concentrated on easily demonstrable abuses such as the gerrymandering of local authorities and the bias displayed by such authorities in appointments and housing allocations. These abuses were almost wholly put right by the reforms of 1968–73, yet the troubles continued. Part of the reason is that further grievances had arisen in the meantime—most notably the heavy-handed security measures used to oppose the IRA offensive. But part of the reason also is that the civil rights movement had not accurately identified all the imbalances existing even before 1968. If we had known as much then as we know now about, for instance, the differential employment patterns of Protestant and Catholic, an earlier beginning might have been made to tackling what has become a major source of grievance in the Catholic community.

On the other side, unionist reactions to the civil rights movement were fuelled by inaccurate perceptions of attitudes in the Catholic community. Many unionists saw Catholics as irremediably hostile to the State, and interpreted the civil rights movement, not as an attempt to secure a square deal within Northern Ireland, but as an attempt to undermine it. Some of them would probably have believed this whatever the evidence; but if the amount of survey and other data now available about Catholic attitudes had been available then, more of them might have been reassured, and therefore more willing to compromise.

As far as southern nationalists are concerned, their perceptions might have been different if the amount of historical scholarship available now had been available then. Although, as we saw in Chapter 6, the traditional nationalist version of history was already beginning to come under scrutiny by the 1960s, it had not yet been systematically examined, and there was still a widespread underestimation in the south about how seriously unionists held their beliefs. If the volume of research now published on the development of unionism had been available then, perhaps perceptions would have been more realistic.

It might be retorted that if Northern Ireland, and Ireland in general, had been capable of producing such research in 1968, then there would never have been so much conflict in the first place. That is probably true, but it does not alter the fact that research puts knowledge in the hands of policy-makers, and of the groups which hope to influence them.

I can make the point best by using, for one last time, my cartographic analogy. I suggested above that researchers are like cartographers trying to map the surface of a planet of highly irregular but unknown shape. Their results will certainly be distorted, but no one knows how much or in what way. None the less, there is little doubt that space explorers would prefer to have maps of uncertain reliability than to have no maps at all. Similarly, policy-makers would rather have some information than none at all. It is the modest but undeniable contribution of researchers that they can provide such information.

HOW CAN FUTURE RESEARCH BE MADE MORE FRUITFUL?

I ended the last section on a mildly optimistic note. I concluded that research in Northern Ireland might be of some use after all. However, a question remains: is there any way of helping researchers to do better?

I can offer one suggestion, but before making it I must attempt a brief foray into the philosophy of the sciences, social and natural. I have already mentioned the philosopher of science Thomas S. Kuhn. He applied the term 'paradigm' to a body of accepted theory on which research in a given area is predicated. He saw science as developing not just cumulatively, but in a series of leaps. He saw a paradigm as winning acceptance because it explained what scientists regarded as the leading problems in that particular field. But no paradigm settles all problems. As a science develops, so more and more phenomena are discovered which the prevailing paradigm fails to explain (Kuhn 1970, 52–65). These cause discomfort and a need for new theories, until eventually a new paradigm emerges which is thought by the relevant scientific community to solve what it now considers the most important problems (pp. 77–91).

Philosophers of science dispute among themselves as to how well Kuhn describes how science develops. Whatever about science in general, Kuhn's picture does seem to describe quite well what has happened in the scholarly study of Northern Ireland. I suggested at the end of Chapter 7 that the traditional nationalist and traditional unionist interpretations shared the same paradigm. Though they disagreed on the answers they gave to the question, they agreed on what was the important question to ask. It was: 'which external actor is mainly responsible for the problem in Northern Ireland—is it Britain or the Republic?' They emphasized in their analysis the external relations of Northern Ireland.

Both the traditional nationalist and traditional unionist interpretations have lost their popularity. As the previous discussion has shown, the most popular view now is what I have called the internal-conflict interpretation. According to this interpretation, the crucial conflict is between the communities in Northern Ireland. Though this conflict is influenced by the relations which Northern Ireland has with Britain on the one hand and the Republic on the other, those relations are not the heart of it. There would still be tensions between the two communities no matter what wider framework was adopted for the region. This interpretation can be considered the dominant paradigm over the last twenty years. As was shown in Chapter 9, it underpins a substantial majority of the writings on Northern Ireland. Indeed most of the work surveyed in Part I, on the nature of the community divide, can be seen as exploring the implications of this paradigm.

The shift to the internal-conflict paradigm was certainly an improvement. It led researchers on Northern Ireland to look into aspects which had been often neglected. But the fact that disagreement continues about the nature of the conflict shows that the paradigm has not solved all difficulties. Perhaps the time has come when we should start looking for a new paradigm.

What shape a new paradigm is likely to take I do not know. Kuhn (1970, 90) suggests that the fundamental innovations of a new paradigm are almost always due to either very young men or to men very new to the field. I can hardly claim to fall into either of those categories, so it is unlikely that the new paradigm will come from me. All the same, I should like to draw attention to a factor that has recurred in the preceding discussion. This is the contrast between one part of Northern Ireland and another. Areas only a few miles from each other can differ enormously—in religious mix, in economic circumstances, in the level of violence, in political attitudes. This means that the nature and intensity of the conflict can vary widely. That in turn means that the nature of a settlement likely to bring peace can vary widely too. Perhaps the next stage in the development of research in Northern Ireland will be a greater concentration on these sub-regional variations.

However, this suggestion is only tentative. What I suggest with more confidence is that the internal-conflict interpretation is beginning to outlive its usefulness. I suspect that even now researchers are articulating the theories which will lead to a new paradigm. In retrospect the importance of this book may lie in the fact that it surveys a distinct era in research on Northern Ireland. It covers a period of twenty years or so in which the internal-conflict interpretation has been dominant.

Appendix A. The CSSRI Research Programme

In the Preface I referred to the programme of research into the Northern Ireland conflict initiated by the Committee for Social Science Research in Ireland (CSSRI). Since no report on this programme has so far been published, I shall provide such a report here. I shall include some information on the CSSRI itself.

The Committee for Social Science Research in Ireland had its origins in 1973, when the Ford Foundation made a grant of $250,000 to help develop the social sciences in Ireland. A committee of economists, sociologists, and political scientists from both parts of Ireland was set up to administer the grant. The chairman was Professor R. D. C. Black, an economist at the Queen's University of Belfast. I was one of the fourteen original members. To begin with we operated under the ponderous title of 'The Committee for the Administration of the Ford Foundation Grant for Social Science Research in Ireland'. I think I am right in saying that no member of the committee had previous experience of serving on a research council or grant-giving body, so to a great extent we were learning as we went along. In our early days our approach was relatively passive. We circulated universities and research institutes, inviting them to submit proposals for specific research projects in the social sciences, and awarded grants to those that we thought most deserving. In so far as we had a focus, it was Europe. The Republic of Ireland and the United Kingdom had just joined the European Community, and this was expected to have effects which would be worth examining.

The next development came in June 1974 when the chairman of the committee reported to us on a visit he had recently made to the United States. He warned us that we were unlikely to receive further funding unless we developed a coherent programme based on a particular problem or problems. During the second half of 1974, the committee discussed what problem(s) it might choose. A number of ideas were discussed before the committee reached a decision at its meeting on 7 December 1974. The key factor, as I remember it, was an impassioned plea from Professor Norman Gibson of the New University of Ulster. He argued that there was no more important problem on the island than the conflict going on in the north, and that we ought therefore to concentrate our resources on that subject. His argument was accepted.

The first attempt at developing a programme of research took the form of approaches, by individual members of the committee, to scholars who were known to have appropriate interests, asking them to submit proposals in the general area of the conflict. This process, which took up the first part of

1975, proved disappointing. Most of those approached already had research commitments, and, while they generally expressed interest, they failed, even though funding was promised, to make submissions. Only one firm proposal emerged from this phase—John Darby of the New University of Ulster put forward a project for examining the segregated education system in Northern Ireland.

At its meeting on 12 June 1975, therefore, the committee decided on a different approach. As one of its members, I was mandated to examine the existing literature, identify research needs, propose an integrated programme for meeting them, and find researchers willing to undertake the programme. I spent the second half of 1975 on this task. I was helped by a lively workshop, held at Wynn's Hotel in Dublin on 17–18 October under the chairmanship of Professor Edmund Dougan of University College Galway, and attended by fifteen social scientists with varying backgrounds and interests. The advice which emerged from this workshop, and which was subsequently endorsed by the full committee at a meeting on 12 December 1975, was that two main types of research should be encouraged—attitude surveys and participant-observation studies.

The new focus in the committee's policy appeared to enhance its fundraising capacities. The Ford Foundation gave a further grant. A number of other grants were received from various sources, most of them earmarked for the conflict-research programme. To recognize the fact that the committee no longer dispensed funds solely from the Ford Foundation, it changed its name in 1977 to the shorter 'Committee for Social Science Research in Ireland'.

The committee set up a subcommittee to co-ordinate its programme of research into the conflict. I was the convenor. The members were the project directors, with the addition of Professor Damian Hannan of the Economic and Social Research Institute, Dublin. This subcommittee met eight times, and its meetings proved a useful forum for the exchange of ideas. Research assistants were also invited, and other scholars with relevant interests when appropriate.

THE RESEARCH PROGRAMME

The following paragraphs list the projects supported by the committee. Though suggestions for the programme came from me, decisions were taken by the committee as a whole. The name of the principal investigator, the date of commencement, and the results are given in each case. It will be noted that the dates of commencement vary. This is because increases in the committee's funds made possible additions to the projects (nos. 1, 2, 3, 5, and 7) initially sponsored.

1. *A study of the effects of segregated education* (John Darby, The New University of Ulster, commenced 1975). As mentioned above, this project was the only one to materialize from the committee's first trawl for projects, in the first half of 1975. It did not fit into the committee's subsequent scheme for favouring (*a*) attitude surveys and (*b*) participant-observation studies, but since it had arisen as a result of the committee's invitation to submit a proposal, and since it was a worthwhile project in its own right, the committee included it in its conflict-research programme. The research was rapidly completed, and issued in a book (Darby *et al.*, *Education and Community in Northern Ireland: Schools Apart?* (1977)). That ended the CSSRI's involvement in the project, but it is worth mentioning that it aroused enough interest for further research in the same area to be funded from other sources. As a result of this further work, two other books have been published by scholars connected with Professor Darby's original research project: Dunn *et al.*, *Schools Together?* (1984) and Dominic Murray, *Worlds Apart: Segregated Schools in Northern Ireland* (1985).

2. *Analysis of the attitudes of Irish males* (John Jackson, Trinity College Dublin, commenced 1975). As mentioned in Chapter 1, Professor Jackson had already collected in 1973–4 a mass of survey data in the course of a study of occupational mobility among Irish males. The sample was very large—2,416 in Northern Ireland, and 2,291 in the Republic—and the questionnaire included many items of political interest. While the committee would ideally have wished to support a survey of the total population of the island, it did not have the resources to fund such a survey. In the meantime, the material in Professor Jackson's survey was a valuable substitute, analysis of which had been held up by shortage of funds. The grant from the committee enabled some of his material to be examined. Six duplicated reports were circulated in 1976.

3. *An attitude survey in the Republic of Ireland* (Earl Davis, Economic and Social Research Institute, Dublin, and Richard Sinnott, University College Dublin; commenced 1975). The bulk of the costs of this project were found by the Economic and Social Research Institute; the grant from the CSSRI did, however, fund the salary of a research fellow for one year, and enable the planning to be done. The survey took place in 1978 and the results were published in Davis and Sinnott, *Attitudes in the Republic of Ireland Relevant to the Northern Ireland Problem*, i (1979). It is only fair to add that some aspects of this report aroused controversy. However, it was the interpretation of the data, rather than the data themselves, which was in contention. (For a discussion of some of the issues, by both critics of the research and its defenders, see Davis *et al.*, *Some Issues in the Methodology of Attitude Research* (1980). See also an exchange of views in the periodical *Studies*: McKeown (1980) and Davis and Sinnott (1980).)

4. *An attitude survey in Northern Ireland* (Edward Moxon-Browne, the

Queen's University of Belfast, commenced 1977). It was obviously desirable to have a survey in Northern Ireland matching that in the Davis–Sinnott survey in the Republic; but surveys are expensive and the committee did not at the outset have the funds to bear the cost of one. However in 1977 it received a windfall when a drop in the value of sterling enhanced the value of its dollar grant. With the proceeds it was able to provide the greater part of the funding for this survey which, as preceding chapters have shown, is one of the major academic surveys to have been undertaken in Northern Ireland. Field-work took place in 1978, and the main results were published in Edward Moxon-Browne, *Nation, Class and Creed in Northern Ireland* (1983). Some of the findings on security issues were published in a separate paper (Moxon-Browne 1981). The value of this survey was increased by the fact that planning for it took place in tandem with the Davis–Sinnott survey, and a number of the same questions were asked in both surveys.

5. *A study of a Northern Ireland market town* (John Hickey, New University of Ulster, commenced 1975). It was intended that this should be a participant-observation study. However, there were difficulties in finding a research assistant prepared to live in the town in question. Eventually the money was spent on a small-scale attitude survey. The results have been published in the appendix to John Hickey, *Religion and the Northern Ireland Problem* (1984).

6. *A study of a second Northern Ireland market town* (John Blacking, the Queen's University of Belfast, commenced 1979). This was successfully launched as a participant-observation study. Substantial research has been done and a book is under way. Some preliminary findings have been published in an article by Blacking, Byrne, and Ingram, 'Looking for Work in Larne: A Social Anthropological Study' (1989).

7. *An appraisal of interpretations of the Northern Ireland conflict* (John Whyte, the Queen's University of Belfast, commenced 1975). This was a small-scale piece of research, intended as a background paper to the other projects. It resulted in a journal article: Whyte, 'Interpretations of the Northern Ireland Problem: An Appraisal' (1978).

8. *An appraisal of research into the Northern Ireland conflict* (John Whyte, the Queen's University of Belfast and subsequently University College Dublin, commenced 1980). This was a natural follow-on from project no. 7, and has issued in the present book. It has taken much longer to complete than I would have dreamt at the outset: the reasons are given in the introduction. Along the way I produced a number of other papers (Whyte 1981*b*, 1983*a*,*b*,*c*, 1986, 1988).

The above account is based partly on the final report of the Committee for Social Science Research in Ireland (1988), and partly on my recollections as a member of the committee from its inception to its winding-up.

There have been hundreds of individual research projects in Northern

Ireland, but to my knowledge the CSSRI's venture is one of the only two *programmes* of research to have been developed. The other one was launched in the early 1980s by the Social Science Research Council, and was expressly targeted on aspects of Northern Ireland other than the conflict, though in practice it often proved difficult to keep the conflict out. Some of the results from this programme have been published in a book edited by Richard Jenkins, *Northern Ireland: Studies in Social and Economic Life* (Jenkins 1989). The programme itself is appraised in Jenkins's preface to that book.

Appendix B. *Opinion Polls in Northern Ireland, 1973–1988*

This appendix lists the surveys which were used for the sections on 'Attitudes to Particular Constitutional Arrangements, 1973–88' and on 'Law and Order' in Chapter 4. In most cases I have been able to work from the original report provided by the market-research organization to its customer, but where a report has been published in a newspaper or periodical, I give the reference. I have to thank the various market-research organizations, and their clients, for making reports available to me. I have also to thank Professor Richard Rose of Strathclyde University and Mr Adrian Guelke of the Queen's University of Belfast for kindly providing copies of reports from their own holdings, in order to fill gaps in my files.

1. May 1973. Carrick James Market Research, for *Fortnight* and the *Sunday Times*. Reported in *Fortnight*, 21 May 1973.
2. April 1974. National Opinion Polls, for the BBC. Reported in the *Belfast Telegraph*, 19 April 1974.
3. June 1974. Opinion Research Centre, for ITN.
4. March 1976. National Opinion Polls, for the BBC and the *Belfast Telegraph*. Reported in the *Belfast Telegraph*, 19 March 1976.
5. January 1978. Opinion Research Centre, for UTV.
6. 1978. Edward Moxon-Browne. Reported in Moxon-Browne (1981, 1983).
7. July 1979. Opinion Research Centre, for ITN. Reported in *New Society*, 6 September 1979.
8. September 1980. Carrick James, for *Fortnight* and RTE. Reported in *Fortnight*, 178, October–November 1980.
9. June 1981. Market and Opinion Research International, for the *Sunday Times*. Reported in *New Society*, 24 September 1981.
10. February 1982. National Opinion Polls, for UTV.
11. May 1982. Market Research Bureau of Ireland, for the *Irish Times*. Reported in the *Irish Times*, 25 May 1982.
12. October 1982. Ulster Marketing Surveys, for the BBC.
13. May 1983. Market Research Bureau of Ireland, for the *Irish News*. Reported in the *Irish News*, 6 June 1983.
14. December 1983. Market Research Bureau of Ireland, for the BBC.
15. May 1984. Market and Opinion Research International, for LWT. Reported in LWT (1984).
16. May 1984. Market Research Bureau of Ireland, for the *Irish Times*. Reported in the *Irish Times*, 22 May 1984.

17. January 1985. Price Waterhouse Associates for the *Belfast Telegraph*. Reported in the *Belfast Telegraph*, 6 February 1985.
18. May 1985. Ulster Marketing Surveys, for the BBC. Reported in the *Irish Independent*, 14 May 1985.
19. January 1986. Coopers and Lybrand, for the *Belfast Telegraph*. Reported in the *Belfast Telegraph*, 15 January 1986.
20. June 1986. David J. Smith, for the Standing Advisory Commission on Human Rights. Reported in Smith 1987*b*.
21. May 1987. Coopers and Lybrand, for UTV.
22. March 1988. Coopers and Lybrand, for *Fortnight* and UTV. Reported in *Fortnight*, 261, April 1988.
23. September 1988. Coopers and Lybrand, for the *Belfast Telegraph*. Reported in the *Belfast Telegraph*, 4 and 5 October 1988.
24. September 1988. Marketing Research Consultancy for UTV.
25. February 1989. Ulster Marketing Surveys for *Sunday Life*. Reported in *Sunday Life*, 19 and 26 February 1989.

Bibliography

Adams, Gerry (1982), *Falls Memories* (Dingle: Brandon Books).

——(1986), *The Politics of Irish Freedom* (Dingle: Brandon Books).

——(1988), *A Pathway to Peace* (Cork: Mercier).

Adamson, Ian (1974), *Cruthin: The Ancient Kindred* (Newtownards: Nosmada Books).

——(1981), *The Identity of Ulster* (Belfast: the author).

Akenson, Donald Harmon (1973), *Education and Enmity: The Control of Schooling in Northern Ireland 1920–50* (Newton Abbot: David & Charles).

——(1975), *A Mirror to Kathleen's Face: Education in Independent Ireland, 1922–1960* (Montreal: McGill-Queen's University Press).

——(1979), *Between Two Revolutions: Islandmagee, County Antrim 1798–1920* (Dublin: Academy Press).

Alcock, A. E. (1982), 'The South Tyrol Package Agreement of 1969 and its Effect on Ethnic Relations in the Province of Bolzano', *Irish Studies in International Affairs*, 1(3), 47–54.

Alevy, Daniel I., *et al.* (1974), 'Rationale, Research, and Role Relations in the Stirling Workshop', *Journal of Conflict Resolution*, 18(2)(June), 276–84.

Alford, Robert R. (1964), *Party and Society: The Anglo-American Democracies* (London: Murray).

Alliance (1985), *What Future for Northern Ireland? Report of the Alliance Commission on Northern Ireland* (London: Alliance).

Anglo-Irish Agreement (1985), (Dublin: Stationery Office). Also published as: *Agreement between the Government of the United Kingdom of Great Britain and Northern Ireland and the Government of the Republic of Ireland* (London: HMSO, Cmnd. 9657).

Antipode (1980), 12(1). Special issue on Ireland.

Arthur, Andrew (1974), 'Attitude Change and "Neuroticism" among Northern Irish Children Participating in Joint-Faith Holidays' (Queen's University of Belfast, M.Sc. thesis).

Arthur, Paul (1987), *Government and Politics of Northern Ireland*, 2nd edn. (London: Longman).

Aughey, Arthur (1989), *Under Siege: Ulster Unionism and the Anglo-Irish Agreement* (Belfast: Blackstaff).

Aunger, Edmund A. (1975), 'Religion and Occupational Class in Northern Ireland'; *Economic and Social Review*, 7(1)(Oct.), 1–18.

Aunger, Edmund A. (1981), *In Search of Political Stability: A Comparative Study of New Brunswick and Northern Ireland* (Montreal: McGill-Queen's University Press).

Austin, Roger (1986), 'The Dividing Line', *Junior Education*, Nov., pp. 12–13.

Austin, William G., and Stephen Worchel (1979), *The Social Psychology of Intergroup Relations* (Belmont, Calif.: Wadsworth).

Bailey, Sydney D. (1988), *Human Rights and Responsibilities in Britain and Ireland: A Christian Perspective* (Basingstoke: Macmillan).

Baker, John (1980), Sermon preached in Westminster Abbey, Matins, Advent Sunday, 30 Nov. (I have to thank the Bishop of Salisbury for providing me with copies of this and other statements that he has made on the Northern Ireland problem).

——(1982), 'Ireland and Northern Ireland', *The Furrow*, 33(1)(Jan.), 13–21.

Bakvis, Herman (1981), *Catholic Power in The Netherlands* (Montreal: McGill-Queen's University Press).

Bambery, Chris (1986), *Ireland's Permanent Revolution* (London: Bookmarks).

Barrington, Donal (1959), *Uniting Ireland*, Pamphlet no. 1 (Dublin: Tuairim).

Barrington, Ruth (1987), *Health, Medicine & Politics in Ireland 1900–1970* (Dublin: Institute of Public Administration).

Barritt, Denis P. (1982), *Northern Ireland: A Problem to Every Solution* (London: Quaker Peace & Service).

——and Charles F. Carter (1962), *The Northern Ireland Problem* (2nd edn. 1972; London: Oxford University Press).

Barton, Brian (1988), *Brookeborough: The Making of a Prime Minister* (Belfast: Queen's University, Institute of Irish Studies).

Beattie, Geoffrey W. (1979), 'The "Troubles" in Northern Ireland', *Bulletin of the British Psychological Society*, 32 (June), 249–52.

Beckett, Ian F. W. (1986), *The Army and the Curragh Incident 1914* (London: Bodley Head for the Army Records Society).

——and Keith Jeffery (1989), 'The Royal Navy and the Curragh Incident', *Historical Research*, 62(147)(Feb.), 54–69.

Belfrage, Sally (1987), *The Crack: A Belfast Year* (London: André Deutsch).

Bell, Desmond (1987), 'Acts of Union: Youth Sub-Culture and Ethnic Identity amongst Protestants in Northern Ireland', *British Journal of Sociology*, 38(2), 158–83.

Bell, Geoffrey (1976), *The Protestants of Ulster* (London: Pluto).

——(1982), *Troublesome Business: The Labour Party and the Irish Question* (London: Pluto).

——(1984), *The British in Ireland: A Suitable Case for Withdrawal* (London: Pluto).

[Bennett] (1979), *Report of the Committee of Inquiry into Police Interrogation Procedures in Northern Ireland* (the Bennett Report) (London: HMSO, Cmnd. 7497).

Bew, Paul, and Henry Patterson (1985), *The British State and the Ulster Crisis: From Wilson to Thatcher* (London: Verso).

——Peter Gibbon, and Henry Patterson (1979), *The State in Northern Ireland, 1921–72: Political Forces and Social Classes* (Manchester: Manchester University Press).

[BICO] (1971*a*), *On the Democratic Validity of the Northern Ireland State*, British and Irish Communist Organisation, Policy Statement no. 2 (Belfast: BICO).

[BICO] (1971*b*), *The Two Irish Nations: A Reply to Michael Farrell* (Belfast: BICO).

[BICO] (1972*a*), *The Home Rule Crisis, 1912–1914*, 2nd edn. (Belfast: BICO).

[BICO] (1972*b*), *The Economics of Partition*, 4th edn. (Belfast: BICO).

[BICO] (1973), *'Ulster as it Is': A Review of the Development of the Catholic/Protestant Political Conflict in Belfast between Catholic Emancipation and the Home Rule Bill* (Belfast: BICO).

[BICO] (1975), *Imperialism*, British and Irish Communist Organisation, Policy Statement no. 8 (Belfast: BICO).

[BICO] (1977), *Against Ulster Nationalism*, 2nd edn. (Belfast: BICO).

Biggs-Davison, John (n.d.: 1982?), *Ulster: Six British Counties*, Salisbury Papers no. 10 (London: The Salisbury Group).

Birrell, Derek (1972), 'Relative Deprivation as a Factor in Conflict in Northern Ireland', *Sociological Review*, NS 20(3), 317–43.

——and Alan Murie (1980), *Policy and Government in Northern Ireland: Lessons of Devolution* (Dublin: Gill and Macmillan).

Blacking, John, Kieran Byrne, and Kate Ingram (1989), 'Looking for Work in Larne: A Social Anthropological Study', in Donnan and MacFarlane (1989), 67–89.

Blackman, Tim, Eileen Evason, Martin Melaugh, and Roberta Woods (1989), 'Housing and Health: A Case Study of Two Areas in West Belfast', *Journal of Social Policy*, 18(1)(Jan.), 1–26.

Blanshard, Paul (1954), *The Irish and Catholic Power* (London: Verschoyle).

Blythe, Ernest (1955). See de Blaghd (1955).

Boal, F. W. (1969), 'Territoriality on the Shankill–Falls Divide, Belfast', *Irish Geography*, 6(1), 30–50.

——(1971), 'Territoriality and Class: A Study of Two Residential Areas in Belfast', *Irish Geography*, 6(3), 229–48.

——and J. Neville H. Douglas (1982), *Integration and Division: Geographical Perspectives on the Northern Ireland Problem* (London: Academic Press).

Boal, F. W. and David Livingstone (1986), 'Protestants in Belfast: A View from the Inside', *Contemporary Review*, 248(1433)(Apr.), 169–75.

——P. Doherty, and D. G. Pringle (1974), *The Spatial Distribution of Some Social Problems in the Belfast Urban Area*, Northern Ireland Community Relations Commission Research Paper (Belfast: Northern Ireland Community Relations Commission).

——Russell C. Murray, and Michael A. Poole (1976), 'Belfast: The Urban Encapsulation of a National Conflict', in Susan C. Clarke and Jeffrey L. Obler (eds.), *Urban Ethnic Conflict: A Comparative Perspective*, Comparative Urban Studies Monograph no. 3 (Chapel Hill; NC: Institute for Research in Social Science, University of North Carolina), 77–131.

Boehringer, G. H., V. Zeruolis, J. Bayley, and K. Boehringer (1974), 'Stirling: The Destructive Application of Group Techniques to a Conflict', *Journal of Conflict Resolution*, 18(2)(June), 257–75.

Boserup, Anders (1972), 'Contradictions and Struggles in Northern Ireland', *Socialist Register*, 157–92.

Bowen, Kurt (1983), *Protestants in a Catholic State: Ireland's Privileged Minority* (Montreal: McGill-Queen's University Press).

Bowman, John (1982), *De Valera and the Ulster Question 1917–1973* (Oxford: Clarendon Press).

Boyce, D. G. (1972), *Englishmen and Irish Troubles: British Public Opinion and the Making of Irish Policy 1918–22* (London: Jonathan Cape).

——(1982), *Nationalism in Ireland* (London: Croom Helm).

Boyd, Andrew (1969), *Holy War in Belfast* (Tralee: Anvil Books).

——(1984), *Have the Trade Unions Failed the North?* (Cork: Mercier).

Boyle, Kevin, and Tom Hadden (1985), *Ireland: A Positive Proposal* (Harmondsworth: Penguin).

Boyle, J., J. Jackson, B. Miller, and S. Roche (1976), 'Attitudes in Ireland', Report no. 1, 'Summary Tables of Attitudes in N. Ireland' (Belfast: Committee for the Administration of the Ford Foundation Grant for Social Research in Ireland).

Brett, C. E. B. (1986), *Housing a Divided Community* (Dublin: Institute of Public Administration, in association with the Institute of Irish Studies, Queen's University of Belfast).

Brewer, John D., Adrian Guelke, Ian Hume, Edward Moxon-Browne, and Rick Wilford (1988), *The Police, Public Order and the State: Policing in Great Britain, Northern Ireland, the Irish Republic, the USA, Israel, South Africa and China* (Basingstoke: Macmillan).

Brooke, Peter (1987), *Ulster Presbyterianism* (Dublin: Gill and Macmillan).

Bruce, Steve (1986), *God Save Ulster! The Religion and Politics of Paisleyism* (Oxford: Clarendon Press).

Buchanan, R. H., and B. M. Walker (eds.) (1987), *Province, City & People: Belfast and its Region* (Antrim: Greystone Books in association with the

Northern Ireland Committee of the British Association for the Advancement of Science).

Buckland, Patrick (1972), *Irish Unionism, i, The Anglo-Irish and the New Ireland* (Dublin: Gill and Macmillan).

——(1973), *Irish Unionism, ii, Ulster Unionism and the Origins of Northern Ireland 1886–1922* (Dublin: Gill and Macmillan).

——(1979), *The Factory of Grievances: Devolved Government in Northern Ireland 1921–1939* (Dublin: Gill and Macmillan).

——(1981), *A History of Northern Ireland* (Dublin: Gill and Macmillan).

Buckley, Anthony D. (1982), *A Gentle People: A Study of a Peaceful Community in Ulster* (Cultra, Co. Down: Ulster Folk and Transport Museum).

——(1983), 'Playful Rebellion: Social Control and the Framing of Experience in an Ulster Community', *Man*, NS 18(2), 383–95.

——(1984), 'Walls within Walls: Religion and Rough Behaviour in an Ulster Community', *Sociology*, 18(1), 19–32.

——(1988), 'Collecting Ulster's Culture: Are There *Really* Two Traditions?', in Alan Gailey (ed.), *The Use of Tradition: Essays Presented to G. B. Thompson* (Cultra, Co. Down: Ulster Folk and Transport Museum), 49–60.

Budge, Ian, and Cornelius O'Leary (1973), *Belfast: Approach to Crisis: A Study of Belfast Politics, 1613–1970* (London; Macmillan).

Bufwack, Mary F. (1982), *Village without Violence: An Examination of a Northern Irish Community* (Cambridge, Mass.: Schenkman).

Bulmer, Martin, with Keith G. Banting, Stuart S. Blume, Michael Carley, and Carol H. Weiss (1986), *Social Science and Social Policy* (London: Allen and Unwin).

Burton, Frank (1978), *The Politics of Legitimacy: Struggles in a Belfast Community* (London: Routledge and Kegan Paul).

Byron, Reginald, and Roy Dilley (1989), 'Social and Micro-Economic Processes in the Northern Ireland Fishing Industry', in Jenkins (1989), 56–65.

Cairns, Ed (1980), 'The Development of Ethnic Discrimination in Children in Northern Ireland', in Harbison (1980), 115–27.

——(1982), 'Intergroup Conflict in Northern Ireland', in Henri Tajfel (ed.), *Social Identity and Intergroup Relations* (Cambridge: Cambridge University Press), 277–97.

——(1987), *Caught in Crossfire: Children and the Northern Ireland Conflict* (Belfast: Appletree).

——(1989), 'Social Identity and Inter-group Conflict in Northern Ireland: A Developmental Perspective', in Harbison (1989), 115–30.

Callaghan, James (1973), *A House Divided: The Dilemma of Northern Ireland* (London: Collins).

Callaghan, James (1987), *Time and Chance* (London: Collins).

Calvert, Harry (1972), *The Northern Ireland Problem* (London: United Nations Association).

[Cameron] (1969), *Disturbances in Northern Ireland: Report of the Commission Appointed by the Governor of Northern Ireland* (the Cameron Report) (Belfast: HMSO, Cmd. 532).

Campaign for Social Justice (1964), *Northern Ireland: The Plain Truth*, 1st edn. (Dungannon: Campaign for Social Justice in Northern Ireland).

——(1969), *Northern Ireland: The Plain Truth*, 2nd edn. (Dungannon: Campaign for Social Justice in Northern Ireland).

Campbell, Colin (1978), 'Social Relations in Glenarm, a Northern Ireland Village' (Queen's University of Belfast, MA thesis).

Campbell, Gregory (n.d.), *Discrimination: The Truth* (Derry: the author).

Canning, David, Barry Moore, and John Rhodes (1987), 'Economic Growth in Northern Ireland: Problems and Prospects', in Teague (1987), 211–35.

Capotorti, Francesco (1979), *Study on the Rights of Persons Belonging to Ethnic, Religious and Linguistic Minorities*, UN doc. E/CN4/Sub.2/432/Rev.2 (New York: United Nations).

Carr, Alan (1974), *The Belfast Labour Movement 1885–1893* (Belfast: Athol Books).

Carson, William A. (1957), *Ulster and the Irish Republic* (Belfast: Cleland).

Cathcart, Rex (1984), *The Most Contrary Region: The BBC in Northern Ireland 1924–1984* (Belfast: Blackstaff).

Cavanagh, Colm (1981), 'How We All Became Sectarian', in *Community Work in a Divided Society* (Belfast: Farset Co-operative Press), 33–6.

Cecil, Rosanne, John Offer, and Fred St Leger (1987), *Informal Welfare: A Sociological Study of Care in Northern Ireland* (Aldershot: Gower).

Chambers, Gerald (1987), *Equality and Inequality in Northern Ireland*, Pt. 2: *The Workplace*, Policy Studies Institute Occasional Paper no. 39 (London: Policy Studies Institute).

Clancy, Patrick, Sheelagh Drudy, Kathleen Lynch, and Liam O'Dowd (eds.) (1986), *Ireland: A Sociological Profile* (Dublin: Institute of Public Administration in association with the Sociological Society of Ireland).

Clarke, Desmond (1985), *Church and State: Essays in Political Philosophy* (Cork: Cork University Press).

Cohen, Anthony P. (ed.) (1982), *Belonging: Identity and Social Organization in British Rural Cultures* (Manchester: Manchester University Press).

Collins, Martin (ed.) (1985), *Ireland after Britain* (London: Pluto Press in association with Labour and Ireland).

Collins, Tom (1983), *The Centre Cannot Hold: Britain's Failure in Northern Ireland* (Dublin: Bookworks Ireland).

Committee for Social Science Research in Ireland (1988), *Report on*

Research Awards in the Disciplines of Economics, Politics and Social Science and under the Conflict Programme for the Period 1974–1987 (Dublin: Trinity College, Department of Economics).

Compton, Paul (1976), 'Religious Affiliation and Demographic Variability in Northern Ireland', *Institute of British Geographers: Transactions*, NS 1(4), 433–52.

——(1978), *Northern Ireland: A Census Atlas* (Dublin: Gill and Macmillan).

——(1980), 'The Other Crucial Factors Why Catholics Don't Get More Jobs', *Belfast Telegraph*, 28 Oct., p. 8.

——(ed.) (1981), *The Contemporary Population of Northern Ireland and Population-Related Issues* (Belfast: Queen's University, Institute of Irish Studies).

——(1985), 'An Evaluation of the Changing Religious Composition of the Population in Northern Ireland', *Economic and Social Review*, 16(3)(Apr.), 201–24.

——(1987), 'Population', in Buchanan and Walker (1987), 237–61.

——(1988), Letter in *Fortnight*, 259 (Feb.), 19.

——and John Coward (1989), *Fertility and Family Planning in Northern Ireland* (Aldershot: Avebury).

——and John F. Power (1986), 'Estimates of the Religious Composition of Northern Ireland Local Government Districts in 1981 and Change in the Geographical Pattern of Religious Composition between 1971 and 1981', *Economic and Social Review*, 17(2)(Spring), 87–105.

——R. J. Cormack and R. D. Osborne (1988), 'Discrimination Research "Flawed"', *Fortnight*, 258 (Jan.), 11–12.

Conroy, John (1988), *War as a Way of Life: A Belfast Diary* (London: Heinemann).

Cooney, John (1986), *The Crozier and the Dáil: Church and State in Ireland 1922–1986* (Cork: Mercier).

Corken, James Peter (1989), 'The Development of the Teaching of Irish History in Northern Ireland in its Institutional and Political Context' (Queen's University of Belfast, MA thesis).

Cormack, R. J., and R. D. Osborne (eds.) (1983), *Religion, Education and Employment: Aspects of Equal Opportunity in Northern Ireland* (Belfast: Appletree).

—— ——(1987), 'Fair Shares, Fair Employment: Northern Ireland Today', *Studies*, 76(303), 273–85.

—— ——(1988), Letter in *Fortnight*, 259 (Feb.), 19.

—— ——(1989), 'Employment and Discrimination in Northern Ireland', *Policy Studies*, 9(3)(Spring), 49–54.

——and E. P. Rooney (1984), 'Religion and Employment in Northern Ireland: 1911–1971', Department of Social Studies, Queen's University, Belfast.

Cormack, R. J., R. D. Osborne, and W. T. Thompson (1980), *Into Work? Young School Leavers and the Structure of Opportunity in Belfast*, Fair Employment Agency, Research Paper no. 5 (Belfast: FEA).

Covello, Vincent T., and Jacqueline A. Ashby (1980), 'Inequality in a Divided Society: An Analysis of Data from Northern Ireland', *Sociological Focus*, 13(2)(Apr.), 87–98.

Coward, John (1986), 'Demographic Structure and Change', in Clancy *et al.* (1986), 176–97.

Cox, W. Harvey (1985), 'Who Wants a United Ireland?', *Government and Opposition*, 20(1)(Winter), 29–47.

——(1987), 'Public Opinion and the Anglo-Irish Agreement', *Government and Opposition*, 22(3)(Summer), 336–51.

Critchley, Julian (1972), *Ireland: A New Partition*, Bow Group Occasional Paper (London: Bow Publications).

Cronin, Seán (1980), *Irish Nationalism: A History of its Roots and Ideology* (Dublin: Academy Press).

Crotty, Raymond (1986), *Ireland in Crisis: A Study in Capitalist Colonial Underdevelopment* (Dingle: Brandon).

Crozier, Maurna (1989), '"Powerful Wakes": Perfect Hospitality', in Curtin and Wilson (1989), 70–91.

Curran, Frank (1986), *Derry: Countdown to Disaster* (Dublin: Gill and Macmillan).

Curtin, Chris, and Thomas M. Wilson (eds.) (1989), *Ireland from Below: Social Change and Local Communities* (Galway: Galway University Press).

Daly, Mary (1981), *An Economic and Social History of Ireland since 1800* (Dublin: Educational Company of Ireland).

Dangerfield, George (1977), *The Damnable Question: A Study in Anglo-Irish Relations* (London: Constable).

Darby, John (1976), *Conflict in Northern Ireland: The Development of a Polarised Community* (Dublin: Gill and Macmillan).

——(ed.) (1983), *Northern Ireland: The Background to the Conflict* (Belfast: Appletree).

——(1986), *Intimidation and the Control of Conflict in Northern Ireland* (Dublin: Gill and Macmillan).

——and Seamus Dunn (1987), 'Segregated Schools: The Research Evidence', in Osborne *et al.* (1987), 85–97.

——and Geoffrey Morris (1974), *Intimidation in Housing*, Northern Ireland Community Relations Commission, Research Paper (Belfast: Northern Ireland Community Relations Commission).

——D. Murray, D. Batts, S. Dunn, S. Farren, and J. Harris (1977), *Education and Community in Northern Ireland: Schools Apart?* (Coleraine: New University of Ulster).

Davey, Ray (n.d.), *Take Away This Hate: The Story of a Search for Community* (Corrymeela: Corrymeela Press).

Davis, E. E., and R. Sinnott (1979), *Attitudes in the Republic of Ireland Relevant to the Northern Ireland Problem*, i, *Descriptive Analysis and Some Comparisons with Attitudes in Northern Ireland and Great Britain*, (no vol. ii; Dublin: Economic and Social Research Institute).

——— (1980), 'The Controversy Concerning Attitudes in the Republic to the Northern Ireland Problem', *Studies*, 69 (Autumn–Winter), 179–92.

——*et al.* (1980), *Some Issues in the Methodology of Attitude Research*, Economic and Social Research Institute, Policy Research Series, no. 3 (Dublin: Economic and Social Research Institute).

De Blaghd, Earnán (1955), *Briseadh na Teorann* (Dublin: Sáirséal agus Dill).

Dent, Martin (1988), 'The Feasibility of Shared Sovereignty (and Shared Authority)', in Townshend (1988), 128–56.

De Paor, Liam (1970), *Divided Ulster* (Harmondsworth: Penguin).

——— (1971), *Divided Ulster*, Pelican rev. edn. (Harmondsworth: Penguin).

——— (1986), *The Peoples of Ireland: From Prehistory to Modern Times* (London: Hutchinson).

Department of Economic Development (1986), *Equality of Opportunity in Employment in Northern Ireland: Future Strategy Options, a Consultative Paper* (Belfast: HMSO).

Devlin, Bernadette (1969), *The Price of my Soul* (London: Pan).

Dewar, Revd M. W., Revd John Brown, and Revd S. E. Long (1967), *Orangeism: A New Historical Appreciation* (Belfast: Grand Orange Lodge of Ireland).

Dilley, Roy (1989), 'Boat Owners, Patrons and State Policy in the Northern Ireland Fishing Industry', in Donnan and McFarlane (1989), 122–47.

Donnan, Hastings, and Graham McFarlane (eds.) (1989), *Social Anthropology and Public Policy in Northern Ireland* (Aldershot: Avebury).

Doob, Leonard W., and William J. Foltz (1973), 'The Belfast Workshop: An Application of Group Techniques to a Destructive Conflict', *Journal of Conflict Resolution*, 17(3)(Sept.), 489–512.

——— (1974), 'The Impact of a Workshop upon Grass-Roots Leaders in Belfast', *Journal of Conflict Resolution*, 18(2)(June), 237–56.

Douglas, J. Neville H., and Frederick W. Boal (1982), 'The Northern Ireland Problem', in Boal and Douglas (1982), 1–18.

Dunn, Seamus, John Darby, and Kenneth Mullan (1984), *Schools Together?* (Coleraine: University of Ulster, Centre for the Study of Conflict).

Dwyer, T. Ryle (1980), *Eamon de Valera* (Dublin: Gill and Macmillan).

——— (1982*a*), *De Valera's Darkest Hour: In Search of National Independence, 1919–1932* (Cork, Mercier).

——— (1982*b*), *De Valera's Finest Hour: In Search of National Independence, 1932–1959* (Cork: Mercier).

Edwards, Owen Dudley (1970), *The Sins of our Fathers: Roots of Conflict in Northern Ireland* (Dublin: Gill and Macmillan).

Edwards, Ruth Dudley (1977), *Patrick Pearse: The Triumph of Failure* (London: Faber and Faber).

Elliott, S., and F. J. Smith (1986), *Northern Ireland: The District Council Elections of 1985* (Belfast: Queen's University).

——and Richard A. Wilford (1983), *The 1982 Northern Ireland Assembly Election*, Studies in Public Policy, no. 119 (Glasgow: University of Strathclyde, Centre for the Study of Public Policy).

Ellis, Ian M. (1984), *Peace and Reconciliation Projects in Ireland*, 2nd edn. (Belfast and Dublin: Co-operation North).

Eversley, David (1989), *Religion and Employment in Northern Ireland* (London: Sage).

——and Valerie Herr (1985), *The Roman Catholic Population of Northern Ireland in 1981: A Revised Estimate* (Belfast: Fair Employment Agency).

Fair Employment Agency (1988), *Eleventh Report and Statement of Accounts of the Fair Employment Agency for Northern Ireland* (London: HMSO).

Fairleigh, John (1975), 'Personality and Social Factors in Religious Prejudice', in Fairleigh *et al.* (1975), 3–13.

——*et al.* (1975), *Sectarianism—Roads to Reconciliation: Papers Read at the 22nd Annual Summer School of the Social Study Conference, St Augustine's College, Dungarvan, 3rd–10th August 1974* (Dublin: Three Candles).

Fanning, Ronan (1989), 'Britain, Ireland and the End of the Union', in *Ireland After the Union: Proceedings of the Second Joint Meeting of the Royal Irish Academy and the British Academy, London, 1986* (Oxford: Oxford University Press), 105–20.

Farrell, Michael (1976), *Northern Ireland: The Orange State*, 1st edn. (London: Pluto).

——(1980), *Northern Ireland: The Orange State*, 2nd edn. (London: Pluto).

——(1983), *Arming the Protestants: The Formation of the Ulster Special Constabulary and the Royal Ulster Constabulary 1920–27* (London: Pluto).

——(ed.) (1988), *Twenty Years On* (Dingle: Brandon).

Faughnan, Seán (1988), 'The Jesuits and the Drafting of the Irish Constitution of 1937', *Irish Historical Studies*, 26(101)(May), 79–102.

Faulkner, Brian (1978), *Memoirs of a Statesman* (London: Weidenfeld and Nicolson).

Fee, Frank (1980), 'Responses to a Behavioural Questionnaire of a Group of Belfast Children', in Harbison (1980), 31–42.

——(1983), 'Educational Change in Belfast Schoolchildren 1975–1981', in Harbison (1983), 44–58.

Fennell, Desmond (ed.) (1968), *The Changing Face of Catholic Ireland* (London: Geoffrey Chapman).

——(1983), *The State of the Nation: Ireland since the Sixties* (Swords: Ward River).

——(1985), *Beyond Nationalism: The Struggle against Provinciality in the Modern World* (Swords: Ward River).

——(1986), *Nice People and Rednecks: Ireland in the 1980s* (Dublin: Gill and Macmillan).

——(1989), *The Revision of Irish Nationalism* (Dublin: Open Air).

Fields, Rona (1977), *Society under Siege: A Psychology of Northern Ireland* (Philadelphia, Pa.: Temple University Press).

FitzGerald, Garret (1972), *Towards a New Ireland* (London: Charles Knight).

——(1982), *Irish Identities*, The Richard Dimbleby Lecture (London: BBC).

Fogarty, Michael, Liam Ryan, and Joseph Lee (1984), *Irish Values & Attitudes: The Irish Report of the European Value Systems Study* (Dublin: Dominican Publications).

Fraser, Morris (1973), *Children in Conflict* (London: Secker and Warburg).

Fraser, T. G. (1986), *Partition in Ireland, India and Palestine: Theory and Practice* (London: Macmillan).

Gafikin, Frank, and Mike Morrissey (1987), 'Poverty and Politics in Northern Ireland', in Teague (1987), 136–59.

Gallagher, Anthony M. (1982), 'Intergroup Relations and Political Attitudes in Northern Ireland' (Queen's University of Belfast, M.Sc. thesis).

Gallagher, Eric, and Stanley Worrall (1982), *Christians in Ulster, 1968–80* (Oxford: Oxford University Press).

Gallagher, Frank (1957), *The Indivisible Island: The History of the Partition of Ireland* (London: Gollancz).

Gallagher, Michael (1982), *The Irish Labour Party in Transition 1957–1982* (Dublin: Gill and Macmillan).

Gallagher, Tom (1981), 'Religion, Reaction and Revolt in Northern Ireland: The Impact of Paisleyism in Ulster', *Journal of Church and State*, 23(3)(Autumn), 423–44.

Galliher, John F., and Jerry L. DeGregory (1985), *Violence in Northern Ireland: Understanding Protestant Perspectives* (Dublin: Gill and Macmillan).

Galway, R. (1978), 'The Perception and Manipulation of the Religious Identities in a Northern Irish Community' (Queen's University of Belfast, MA thesis).

Garvin, Tom (1988), 'The North and the Rest: The Politics of the Republic of Ireland', in Townshend (1988), 95–109.

Gibbon, Peter (1975), *The Origins of Ulster Unionism: The Formation of Popular Protestant Politics and Ideology in Nineteenth-Century Ireland* (Manchester: Manchester University Press).

Gibbon, Peter (1977), 'Some Basic Problems of the Contemporary Situation', *Socialist Register*, pp. 81–7.

Gibson, Norman (1971), 'The Northern Problem: Religious or Economic or What?', *Community Forum*, 1(1)(Spring), 2–5.

Gilmour, David (1983), *Lebanon: The Fractured Country* (London: Sphere).

Girvin, Brian (1986*a*), 'Social Change and Moral Politics: The Irish Constitutional Referendum 1983', *Political Studies*, 34(1)(Mar.), 61–81.

——(1986*b*), 'National Identity and Conflict in Northern Ireland', in Brian Girvin and Roland Sturm (eds.), *Politics and Society in Contemporary Ireland* (Aldershot: Gower), 105–34.

——(1987), 'The Divorce Referendum in the Republic, June 1986', *Irish Political Studies*, 2, 93–9.

Glassie, Henry (1982), *Passing the Time: Folklore and History of an Ulster Community* (Dublin: O'Brien).

Goudsblom, Johan (1967), *Dutch Society* (New York: Random House).

Graham, Donald (1984), 'Discrimination in Northern Ireland: The Failure of the Fair Employment Agency', *Critical Social Policy* (Summer), 40–54.

Gray, Tony (1972), *The Orange Order* (London: Bodley Head).

Greaves, C. Desmond (1972), *The Irish Crisis* (London: Lawrence and Wishart).

Gree, John E. (1985), 'Viewing "the Other Side" in Northern Ireland: Openness and Attitudes to Religion among Catholic and Protestant Adolescents', *Journal for the Scientific Study of Religion*, 24(3), 275–92.

Gudgin, Graham (1989), 'Prospects for the Northern Ireland Economy: The Role of Economic Research', in Jenkins (1989), 69–84.

Guelke, Adrian (1988), *Northern Ireland: The International Perspective* (Dublin: Gill and Macmillan).

Gwynn, Denis (1950), *The History of Partition (1912–1925)* (Dublin: Brown and Nolan).

Haagerup, N. J., rapporteur (1984), *Report Drawn up on behalf of the Political Affairs Committee on the Situation in Northern Ireland*, European Parliament Working Documents, 1983–1984, document 1-1526/83, 19 Mar. (the Haagerup Report).

Hall, Michael (1986), *Ulster: The Hidden History* (Belfast: Pretani).

Harbinson, John F. (1973), *The Ulster Unionist Party, 1882–1973: Its Development and Organisation* (Belfast: Blackstaff).

Harbison, Jeremy and Joan (eds.) (1980), *A Society under Stress: Children and Young People in Northern Ireland* (Shepton Mallet: Open Books).

Harbison, Joan (ed.) (1983), *Children of the Troubles: Children in Northern Ireland* (Belfast: Stranmillis College, Learning Resources Unit).

——(ed.) (1989), *Growing up in Northern Ireland* (Belfast: Stranmillis College, Learning Resources Unit).

Harris, Rosemary (1972), *Prejudice and Tolerance in Ulster: A Study of*

Neighbours and 'Strangers' in a Border Community (Manchester: Manchester University Press).

Harrison, Henry (1939), *Ulster and the British Empire, 1939: Help or Hindrance?* (London: Robert Hale).

Hartz, Louis (1964), *The Founding of New Societies: Studies in the History of the United States, Latin America, South Africa, Canada, and Australia* (New York: Harcourt, Brace and World).

Hastings, Max (1970), *Ulster 1969: The Fight for Civil Rights in Northern Ireland* (London: Gollancz).

Hechter, Michael (1975), *Internal Colonialism: The Celtic Fringe in British National Development, 1536–1966* (London: Routledge and Kegan Paul).

Heskin, Ken (1980), *Northern Ireland: A Psychological Analysis* (Dublin: Gill and Macmillan).

——(1981), 'Societal Disintegration in Northern Ireland: Fact or Fiction?', *Economic and Social Review*, 12(2)(Jan.), 97–113.

——(1985), 'Societal Disintegration in Northern Ireland: A Five-Year Update', *Economic and Social Review*, 16(3)(Apr.), 187–99.

Heslinga, M. W. (1962), *The Irish Border as a Cultural Divide* (repr. 1971; Assen: van Gorcum).

Hewitt, Christopher (1981), 'Catholic Grievances, Catholic Nationalism and Violence in Northern Ireland during the Civil Rights Period: A Reconsideration', *British Journal of Sociology*, 32(3)(Sept.), 362–80.

——(1983), 'Discrimination in Northern Ireland: A Rejoinder', *British Journal of Sociology*, 34(3), 446–51.

——(1985), 'Catholic Grievances and Violence in Northern Ireland', *British Journal of Sociology*, 36(1), 102–5.

——(1987), 'Explaining Violence in Northern Ireland', *British Journal of Sociology*, 38(1), 88–93.

Hickey, John (1984), *Religion and the Northern Ireland Problem* (Dublin: Gill and Macmillan).

Hogan, G. W. (1987), 'Law and Religion: Church–State Relations in Ireland from Independence to the Present Day', *American Journal of Comparative Law*, 35(1)(Winter), 47–96.

Howe, Leo (1989*a*), 'Unemployment: Doing the Double and Labour Markets in Belfast', in Curtin and Wilson (1989), 144–64.

——(1989*b*), '"Doing the Double" or Doing Without: The Social and Economic Context of Working "On the Side" in Northern Ireland', in Jenkins (1989), 164–77.

Hunter, John (1982), 'An Analysis of the Conflict in Northern Ireland', in Rea (1982), 9–59.

Hurley, Michael (ed.) (1970), *Irish Anglicanism 1869–1969* (Dublin: Allen Figgis).

Inglis, Tom (1987), *Moral Monopoly: The Catholic Church in Modern Irish Society* (Dublin: Gill and Macmillan).

Institute for Representative Government (1989), *Fair Employment or Social Engineering? Submission to the Department of Economic Development on the White Paper, 'Fair Employment in Northern Ireland'* (Belfast: Institute for Representative Government).

Irish Episcopal Conference (1984), *Submission to the New Ireland Forum* (Dublin: Veritas).

Irish Information Partnership (1989), 'Information Service on Northern Ireland Conflict and Anglo-Irish Affairs. Extracts from Forthcoming Edition of Agenda: Summary Tables', 11 Aug. (London: Irish Information Partnership).

Jackson, Harold (1971), *The Two Irelands: A Dual Study of Inter-Group Tensions*, Minority Rights Group, Report no. 2 (London: Minority Rights Group).

Jackson, T. A. (1946), *Ireland Her Own: An Outline History of the Irish Struggle for National Freedom and Independence* (London: Cobbett).

Jahoda, Gustav, and Susan Harrison (1975), 'Belfast Children: Some Effects of a Conflict Environment', *Irish Journal of Psychology*, 3(1), 1–19.

Jalland, Patricia (1980), *The Liberals and Ireland: The Ulster Question in British Politics to 1914* (Brighton: Harvester).

Jenkins, Richard (1982), *Hightown Rules: Growing up in a Belfast Estate* (Leicester: National Youth Bureau).

——(1983), *Lads, Citizens and Ordinary Kids: Working-Class Youth Life-Styles in Belfast* (London: Routledge and Kegan Paul).

——(1984), 'Bringing it all Back Home: An Anthropologist in Belfast', in Colin Bell and Helen Roberts (eds.), *Social Researching: Politics, Problems, Practice* (London: Routledge and Kegan Paul), 147–64.

——(1986), 'Northern Ireland: In What Sense "Religions" in Conflict?' in Richard Jenkins and Hastings Donnan & Graham McFarlane, *The Sectarian Divide in Northern Ireland Today*, Royal Anthropological Institute of Great Britain and Ireland, Occasional Paper no. 41 (London: Royal Anthropological Institute of Great Britain and Ireland), 1–21.

——(ed.) (1989), *Northern Ireland: Studies in Social and Economic Life* (Aldershot: Avebury, in association with the Economic and Social Research Council).

Johnson, David (1985), *The Interwar Economy in Ireland*, Studies in Irish Economic and Social History, no. 4. (Dundalk: Dundalgan Press for Economic and Social History Society of Ireland).

Jones, Emrys (1956), 'The Distribution and Segregation of Roman Catholics in Belfast', *Sociological Review*, 4, 167–89.

——(1960), *A Social Geography of Belfast* (London: Oxford University Press).

Jones, Thomas (1971), *Whitehall Diary*, iii, *Ireland 1918–1925*, ed. Keith Middlemas (London: Oxford University Press).

Jowell, Roger, and Colin Airey (eds.) (1984), *British Social Attitudes: The 1984 Report* (Aldershot: Gower).

Kee, Robert (1972), *The Green Flag: A History of Irish Nationalism* (London: Weidenfeld and Nicolson).

Kelley, Jonathan, and Ian McAllister (1984), 'The Genesis of Conflict: Religion and Status Attainment in Ulster, 1968', *Sociology*, 18(2)(May) 171–90.

Kennedy, Dennis (1988), *The Widening Gulf: Northern Attitudes to the Independent Irish State 1919–49* (Belfast: Blackstaff).

Kennedy, Kieran A., Thomas Giblin, and Deirdre McHugh (1988), *The Economic Development of Ireland in the Twentieth Century* (London: Routledge).

Kennedy, Liam (1986), *Two Ulsters: A Case for Repartition* (Belfast: the author).

Kennedy, Robert E., Jr. (1973), *The Irish: Emigration, Marriage, and Fertility* (Berkeley: University of California Press).

Kenny, Anthony (1986), *The Road to Hillsborough: The Shaping of the Anglo-Irish Agreement* (Oxford: Pergamon).

Keogh, Dermot (1986), *The Vatican, the Bishops and Irish Politics 1919–39* (Cambridge: Cambridge University Press).

——(1987), 'The Constitutional Revolution: An Analysis of the Making of the Constitution', *Administration*, 35(4) (special number, 'The Constitution of Ireland, 1937–1987'), 4–84.

[Kilbrandon] (1984), *Northern Ireland: Report of an Independent Inquiry, Chairman Lord Kilbrandon* (the Kilbrandon Report) (London: Independent Inquiry).

Kirk, Thomas (1967), 'The Religious Distribution of Lurgan with Special Reference to Segregational Ecology' (Queen's University of Belfast, MA thesis).

Koneĕni, Vladimir J. (1979), 'The Role of Aversive Events in the Development of Intergroup Conflict', in Austin and Worchel (1979), 85–102.

Kovalcheck, Kassian A. (1987), 'Catholic Grievances in Northern Ireland: Appraisal and Judgment', *British Journal of Sociology*, 38(1), 77–87.

Kremer, John, Robert Barry, and Andrew McNally (1986), 'The Misdirected Letter and the Quasi-questionnaire: Unobtrusive Measures of Prejudice in Northern Ireland', *Journal of Applied Social Psychology*, 16(4), 303–9.

Kuhn, Thomas S. (1970), *The Structure of Scientific Revolutions*, 2nd edn. (Chicago: University of Chicago Press).

Kuper, Leo (1981), *Genocide: Its Political Use in the Twentieth Century* (Harmondsworth: Penguin).

Labour Party (1987), *New Rights, New Prosperity and New Hope for Northern Ireland: A Policy Statement of the National Executive Committee of the Labour Party* (London: Labour Party).

——(1988), *Towards a United Ireland. Reform and Harmonisation: A Dual Strategy for Irish Unification* (London: Labour Party).

Laffan, Michael (1983), *The Partition of Ireland 1911–1925* (Dundalk: Dublin Historical Association).

Larsen, Sidsel Saugestad (1982*a*), 'The Two Sides of the House: Identity and Social Organisation in Kilbroney, Northern Ireland', in Cohen (1982), 131–63.

——(1982*b*), 'The Glorious Twelfth: A Ritual Expression of Collective Identity', in Cohen (1982), 278–91.

Lawlor, Sheila (1983), *Britain and Ireland 1914–23* (Dublin: Gill and Macmillan).

Lawrence, R. J. (1965), *The Government of Northern Ireland: Public Finance and Public Services 1921–1964* (Oxford: Clarendon Press).

Lee, Joseph (1968), 'Some Aspects of Modern Irish Historiography', in Ernst Schulin (ed.), *Gedenkschrift Martin Göhring: Studien zur europäischen Geschichte* (Wiesbaden: Franz Steiner), 431–43.

——and Gearóid Ó Tuathaigh (1982), *The Age of de Valera* (Dublin: Ward River Press in association with Radio Telefís Éireann).

Lee, Raymond M. (1979), 'Interreligious Courtship in Northern Ireland', in Mark Cook and Glenn Wilson (eds.), *Love and Attraction: An International Conference* (Oxford: Pergamon), 167–9.

Lennon, Brian (1984), 'A Wider View from a Local Housing Estate', *Studies*, 73(292), 309–17.

Leyton, Elliott (1974), 'Opposition and Integration in Ulster', *Man*, NS 9, 185–98.

——(1975), *The One Blood: Kinship and Class in an Irish Village*, Newfoundland Social and Economic Studies no. 15 (St John's: Memorial University of Newfoundland, Institute of Social and Economic Research).

Lijphart, Arend (1971), *Class Voting and Religious Voting in the European Democracies*, Survey Research Centre, Occasional Paper no. 8 (Glasgow: University of Strathclyde).

——(1975*a*), *The Politics of Accommodation: Pluralism and Democracy in The Netherlands*, 2nd edn. (Berkeley: University of California Press).

——(1975*b*), Review article, 'The Northern Ireland Problem: Cases, Theories, and Solutions', *British Journal of Political Science*, 5, 83–106.

——(1977), *Democracy in Plural Societies: A Comparative Exploration* (New Haven, Conn.: Yale University Press).

Long, Revd S. E. (1967), '"The Union: Pledge and Progress" 1886–1967', in Dewar *et al.* (1967), 147–200.

Longford, The Earl of, and Thomas P. O'Neill (1970), *Eamon de Valera* (Dublin: Gill and Macmillan).

——and Anne McHardy (1981), *Ulster* (London: Weidenfeld and Nicolson).

Loughlin, James (1986), *Gladstone, Home Rule and the Ulster Question 1882–93* (Dublin: Gill and Macmillan).

Lustick, Ian (1985), *State-Building Failure in British Ireland and French Algeria* (Berkeley, Calif.: Institute of International Studies).

LWT (1984), *From the Shadow of the Gun: The Search for Peace in Northern Ireland* (London: London Weekend Television).

Lyons, F. S. L. (1977), *Charles Stewart Parnell* (London: Collins).

McAllister, Ian (1975), *The 1975 Northern Ireland Convention Election*, University of Strathclyde, Survey Research Centre, Occasional Paper no. 14 (Glasgow: University of Strathclyde).

——(1977), *The Northern Ireland Social Democratic and Labour Party: Political Opposition in a Divided Society* (London: Macmillan).

——(1982), 'The Devil, Miracles and the Afterlife: The Political Sociology of Religion in Northern Ireland', *British Journal of Sociology*, 33(3)(Sept.), 330–47.

——(1983), 'Religious Commitment and Social Attitudes in Ireland', *Review of Religious Research*, 25(1)(Sept.), 3–20.

——and Brian Wilson (1978), 'Bi-confessionalism in a Confessional Party System: The Northern Ireland Alliance Party', *Economic and Social Review*, 9(4)(Apr.), 207–25.

McAnallen, Martin (1977), 'Minority Interaction in a Small Northern-Irish Village' (Queen's University of Belfast, MA thesis).

McAteer, Fergus (1972), *Won't You Please Sit Down?* (Derry: the author).

McCann, Eamonn (1974), *War and an Irish Town*, 1st edn. (Harmondsworth: Penguin).

——(1980), *War and an Irish Town*, 2nd edn. (London: Pluto).

McCartney, R. L., Sean Hall, Bryan Somers, Gordon Smyth, H. L. McCracken, and Peter Smith (1981), 'The Unionist Case' (Belfast: typescript).

McCashin, Anthony (1982), 'Social Policy: 1957–82', in *Administration*, 30(2–3) (special number, 'Unequal Achievement: The Irish Experience 1957–1982'), 203–23.

McClean, Raymond (1983), *The Road to Bloody Sunday* (Swords: Ward River).

McCluskey, Conn (1989), *Up off their Knees: A Commentary on the Civil Rights Movement in Northern Ireland* (Galway: Conn McCluskey and Associates).

McCreary, Alf (1975), *Corrymeela: The Search for Peace* (Belfast: Christian Journals).

McCrudden, C. (1983), 'The Experience of the Legal Enforcement of the Fair Employment (Northern Ireland) Act 1976', in Cormack and Osborne (1983), 201–21.

MacDonald, Michael (1986), *Children of Wrath: Political Violence in Northern Ireland* (Cambridge: Polity).

McFarlane, W. Graham (1978), 'Gossip and Social Relationships in a Northern Irish Village' (Queen's University of Belfast, Ph.D. thesis).

——(1979), 'Mixed Marriages in Ballycuan, Northern Ireland', *Journal of Comparative Family Studies*, 10(2)(Summer), 191–205.

——(1989), 'Dimensions of Protestantism: The Working of Protestant Identity in a Northern Irish Village', in Curtin and Wilson (1989), 23–45.

MacIver, Martha Abele (1987), 'Ian Paisley and the Reformed Tradition, *Political Studies*, 35(3)(Sept.), 359–78.

McKee, Eamonn (1986), 'Church–State Relations and the Development of Irish Health Policy: The Mother-and-Child Scheme, 1944–53', *Irish Historical Studies*, 25(98)(Nov.), 159–94.

McKeown, Ciaran (1984), *The Passion of Peace* (Belfast: Blackstaff).

McKeown, Kieran (1980), 'A Critical Examination of Some Findings of the Davis and Sinnott Report', *Studies*, 69(274)(Summer), 113–20.

McKeown, Michael (1986), *The Greening of a Nationalist* (Lucan: Murlough).

——(1989), *Two Seven Six Three: An Analysis of Fatalities Attributable to Civil Disturbances in Northern Ireland in the Twenty Years between July 13, 1969 and July 12, 1989* (Lucan: Murlough).

MacLaughlin, James G., and John A. Agnew (1986), 'Hegemony and the Regional Question: The Political Geography of Regional Industrial Policy in Northern Ireland, 1945–1972', *Annals of the Association of American Geographers*, 76(2), 247–61.

McLoone, James (ed.) (1985), *Being Protestant in Ireland* (Belfast and Dublin: Co-operation North in association with the Social Study Conference).

McMahon, Deirdre (1984), *Republicans and Imperialists: 'Anglo-Irish Relations in the 1930s* (New Haven, Conn.: Yale University Press).

McNabb, Patrick (1971), 'A People under Pressure', Paper presented to Lancaster University Conference on Northern Ireland.

McNeill, Ronald (1922), *Ulster's Stand for Union* (London: John Murray).

MacRae, John (1966), 'Polarisation in Northern Ireland: A Preliminary Report' (Lancaster: Peace Research Centre, photocopied document).

McWhirter, Liz (1983a), 'Contact and Conflict: The Question of Integrated Education', *Irish Journal of Psychology*, 6(1), 13–27.

——(1983*b*), 'Looking Back and Looking Forward: An Inside Perspective', in Harbison (1983), 127–57.

Mair, Peter (1987), 'Breaking the Nationalist Mould: The Irish Republic and the Anglo-Irish Agreement', in Teague (1987), 81–110.

Mansergh, N. (1974), 'The Government of Ireland Act, 1920: Its Origins and Purposes. The Working of the "Official" Mind', in J. G. Barry (ed.), *Historical Studies*, ix, *Papers Read before the Irish Conference of Historians, Cork, 29–31 May 1971* (Belfast: Blackstaff), 19–48.

Marrinan, Patrick (1973), *Paisley: Man of Wrath* (Tralee: Anvil Books).

Martin, John (1982), 'The Conflict in Northern Ireland: Marxist Interpretations', *Capital and Class*, 18(Winter), 56–71.

Marx, Karl, and Frederick Engels (1971), *On Ireland* (London: Lawrence and Wishart).

Miller, David (1978), *Queen's Rebels: Ulster Loyalism in Historical Perspective* (Dublin: Gill and Macmillan).

Miller, Robert (1978), *Attitudes to Work in Northern Ireland*, Fair Employment Agency, Research Paper no. 2 (Belfast: FEA).

——(1983), 'Religion and Occupational Mobility', in Cormack and Osborne (1983), 64–77.

——(1986), 'Social Stratification and Mobility', in Clancy *et al.* (1986), 221–43.

——(1988), 'Evaluation Research "Ulster Style": Investigating Equality of Opportunity in Northern Ireland', *Network: Newsletter of the British Sociological Association*, 42(Oct.), 4–7.

——and Robert Osborne (1980), 'Why Catholics Don't Get More Jobs: A Reply', *Belfast Telegraph*, 4 Nov., p. 12.

Mogey, John M. (1947), *Rural Life in Northern Ireland: Five Regional Studies Made for the Northern Ireland Council of Social Service (inc.)* (London: Oxford University Press).

Moloney, Ed, and Andy Pollak (1986), *Paisley* (Swords: Poolbeg).

Moody, T. W., and J. C. Beckett (1954, 1957) *Ulster since 1800*, 2 vols. (London: BBC).

Moore, Jonathon (1988), 'Historical Revisionism and the Irish in Britain', *Linen Hall Review*, 5(3)(Autumn), 14–15.

Morgan, Austen (1978), 'Politics, the Labour Movement and the Working Class in Belfast 1905–1923' (Queen's University of Belfast, Ph.D. thesis).

——(1988), *James Connolly: A Political Biography* (Manchester: Manchester University Press).

——and Bob Purdie (eds.) (1980), *Ireland: Divided Nation, Divided Class* (London: Ink Links).

Moxon-Browne, E. (1981), 'The Water and the Fish: Public Opinion and the Provisional IRA in Northern Ireland', in Paul Wilkinson (ed.), *British Perspectives on Terrorism* (London: George Allen & Unwin), 41–72.

Moxon-Browne, E. (1983), *Nation, Class and Creed in Northern Ireland* (Aldershot: Gower).

Moynihan, Maurice (ed.) (1980), *Speeches and Statements by Eamon de Valera 1917–73* (Dublin: Gill and Macmillan).

Munck, Ronnie (1985), *Ireland: Nation, State, and Class Conflict* (Boulder, Colo.: Westview).

Murphy, Dervla (1978), *A Place Apart* (London: John Murray).

——(1984), *Changing the Problem: Post-Forum Reflections*, Lilliput Pamphlets no. 3 (Gigginstown: Lilliput).

Murray, Dominic (1985), *Worlds Apart: Segregated Schools in Northern Ireland* (Belfast: Appletree).

——and John Darby (1980), *The Vocational Aspirations and Expectations of School Leavers in Londonderry and Strabane*, Fair Employment Agency, Research Paper no. 6 (Belfast: FEA).

Nairn, Tom (1977), *The Break-Up of Britain* (London: NLB).

Nelson, Sarah (1975), 'Protestant "Ideology" Considered: The Case of "Discrimination"', in Ivor Crewe (ed.), *British Political Sociology Yearbook*, ii, *The Politics of Race* (London: Croom Helm), 155–87.

——(1984), *Ulster's Uncertain Defenders: Protestant Political, Paramilitary and Community Groups and the Northern Ireland Conflict* (Belfast: Appletree).

New Ireland Forum (1983–4), *Report of Proceedings*, nos. 1–13 (Dublin: Stationery Office).

——(1984*a*), *Report* (Dublin: Stationery Office).

——(1984*b*), *The Macroeconomic Consequences of Integrated Economic Policy, Planning and Co-ordination of Ireland*, A study prepared for the New Ireland Forum by Davy Kelleher McCarthy Ltd., economic consultants, and commentary on the study by Professor Norman Gibson and Professor Dermot McAleese (Dublin: Stationery Office).

New Ulster Movement (1971*a*), *The Reform of Stormont* (Belfast: New Ulster Movement).

——(1971*b*), *A Commentary on the Programme of Reforms for Northern Ireland* (Belfast: New Ulster Movement).

——(1971*c*), *The Way Forward* (Belfast: New Ulster Movement).

——(1972*a*), *Two Irelands or One?* (Belfast: New Ulster Movement).

——(1972*b*), *Violence and Northern Ireland* (Belfast: New Ulster Movement).

——(1972*c*), *A New Constitution for Northern Ireland* (Belfast: New Ulster Movement).

——(1973), *Tribalism or Christianity in Ireland?* (Belfast: New Ulster Movement).

New Ulster Political Research Group (1979), *Beyond the Religious Divide* (Belfast: New Ulster Political Research Group).

North-Eastern Boundary Bureau (1923), *Handbook of the Ulster Question* (Dublin: Stationery Office).

Northern Friends Peace Board (1969), *Orange and Green: A Quaker Study of Community Relations in Northern Ireland* (Sedbergh: Northern Friends Peace Board).

Northern Ireland Assembly (1984), *Report: The Investigation by the Fair Employment Agency for Northern Ireland into the Non-industrial Northern Ireland Civil Service* (Belfast: HMSO).

Northern Ireland Census 1981: Religion Report (1984) (Belfast: HMSO).

Northern Ireland Office (1972), *The Future of Northern Ireland: A Paper for Discussion* (London: HMSO).

O'Brien, Conor Cruise (1972), *States of Ireland* (London: Hutchinson).

——(1980), *Neighbours: The Ewart-Biggs Memorial Lectures 1978–1979* (London: Faber and Faber).

O'Carroll, John P., and John A. Murphy (eds.) (1983), *De Valera and his Times* (Cork: Cork University Press), 1983.

O'Connell, James (1988), 'Conflict and Conciliation: A Comparative Approach Related to Three Case Studies—Belgium, Northern Ireland, and Nigeria', in Townshend (1988), 157–91.

O'Donnell, E. E. (1977), *Northern Irish Stereotypes* (Dublin: College of Industrial Relations).

O'Dowd, Liam, Bill Rolston, and Mike Tomlinson (1980), *Northern Ireland: Between Civil Rights and Civil War* (London: CSE Books).

Ó Gadhra, Nollaig (1976), 'Appreciation: Earnán de Blaghd, 1880–1975', *Éire-Ireland*, 11(3), 93–105.

Ó Glaisne, Risteard (1971), *Ian Paisley agus Tuaisceart Éireann* (Dublin: Cló Morainn).

O'Halloran, Clare (1987), *Partition and the Limits of Irish Nationalism: An Ideology under Stress* (Dublin: Gill and Macmillan).

O'Hearn, Denis (1983), 'Catholic Grievances, Catholic Nationalism: A Comment', *British Journal of Sociology*, 34(3), 438–45.

——(1985), 'Again on Discrimination in the North of Ireland: A Reply to the Rejoinder', *British Journal of Sociology*, 36(1), 94–101.

——(1987), 'Catholic Grievances: Comments', *British Journal of Sociology*, 38(1), 94–100.

O'Hegarty, P. S. (1952), *A History of Ireland under the Union, 1801 to 1922* (London: Methuen).

O'Leary, Brendan (1985), 'Explaining Northern Ireland: A Brief Study Guide', *Politics*, 5(1)(Apr.), 35–41.

O'Leary, Cornelius (1986), 'The Irish Referendum on Divorce (1986)', *Electoral Studies*, 6(1), 69–74.

——and Tom Hesketh (1988), 'The Irish Abortion and Divorce Referendum Campaigns', *Irish Political Studies*, 3, 43–62.

Oliver, John (1978*a*), *Ulster Today and Tomorrow*, vol. xliv, broadsheet no. 574 (London: PEP).

——(1978*b*), *Working at Stormont* (Dublin: Institute of Public Administration).

O'Malley, Padraig (1983), *The Uncivil Wars: Ireland Today* (Belfast: Blackstaff).

O'Neill, Terence (1969), *Ulster at the Crossroads* (London: Faber and Faber).

——(1972), *The Autobiography of Terence O'Neill, Prime Minister of Northern Ireland 1963–1969* (London: Rupert Hart-Davis).

Osborne, Robert D. (1978), 'Denomination and Unemployment in Northern Ireland', *Area*, 10(4), 280–3.

——(1980), 'Religious Discrimination and Disadvantage in the Northern Ireland Labour Market', *International Journal of Social Economics*, 7(4), 206–23.

——(1983), 'What About the Other Minority?', *Fortnight*, 196 (Aug.), 14.

——and R. J. Cormack (1983), 'Conclusions' and 'The Last Word' in Cormack and Osborne (1983), 222–33 and 238–42.

—— ——(1985), 'Higher Education: North and South', *Administration*, 33(3), 326–54.

—— ——(1986), 'Unemployment and Religion in Northern Ireland', *Economic and Social Review*, 17(3)(Apr.), 215–23.

—— ——(1987), *Religion, Occupations and Employment 1971–1981*, Fair Employment Agency, Research Paper no. 11 (Belfast: FEA).

—— ——(1989), 'Gender and Religion as Issues in Education, Training and Entry to Work', in Harbison (1989), 42–65.

—— ——N. G. Reid, and A. P. Williamson (1984), 'Class, Sex, Religion and Destination: Participation and Higher Education in Northern Ireland', *Studies in Higher Education*, 9(2), 123–37.

—— ——and R. L. Miller (eds.) (1987), *Education and Policy in Northern Ireland* (Belfast: Queen's University and the University of Ulster, Policy Research Institute).

Paisley, Dr Ian R. K., Ald. Peter Robinson, and Rt. Hon. John D. Taylor (1982), *Ulster: The Facts* (Belfast: Crown Publications).

Paisley, Rhonda (1988), *Ian Paisley, My Father* (Basingstoke: Marshall Pickering).

Palley, Claire (1972), *The Evolution, Disintegration and Possible Reconstruction of the Northern Ireland Constitution* (Repr. from the *Anglo-American Law Review*; London: Barry Rose, in association with the Institute of Irish Studies).

Patterson, Henry (1980), *Class Conflict and Sectarianism: The Protestant Working Class and the Belfast Labour Movement 1868–1920* (Belfast: Blackstaff, an Ulster Polytechnic Book).

Pickvance, T. J. (1975), *Peace through Equity: Proposals for a Permanent Settlement of the Northern Ireland Conflict* (Birmingham: the author).

Poole, Michael A. (1982), 'Religious Residential Segregation in Northern Ireland', in Boal and Douglas (1982), 281–308.

——(1983), 'The Demography of Violence', in Darby (1983), 151–80.

——and F. W. Boal (1973, 'Religious Residential Segregation in Belfast in mid-1969: A Multi-level Analysis', in B. D. Clark and M. D. Gleave (eds.), *Social Patterns in Cities*, Special Publication no. 5, (London: Institute of British Geographers), 1–40.

[PPRU] (1989), *PPRU Monitor*, 1/89, Apr. (Belfast: Department of Finance and Personnel, Policy Planning and Research Unit).

Pringle, D. G. (1985), *One Island, Two Nations? A Political Geographical Analysis of the National Conflict in Ireland* (Letchworth: Research Studies Press).

Prior, James (1986), *A Balance of Power* (London: Hamish Hamilton).

Probert, Belinda (1978), *Beyond Orange and Green: The Political Economy of the Northern Ireland Crisis* (London: Zed).

Project Team (1977), *Belfast: Areas of Special Social Need. Report by Project Team 1976* (Belfast: HMSO).

Randall, Vicky (1986), 'The Politics of Abortion in Ireland', in Joni Lovenduski and Joyce Outshoorn (eds.), *The New Politics of Abortion* (London: Sage), 67–85.

Rea, Desmond (ed.) (1982), *Political Co-operation in Divided Societies: A Series of Papers Relevant to the Conflict in Northern Ireland* (Dublin: Gill and Macmillan).

Reed, David (1984), *Ireland: The Key to the British Revolution* (London: Larkin).

Rees, Merlyn (1985), *Northern Ireland: A Personal Perspective* (London: Methuen).

Road to Partition: 1914–1919, The (1974) (Belfast: Athol Books).

Roberts, David A. (1971), 'The Orange Order in Ireland: A Religious Institution?', *British Journal of Sociology*, 22(3), 269–82.

Roberts, Hugh (1987), 'Sound Stupidity: The British Party System and the Northern Ireland Question', *Government and Opposition*, 22(3)(Summer), 315–35.

Robinson, Alan (1971*a*), 'Education and Sectarian Conflict in Northern Ireland', *The New Era*, 52(1), (Jan.), 384–8.

——(1971*b*), 'If you Lived in Northern Ireland—Would *your* Child be Fighting in the Streets?', *Where*, 57(May), 133–6.

Rolston, Bill (1980), 'The Limits of Trade Unionism', in O'Dowd *et al.* (1980), 68–94.

—(1983), 'Reformism and Sectarianism: The State of the Union after Civil Rights', in Darby (1983), 197–224.

Rolston, B. and Mike Tomlinson (1988), *Unemployment in West Belfast: The Obair Report* (Belfast: Beyond the Pale Publications).

—— ——Liam O'Dowd, Bob Miller, and Jim Smyth (1983), *A Social Science Bibliography of Northern Ireland 1945–1983* (Belfast: Queen's University).

Rose, Richard (1971), *Governing without Consensus: An Irish Perspective* (London: Faber and Faber).

——(1976), *Northern Ireland: A Time of Choice* (London: Macmillan).

——Ian McAllister, and Peter Mair (1978), *Is There a Concurring Majority about Northern Ireland?*, Studies in Public Policy no. 22 (Glasgow: University of Strathclyde, Centre for the Study of Public Policy).

Rowthorn, Bob (1987), 'Northern Ireland: An Economy in Crisis', in Teague (1987), 111–35.

——and Naomi Wayne (1988), *Northern Ireland: The Political Economy of Conflict* (Cambridge: Polity).

Russell, James (1974), 'Sources of Conflict', *Northern Teacher*, 11(3), 3–11.

——and James A. Schellenberg (1976), 'Political Attitude Structure of Schoolboys in Northern Ireland', *Irish Journal of Psychology*, 3(2), 73–86.

Ryan, Desmond (ed.) (1948), *Socialism and Nationalism: A Selection from the Writings of James Connolly* (Dublin: Three Candles).

Ryan, Liam (1979), 'The Church and Politics: The Last Twenty-Five Years', *The Furrow*, 30(1)(Jan.), 3–18.

SACHR (Standing Advisory Commission on Human Rights) (1987), *Religious and Political Discrimination and Equality of Opportunity in Northern Ireland: Report on Fair Employment* (London: HMSO, Cm. 237).

Salters, John (1970), 'Attitudes towards Society in Protestant and Roman Catholic School Children in Belfast' (Queen's University of Belfast, M.Ed. thesis).

Schmitt, David (1980), 'Equal Employment Opportunity as a Technique toward the Control of Political Violence: The Case of Northern Ireland's Fair Employment Agency', *Current Research on Peace and Violence*, 3(1), 33–46.

Shanks, Amanda (1988), *Rural Aristocracy in Northern Ireland* (Aldershot: Avebury).

Shannon, Catherine B. (1988), *Arthur J. Balfour and Ireland, 1874–1922* (Washington: Catholic University of America Press).

Shea, Patrick (1981), *Voices and the Sound of Drums: An Irish Autobiography* (Belfast: Blackstaff).

Shearman, Hugh (1942), *Not an Inch: A Study of Northern Ireland and Lord Craigavon* (London: Faber and Faber).

——(1948), *Anglo-Irish Relations* (London: Faber and Faber).

——(1970), 'Conflict in Northern Ireland', in *Year Book of World Affairs*, 24, 40–53.

——(1982), 'Conflict in Northern Ireland', in *Year Book of World Affairs*, 36, 182–96.

Sheehy, Michael (1955), *Divided We Stand: A Study of Partition* (London: Faber and Faber).

Singleton, Dale (1985), 'Housing and Planning Policy in Northern Ireland: Problems of Implementation in a Divided Community', *Policy and Politics*, 13(3), 305–26.

Smith, David J. (1987*a*), *Equality and Inequality in Northern Ireland*, Pt. 1, *Employment and Unemployment*, PSI Occasional Paper no. 39 (London: Policy Studies Institute).

——(1987*b*), *Equality and Inequality in Northern Ireland*, Pt. 3, *Perceptions and Views*, PSI Occasional Paper no. 39 (London: Political Studies Institute).

——(1988*a*), ' "No Substance" to Criticisms', *Fortnight*, 258 (Jan.) 12.

——(1988*b*), Letter in *Fortnight*, 260 (Mar.), 19.

——(1988*c*), 'Policy and Research: Employment Discrimination in Northern Ireland', *Policy Studies*, 9(1)(July), 41–59.

——and Gerry Chambers (1987), 'Positions, Perceptions, Practice', *Fortnight*, 257 (Dec.), 18–19.

Smith, M. G. (1969), 'Some Developments in the Analytic Framework of Pluralism', in Leo Kuper and M. G. Smith (eds.), *Pluralism in Africa* (Berkeley: University of California Press), 415–58.

Smyth, Clifford (1986), 'The DUP as a Politico-Religious Organization', *Irish Political Studies*, 1, 33–43.

——(1987), *Ian Paisley: Voice of Protestant Ulster* (Edinburgh: Scottish Academic Press).

Smyth, Martin (1975), 'A Protestant Looks at the Republic', in Fairleigh *et al.* (1975), 25–35.

Stewart, A. T. Q. (1977), *The Narrow Ground: Aspects of Ulster, 1609–1969* (London: Faber and Faber).

Strauss, E. (1951), *Irish Nationalism and British Democracy* (London: Methuen).

Sugden, John, and Alan Bairner (1986), 'Northern Ireland: Sport in a Divided Society', in Lincoln Allison (ed.), *The Politics of Sport* (Manchester: Manchester University Press), 90–115.

Sunday Times 'Insight' Team (1972), *Ulster* (Harmondsworth: Penguin).

Tajfel, Henri, and John Turner (1979), 'An Integrative Theory of Intergroup Conflict', in Austin and Worchel (1979), 33–47.

Tapsfield, Joan A. (1983), 'In Search of Truth in Northern Ireland', *The Furrow*, 34(2)(Feb.), 95–8.

Taylor, David (1984), 'Ian Paisley and the Ideology of Ulster Protestantism', in Chris Curtin *et al.* (eds.), *Culture and Ideology in Ireland*, Studies in Irish Society, ii (Galway: Galway University Press), 59–78.

Taylor, Rupert Langley (1986), 'The Queen's University of Belfast and its Relationship to the Troubles: The Limits of Liberalism' (University of Kent at Canterbury, Ph.D. thesis).

——(1988*a*), 'Social Scientific Research on the "Troubles" in Northern Ireland: The Problem of Objectivity', *Economic and Social Review*, 19(2)(Jan.), 123–45.

——(1988*b*), 'The Queen's University of Belfast: The Liberal University in a Divided Society', *Higher Education Review*, 20(2)(Spring), 27–45.

Teague, Paul (ed.) (1987), *Beyond the Rhetoric: Politics, the Economy and Social Policy in Northern Ireland* (London: Lawrence and Wishart).

Todd, Jennifer (1987), 'Two Traditions in Unionist Political Culture', *Irish Political Studies*, 2, 1–26.

Tóibín, Colm (1987), *Walking Along the Border* (London: MacDonald Queen Anne Press).

Tovey, Hilary (1975), 'Religious Group Membership and National Identity Systems', *Social Studies*, 4(2), 124–43.

Townshend, Charles (ed.) (1988), *Consensus in Ireland: Approaches and Recessions* (Oxford: Clarendon Press).

Trew, Karen (1980), 'Sectarianism in Northern Ireland: A Research Perspective', Paper presented at the British Psychological Society, Social Psychology Section Annual Conference, Canterbury, Sept. 1980.

——(1983), 'Group Identification in a Divided Society', in Harbison (1983), 109–19.

——(1986), 'Catholic-Protestant Contact in Northern Ireland', in Miles Hewstone and Rupert Brown (eds.), *Contact and Conflict in Intergroup Encounters* (Oxford: Blackwell), 93–106.

——and L. McWhirter (1982), 'Conflict in Northern Ireland: A Research Perspective', in Peter Stringer (ed.), *Confronting Social Issues* (London: Academic Press), 195–214.

[UK Government] (1982), *Northern Ireland: A Framework for Devolution* (London: HMSO, Cmnd. 8541).

Ulster Unionist Party (1984), *Devolution and the Northern Ireland Assembly: The Way Forward*, Discussion Paper presented by the Ulster Unionist Party's Report Committee, Belfast.

Van der Straeten, Serge, and Philippe Daufouy (1972), 'La Contre-révolution irlandaise', *Les Temps Modernes*, 29ᵉ année, 311, 2069–104.

[Van Straubenzee] (1973), *Report and Recommendations of the Working Party on Discrimination in the Private Sector of Employment* (the Van Straubenzee Report) (Belfast: HMSO, Ministry of Health and Social Services).

Viney, Michael (1965), *The Five Per Cent: A Survey of Protestants in the Republic* (repr. from the *Irish Times*; Dublin).

Violence in Ireland: A Report to the Churches (1976) (Belfast: Christian Journals; Dublin: Veritas Publications).

Waddell, Neil, and Ed Cairns (1986), 'Situational Perspectives on Social Identity in Northern Ireland', *British Journal of Social Psychology*, 25, 25–31.

Walker, B. M. (1989), *Ulster Politics: The Formative Years, 1868–86* (Belfast: Ulster Historical Foundation and Institute of Irish Studies).

Walker, Graham (1985), *The Politics of Frustration: Harry Midgley and the Failure of Labour in Northern Ireland* (Manchester: Manchester University Press).

Wallace, Martin (1970), *Drums and Guns: Revolution in Ulster* (London: Geoffrey Chapman).

——(1971), *Northern Ireland: 50 Years of Self-Government* (Newton Abbot: David & Charles).

——(1982), *British Government in Northern Ireland: From Devolution to Direct Rule* (Newton Abbot: David & Charles).

Wallis, Roy, Steve Bruce and David Taylor (1986), *'No Surrender!' Paisleyism and the Politics of Ethnic Identity in Northern Ireland* (Belfast: Queen's University, Department of Social Studies).

—— —— ——(1987), 'Ethnicity and Evangelicalism: Ian Paisley and Protestant Politics in Ulster', *Comparative Studies in Society and History*, 29, 293–313.

Walmsley, A. J. (1959), *Northern Ireland: Its Policies and Record* (Belfast: Ulster Unionist Council).

Walsh, Brendan M. (1970), *Religion and Demographic Behaviour in Ireland*, Economic and Social Research Institute, Paper no. 55 (Dublin: Economic and Social Research Institute).

——(1975), 'Trends in the Religious Composition of the Population in the Republic of Ireland, 1946–71', *Economic and Social Review*, 6(4)(July), 543–55.

Watt, David (ed.) (1981), *The Constitution of Northern Ireland: Problems and Prospects*, National Institute of Economic and Social Research, Policy Studies Institute, Royal Institute of International Affairs, Joint Studies in Public Policy no. 4 (London: Heinemann).

White, Barry (1984), *John Hume: Statesman of the Troubles* (Belfast: Blackstaff).

White, Jack (1975), *Minority Report: The Anatomy of the Southern Irish Protestant* (Dublin: Gill and Macmillan).

Whyte, John (1978), 'Interpretations of the Northern Ireland Problem: An Appraisal', *Economic and Social Review*, 9(4)(July), 257–82.

——(1980), *Church and State in Modern Ireland 1923–1979*, 2nd edn. (1st edn., covering 1923–70, pub. 1971; Dublin: Gill and Macmillan).

——(1981*a*), *Catholics in Western Democracies: A Study in Political Behaviour* (Dublin: Gill and Macmillan).

——(1981*b*), 'Why is the Northern Ireland Problem so Intractable?', *Parliamentary Affairs*, 34(4)(Autumn), 422–35.

Whyte, John (1983*a*), *Is Research on the Northern Ireland Problem Worth While?*, an Inaugural Lecture delivered before the Queen's University of Belfast on 18 Jan. (Belfast: Queen's University).

——(1983*b*), 'How much Discrimination Was There under the Unionist Regime, 1921–68?', in Tom Gallagher and James O'Connell (eds.), *Contemporary Irish Studies* (Manchester: Manchester University Press), 1–35.

——(1983*c*), 'The Permeability of the United Kingdom–Irish Border: A Preliminary Reconnaissance', *Administration*, 31(3), 300–15.

——(1986), 'How is the Boundary Maintained between the Two Communities in Northern Ireland?', *Ethnic and Racial Studies*, 9(2)(Apr.), 219–34.

——(1988), 'Interpretations of the Northern Ireland Problem', in Townshend (1988), 24–46.

Wilkinson, Paul (1986), 'Maintaining the Democratic Process and Public Support', in Richard Clutterbuck, *The Future of Political Violence: Destabilization, Disorder and Terrorism* (Basingstoke: Macmillan), 177–84.

Wilson, Des (1985), *An End to Silence* (Cork: Mercier).

Wilson, Thomas (ed.) (1955), *Ulster under Home Rule* (London: Oxford University Press).

——(1989), *Ulster: Conflict and Consent* (Oxford: Blackwell).

Wright, Frank (1973), 'Protestant Ideology and Politics in Ulster', *European Journal of Sociology*, 14, 213–80.

——(1981), 'Case Study III: The Ulster Spectrum', in David Carlton and Carlo Schaerf (eds.), *Contemporary Terror: Studies in Sub-State Violence* (London: Macmillan), 153–214.

——(1987), *Northern Ireland: A Comparative Analysis* (Dublin: Gill and Macmillan).

——(1989), 'Northern Ireland and the British-Irish Relationship', *Studies*, 78(310)(Summer), 151–62.

Index